SERIES I YEAR 1

PREACHING WORKBOOK

Jerry L. Schmalenberger

CSS Publishing Company, Inc.
Lima, Ohio

This book is dedicated to those young Bataks on the South China Sea island of Sumatra, Indonesia, for whom I am Ompung: *Reverend Deonal Sinaga, Omega Sitorus, Rospita Siahaan, Benny Sinaga, Todo Tua Sirait, Wilda Simanjuntak, and Santi Hutagaol. Their simple piety and loving devotion inspire me to continue teaching and writing.*

Horas *and* ima tutu

Acknowledgments
Special thanks to Greg Schaefer for typing my handwritten manuscript into a printed computer format and to my wife, Carol Schmalenberger, for doing the final edits and formatting.

Copyright © 2002 by
CSS Publishing Company, Inc.
Lima, Ohio

All rights reserved. No part of this publication may be reproduced in any manner whatsoever without the prior permission of the publisher, except in the case of brief quotations embodied in critical articles and reviews. Inquiries should be addressed to: Permissions, CSS Publishing Company, Inc., P.O. Box 4503, Lima, Ohio 45802-4503.

Some scripture quotations are from the *New Revised Standard Version of the Bible*, copyright 1989 by the Division of Christian Education of the National Council of the Churches of Christ in the USA. Used by permission.

For more information about CSS Publishing Company resources, visit our website at www.csspub.com or e-mail us at custserv@csspub.com or call (800) 241-4056.

Table Of Contents

Sermon Planner/Builder	4
Introduction	5
December	6
January	25
February	36
March	48
April	63
May	81
June	92
July	107
August	119
September	134
October	146
November	158

Sermon Planner/Builder

Date: _____ Cycle/Season: _____ Sunday: _____

Theological clue _____
_____

Psalm/central thought: _____
_____

Collect/prayer concern/focus: _____
_____

Sermon text(s): _____
_____

Summary of sermon text(s): _____
_____
_____
_____
_____
_____
_____
_____

Pastoral perspective: _____
_____
_____
_____
_____

Stories/illustrations: _____
_____
_____
_____
_____

Type of sermon: _____

Sermon plan/sketch: _____
_____
_____
_____
_____
_____
_____

Introduction

How I wish some old war-horse of a preacher who had seen lots of the world and a contemporary life would have prepared a workbook such as this for my use in the early days of my parish ministry and preaching the gospel. It would have enriched and strengthened the thin messages my long-suffering congregation had to endure.

In the pages following I have not tried to provide an academic exegesis of the texts, but I have tried to explore many homiletical approaches examining the readings with the eyes of long experience in living life, experiencing different cultures, and proclaiming the gospel in all sorts of situations and places.

As an homilitician, I have tried to do a little teaching within this volume of theories for effective organization for and delivering of sermons.

My main resources while composing are my many years of preaching and teaching and my homiletical journals carefully kept over forty years. These additional few books I kept at the ready as I wrote:

The New Revised Standard Version of the Bible
William Barclay's *The Daily Study Bible*
The Interpreter's One-Volume Commentary on the Bible
The Bible Knowledge Commentary
Vine's *Expository on Isaiah*
Harper's *Bible Dictionary*
A Dictionary of Quotations from Shakespeare
These Will Preach, a book of metaphors
Macartney's *Illustrations*

Many of the metaphors and stories are from my book, *These Will Preach*, which is a collection from my homiletical journals. Others are from my overseas service as a Professor of Practical Theology and lecturer on discipleship as a Global Mission Volunteer for the Evangelical Lutheran Church in America.

Special thanks to two people who helped with this writing in very significant ways: seminarian and spiritual son Greg Schaefer, who did the input with editing into a computer, and to my faithful wife Carol, who always does the final edit of my works.

Thanks also to CSS Publishing who has been so gracious to publish so much of my work over many years. Because of them, I have had the deep privilege of sharing my thoughts with many. It has been the centerpiece of my very blessed career.

Some years ago I preached in Curran Memorial Church in Sanoyea, Liberia, West Africa. There were no lights in the church except for those which several hundred villagers brought with them. They placed a Coleman gasoline lantern in front of me so the congregation could see my face as I preached. Each time the lantern would run down, a deacon would come forward and pumped it up with the words, "Preach on!" Those words I say to you also. "Preach on!"

— JLS

First Sunday In December

Isaiah 64:1-9   1 Corinthians 1:3-9   Mark 13:24-37

Seasonal Theme   A time of expectation, anticipation, and preparation for the coming again of Jesus in Bethlehem and in our hearts.

Theme For The Day   The hope for, and the joyful anticipation of, the coming again of the Christ into our hearts.

Comments On The Scripture

In the next weeks before Christmas we will read often from the book of Isaiah, the greatest of the Hebrew prophets whose name means "Jehovah is Salvation." From this book and 2 Kings 19 and 20 we can learn a little about him. Born about 765 B.C., his father was named Amoz. Isaiah must have lived in Jerusalem and knew well the liturgy and area of the Temple. Married to a prophetess, the couple named their two sons after Isaiah's preaching themes. He tells us of his call to be a prophet and his prophetic work over forty years, plus the reign of four Judean kings. Unlike many of the prophets, he was a friend of these kings and a well-known figure of his day with a hand in the formation of national policies. Isaiah had a disciple whom he taught and who must have been influenced by Amos and Hosea who were also prophesying in Israel at that time. Isaiah died sometime after 700 B.C. Tradition says he was sawn asunder (Hebrews 11:37).

His main message seemed to be that the time of God's patience was ending. *Harper's Bible Dictionary* states of Isaiah: "... pre-eminently a prophet, embodying high ethical, social, and spiritual qualities which made his utterances the voice of God to the people" (p. 285).

Old Testament Lesson   Isaiah 64:1-9   *The Plea Of The Remnant*

This chapter is a continuing of Isaiah's prayer. He calls upon God to destroy his enemies. There is a wonderful threefold combination here as joy and righteousness and the remembrance of God. The secret is God's presence which becomes the power to serve him. In verse 6 we have a confession of the prophet, thus in verse 7 God hides himself when they come to him. Then comes the wonderful plea to God. You are our Parent! Don't be angry with us or forget our iniquity — *remember we are your people!* (v. 9). Isaiah's reasons for God deserting them were stated earlier: the nation's sins (50:1) and God's commitment to God's word. But because of God's compassion (54:7) and kindness God will restore the nation to himself. They will have to count on God's faithfulness and promises.

New Testament Lesson   1 Corinthians 1:3-9   *How It Ought To Be*

Before taking up the tough subject of the divisions within the Corinthian church, Paul greets them (v. 3) and then he writes them as if they were well-behaved Christians (vv. 4-9). It looks to me as if he was flattering them before the scolding which begins in verse 10. What that bunch of quarreling Christians needed most was in verse 3: God's grace and God's peace. Paul is thankful these are available to these Corinthians even though they don't seem to realize it. They must acknowledge what God has done for them and what they ought to be in Christ. If this is not sarcasm, what a wonderful way to approach a congregation which deserves scolding. I have a hunch that once a congregation takes the steps of acknowledging what God has done for them and what they ought to be in Christ, most or all of the quarreling would disappear.

The Gospel   Mark 13:24-37   *The Necessity Of Watchfulness*

It's a great reading for the sleepy early service people, "Keep awake!"

Mark 13:1-37 is the longest speech of Jesus in Mark. It is about the last days and, according to Mark, was only given to the four senior disciples. These secrets were not meant for Jesus' public teachings. It has been called by some "the little Apocalypse." There is a similarity with Daniel 7-12 and the book of Revelation. Of course it was selected by our church foremothers and forefathers because of its focus on being watchful, alert, and prepared which is the general emphasis of Advent.

We must remember that this is a *pre*-scientific view of the universe.

The coming of the Son of Man is consistent with what the early Christians expected. See Deuteronomy 30:4; Isaiah 13:10, 14:12; Daniel 7:13; and Zechariah 2:6. We can get the same idea in Acts 1:9-11.

Verse 30 is best understood as those things which will take place, not at his second coming, but within his own generation. And they did! Jerusalem did fall and the destruction of the Temple did take place.

There are some truths we can glean from all this puzzling apocalyptic writing:
1. It's risky to forget God and become absorbed in the earthly.
2. It says it is only the devout who can see into history.
3. It speaks about the second coming of Christ. We ought not to forget it and that history is going somewhere.
4. We live in the shadow of eternity and must be prepared for it all the time.

Preaching Possibilities

Each of the three readings for this Sunday can easily stand alone or be put together under the theme of getting ready, anticipating, and being prepared. If used separately, outlines might look like this:

Old Testament

Title: The Power To Serve

The main moves could be:
A. God's presence brings us a profound joy.
B. God's presence brings us a righteousness the world cannot (will not) provide.
C. God's presence brings us a remembrance of God and all God has done for us.
D. Altogether we have, then, the God-given equipment to serve God and God's people.

New Testament

Title: How We "Oughta" Be *or* Oughta-Be Christians

The main sermon moves could be:
A. We "oughta" have God's grace and peace. This ought to be from God to us and then from us to others (v. 3).
B. We "oughta" continue to grow in Christ in our speech and knowledge (v. 5).
C. We "oughta" not lack in any spiritual gifts.
D. We "oughta" be strengthened and blameless (v. 8).
E. We "oughta" acknowledge our call into fellowship with Jesus Christ (v. 9b).
F. Then we can describe how we ought best realize the above results in this congregation.

Gospel

Title: Anticipating His Coming Again

Possible moves in this sermon might be:

Begin by describing your own preparation for the birth of a child.
A. There are many ways we can expect him to come into our lives and congregations this year.
   1. Into our hearts and how that ought change us.
   2. Into our church and how that should re-prioritize our ministry.
   3. Into our community and how that will change how we try to live together and treat each other.
   4. Into our nation and other nations to the unchurched who need to hear of the Savior.

B. So here are some of the ways we can prepare for his birth again this year.
   1. Study the scripture and strengthen our piety.
   2. Pray often on a regular schedule thus renewing our relationship with the Christ.
   3. Gather as a congregation for worship often thus developing a precious fellowship among those who sincerely are anticipating his arrival again.
C. Now frame by returning to how a family prepares for the birth of a new baby.
D. Close by re-reading verses 32-37.

Possible Outline Of Sermon Moves (using all three readings)
A. Begin by describing your own preparation for the birth of a child into your life. You might retell the television ad for Diehard car batteries as they keep the car ready to go in a cold climate.
B. Now move to the three passages of scripture and relate how all of them expected a coming and then a second coming of the Messiah.
   1. So Isaiah would prepare for the birth of the Savior by rediscovering the power of the presence of God in his life enabling him to serve God and God's people. He knew he could count on God's kindness and forgiveness if he would repent of his sins and untruthfulness.
   2. So Paul would prepare by celebrating God's peace and grace (v. 3). He would voice his thankfulness to God for Jesus Christ. He would seek to be further enriched by God (v. 5) and identify the spiritual gifts given to him. And, lo, Jesus is born again in Paul's heart.
   3. Mark would make a great effort to be alert in his discipleship, always on the ready and expecting Christ's arrival and birth again at any time. He would renew his resolve not only to be more faithful in worship attendance but also much more faithful in bringing others. (The one who invites and witnesses is almost always more blessed than the one invited.)
C. Now make your own witness as to how easy it is to prepare for the coming of Jesus again that we miss it when it does happen over and over again.
D. Now frame your sermon by returning to your description of preparing for the birth of a child in your family.
E. Close by reading verses 32-37 of Mark 13.

Prayer For The Day

Prepare our hearts this day, O God, for the birth again of the Christ that we might know the peace and power and joy of his presence there. Help us to live on the alert not only for the awareness of your kingdom breaking in, but also for the needs of others that they too might know the blessings of being loved by you. In Christ's name. Amen.

Possible Metaphors And Stories

"Four-toast Henry" from Myanmar (Burma) was one of the students preparing in Hong Kong to return to his country as a professor in a new seminary. He told me of the preparations which he had to make in order to prepare for the birth of my goddaughter, Katie. He had to prepare food to take along for the stay in the hospital. He had to hire a car to transport his wife the 45 miles to the nearest medical facility. He had to hire a doctor, nurse, and cleaning lady for the time of delivery. He also had to bring along a portable generator and any medicine she would need. It was all in order to be prepared in anticipation of the birth.

At a church meal following a funeral, a man told me they were expecting a baby any time now, so each night in cold, cold Iowa, he removed the battery from his car and kept it in the house where it would be warm and ready to start the car. Might we anticipate the coming of the Christ Child with such eager and careful anticipation?

Charles L. Wallis has written about this season in his book *Speaker's Illustrations for Special Days*. Many of the noble visions of the past have become blurred; but as Christmas approaches, new hope and new faith enter our hearts. The adventure of life is renewed and reinvigorated. We are given, as it were, a new spiritual lease on life; for a spirit of expectancy and enthusiasm comes to those who remember the hope that God in Christ brings to people."

Captain Gerald Coffer of the Air Force told how prisoners of war during the Vietnam war would tap out encouragement to each other by tapping on the cell plumbing. When the guy next to them was really hurting, they would tap out "GB" for "God bless." "GN" meant "Good night." Isaiah would tap out today "GP" for "God is present." Paul would tap out "G and P" for "Grace and peace" and Mark would simply tap "BA," "Be alert." Let us tap out the good news of Christmas to those in prison all around us.

Second Sunday In December

Isaiah 40:1-11	2 Peter 3:8-15a	Mark 1:1-8

Seasonal Theme   A time of expectation, anticipation, and preparation for the coming again of Jesus in Bethlehem and in our hearts.

Theme For The Day   The patience of God and the preparation for the coming again of Jesus into our hearts.

Old Testament Lesson   Isaiah 40:1-11   *Our Mighty Judge And Tender Shepherd*

Up to chapter 40 of the book of Isaiah is full of messages of judgment. But now begins an emphasis on restoration and deliverance. In this chapter we read of God's majesty. The word for comfort in verse 1 literally means "to cause to breathe again." So there is power as well as consolation. God is also promising in these verses that the people's time of trial is almost over.

In verses 3-5 we have "a voice" which was the term for a true prophet. The task was to get the people back into the right relationship with God.

Here is the heart of the passage being read on this day. All four Gospel writers related Isaiah 40:3 to John the Baptist: Matthew 3:1-4; Mark 1:1-4; Luke 1:76-78; and John 1:23. John prepared the way coming out of the desert. In this passage the whole nation was a spiritual wilderness.

In verses 6-8 we have God's voice calling out to Isaiah. Tell them, Isaiah, that people are interim and they change. And because God's word can be trusted, the people will be restored to their land. In verse 10, Isaiah often uses God's arm to refer to God's strength. These two characteristics are often found in this second portion of the book. God's strength and the image of a tender shepherd who carries and leads the weak sheep is a beautiful image of our God warning and loving people. One might translate, today, verse 3 as "roll out the red carpet." While the first part of this passage is judicial, the second part is very conciliatory. From the victor and strong judge we move to the tender shepherd. Nice!

New Testament Lesson   2 Peter 3:8-15a   *In The Meantime*

Verses 13-15a are key to our theme this Sunday. We are to be occupied in watchful waiting. And for us, according to Peter, there will be nothing to fear; but instead, we will experience joy. So this passage tells us that our God is not in a hurry and we ought to be patient and alert in our waiting for the parousia. I sometimes think Jesus never intended to give the impression that the parousia was very near. Perhaps he has already returned in the coming of the Holy Spirit at that glorious Pentecost. Perhaps instead of morbidly guessing about how and when he will return, we ought look for him and his kingdom in our midst already returned!

In verse 15a Peter reminds us that salvation is all wrapped up in that truth that our God is *patient*. Wow! That's a sermon in itself. How patient God has been with us sinners all down through the ages.

The Gospel   Mark 1:1-8   *The Proclamation Of John The Baptist*

We have here the start of John Mark's Gospel and the beginning of the public ministry of John the Baptist, cousin of Jesus. The facts, as we begin, are these:
1. John is the messenger Isaiah promised would announce the coming of Jesus (v. 2).
2. John's message was to repent and be baptized for forgiveness (v. 4).
3. John lived close to the ground as a desert person (v. 6).
4. John pointed beyond himself to the Messiah (v. 7).
5. Jesus' baptism would be far more spiritual than John's (v. 8).

It may not be wise to make too much of John's diet! Both the words "locust" and "wild honey" can be taken two ways. Locusts can mean the little bugs or a nut, the carob, which the poor often eat. The honey can be from wild bees or a kind of sap from certain trees. The point is only that John ate the diet of the very poor. So here is a humble prophet who pointed to someone beyond himself. It will preach.

Preaching Possibilities

All three readings are meant to connect together today. One way to connect them would be:
1. Isaiah 40:3 "A voice cries out: 'In the wilderness prepare....' "
2. 2 Peter 3:13 "We wait (patiently) for a new heaven and a new earth...."
3. Mark 1:3 "Prepare the way of the Lord ... he will baptize you with the Holy Spirit" (and 8)

We could go with an outline using all three something similar to this:
A. The Old Testament tells us God is patient and we should be also. And it says God is not only our judge but also our loving shepherd.
B. The New Testament: God is patient with us and we should be with God and with each other. And while we wait, we ought strive to be found at peace and without sin. And we ought celebrate that God is very patient with us so we can have salvation.
C. The Gospel: In John we have an example of how we should be while we patiently wait. That is, humble, living a life and speaking a verbiage of truth, and always pointing beyond ourselves to our Savior who was born in Bethlehem.

Possible Outline Of Sermon Moves

John the Baptizer is such a delicious character to describe and his message is so relevant for today that I will go with a character sermon. Here are some suggested moves:
A. Introduction: Describe some brave contemporary people who speak the truth regardless of the risk. Or tell of the advance man who comes ahead of a dignitary.
B. Describe John the Baptist as a great prophet who was advance man for Jesus.
   1. The man — tell about his birth and cousin relationship to younger Jesus.
   2. The content — it had been a long time since the people had heard a prophetic voice from God. Isaiah had promised one who would come and announce the Messiah. John is the man.
   3. The message — There is a need for profound sorrow for our sins. Repent, be baptized.
      He was believable because he spoke the truth boldly.
      He pointed to someone beyond himself — the Christ.
      He lived a simple life with the people of the land.
      He was humble and felt unworthy even to be a slave of Jesus.
C. Local application: Talk about what John teaches us about our church and community.
   1. How might we better prepare the way for Jesus to be born in our hearts and the hearts of others in our community?
   2. And what would John renounce today where we live and work and worship and play?
D. Now relate the end of John's life and ministry.
   1. He was in prison and sent his disciples to witness Jesus and his ministry first hand.
   2. He scolds King Herod for his adultery. He was beheaded by King Herod. See Mark 6:14-29.
E. See if you can come up with three or four resolutions which you can challenge the congregation to carry out as together you seek to make this a time of preparing for Jesus again. Then close with a prayer to God for help to do them.

Prayer Of The Day

Prepare our hearts, O God, for your birth in them again. And show us the way to prepare others for your arrival this year as well. In the name of the one who was born long ago in Bethlehem and wants to return to be with us again this year. Amen.

Possible Metaphors And Stories

We have a routine at our townhouse when special company is coming for a visit. The pieces of carpet which protect the main walking areas are all picked up and put out of sight. Some drawers are stuffed with papers which usually lie out. The old magazines are put into the garage. End tables are dusted. Extra rolls of toilet paper are in place. And we use Windex to clean the patio door, etc. How do we prepare for the coming of the Christ into our homes these weeks before Christmas?

At the seminaries where I have taught it has been the same everywhere. When the Bishop or the Board are coming, the faculty all put on suits and ties. The students wear better clothing. Welcome signs are put in place. And the food is much better in the dining hall. At the Lutheran Theological Seminary in Hong Kong, I noticed they polished the brass plaques which listed the donors to the school, just before the Parents' Night was held. We prepare in many ways.

Clarence E. Macartney writes: "A man must live," said the world to John the Baptist. But John answered, "No, a man must *not* live. A man may have to die in order that the true, the high, the spiritual, in him — the person of God — shall live." And here on a silver plate is the head of John the Baptist — to please the whim of a half-naked dancing girl, to satisfy the vengeance of a bad woman! John died, yet in the highest sense John lived — and lives — and the mention of his name today is like an army with banners.

In front of the town hall in Prague, one can see a great monument to John Huss who was burned at the stake in 1415 for heresy. Now in that capital city stands his bronze figure. That's the way it is. One generation burns them and the next builds a monument to the martyr's name. I wondered what a monument to John the Baptist would look like. Perhaps a strong man in simple garb, one defiant hand in the air pointing a finger and a second one cradling his own severed hand. He would stand firm like a linebacker for the Oakland Raiders football team.

From the Center for a New American Dream
Americans Seek Simpler Christmas Season
   91% of Americans feel holidays are too commercial and the idea of peace on earth has been forgotten by too many people.
   27% feel pressured to have a more elaborate or expensive holiday than they'd like.
   39% would save money or pay off debts if they didn't feel pressured to give gifts; 35% would give gifts anyway.
   58% buy fewer gifts or otherwise have simpler holiday celebrations than three years ago.
   33% of those who have simplified the holidays did so to have a celebration more in keeping with their family values; 12% did it to reduce stress; and 11% did it to have more time with friends and family.

Third Sunday In December

Isaiah 61:1-4, 8-11 1 Thessalonians 5:16-24 John 1:6-8, 19-28

Seasonal Theme A time of expectation, anticipation, and preparation for the coming again of Jesus in Bethlehem and into our hearts.

Theme For The Day Paul's advice on being true Christians and a faithful Christian congregation.

Old Testament Lesson Isaiah 61:1-4, 8-11 *Called To A Hope*

This passage, according to Luke, Jesus quoted in his hometown church in Nazareth. It points to one convinced of his call by God to bring the good news — the prophet senses that his call is one of release and hope for his people. Here is a view of the exile — a period of slavery — and then the day of delivery dawns. Not vengeance but, rather, rescue and deliverance. Verse 8 is a great thing to know about God. God loves justice and hates wrongdoing. Verse 10 follows with a promise of rejoicing in such a God. The whole passage is permeated with divine and delicious *hope*.

New Testament Lesson 1 Thessalonians 5:16-24 *Do's And Don'ts*

William Barclay writes that verses 16-18 list three marks of a genuine church: 1) A happy church, 2) a praying church, and 3) a thankful church. The passage is a simple list of good advice to Christians.
1. The *don'ts* are:
    a) don't despise the preacher's words
    b) don't dampen the spirit's manifestation
2. The *do's* are:
    a) rejoice always
    b) pray without ceasing
    c) give thanks in all things
    d) test everything
    e) hold fast to what is good
    f) abstain from all evil
3. As we try to do the above God will sanctify us and we will be held blameless at Jesus' coming.

The Gospel John 1:6-8 and 19-28 *It's John The Baptist Again!*

The writer of John seems to assume that the Jews knew John the Baptist. He also assumes that John was the forerunner of Jesus' public ministry. To many Jews, he was the pre-eminent prophet like Elijah or Moses. John denies all pretensions of authority. Still he is a voice from God (v. 6). He is the first witness and believer in Jesus. Verse 27 indicates John did not think of himself as even worthy of being a slave of Jesus. The point is made again, as in last Sunday's Gospel, that John always pointed to Jesus and never to himself. Jesus was the light. John witnessed to that light but was not the light (v. 8).

Because the Jews believed that Elijah was to be the forerunner of the Messiah, they asked John if he is Elijah. And then if he is a prophet. His answer to who he was is "a voice" and he quotes Isaiah 40:3.

Preaching Possibilities

This Sunday is a second opportunity to preach about John the Baptist. If you did not do so last Sunday, you could use the suggested outline of sermon moves from last week's writing. If you did, you might use the Old Testament Reading and address the social injustices in your community. It might be called *Isaiah's Church*. You could play with naming a congregation St. Isaiah's Methodist (or whatever) church and talk about what he would demand of a congregation named after him.

1. Where members are convinced of their call from God,
2. Where the Good News is proclaimed and celebrated,
3. Where God rescues others rather than judging and condemning them,
4. Where the injustices in the community are exposed for what they really are, and
5. Where the divine hope is evident and lifts us all up rather than beating us down.

Or we could use both the Isaiah and 1 Thessalonians passage and talk about what a "St. Isaiah and Paul Church" would look like.

I'll go with 1 Thessalonians 5:16-24 for a more topical approach.

Possible Outline Of Sermon Moves

Consider using my homiletical formula based on audience response to a sermon.

A. Build a fire — When I write an e-mail or a letter, the last few lines are usually those things I want to say and are rather distilled words. So with Saint Paul.
B. Build a bridge — We all are here in church and have our own ideas of what church and church people ought be like. Paul had his ideas also when he wrote to this little congregation in Thessalonica, which he had begun during his second missionary journey. He had to leave after only a few weeks because of the Jews' opposition. So he wrote them this letter of encouragement and sound advice. We'll want to take it seriously here also.
C. The point is this: we can apply Paul's advice on how to be a sanctified congregation, too.
D. The Thessalonian congregation were told two things they should not do:
   1. Don't despise the preacher's words, and
   2. Don't dampen the spirit's activity.
E. Read verses 19 and 20.
   And they were told these things they ought to be as a congregation:
   1. A happy congregation
   2. A praying congregation, and
   3. A thankful congregation.
F. Talk about each of these and their implications for your congregation. Read verses 16-18.
G. Example: Choose from the stories listed below.
H. So What? Now propose some new steps for the congregation to consider for improvement, such as establishing a prayer group or a social ministry committee.
I. Frame: Then return to the opening few sentences and the fact we all have different ideas about being a church. Perhaps Paul's is our best guidance. Close with the reading of verses 16-24 and then have a member of the church's governing board pray for each of the above points to be true here.

Prayer Of The Day

Help us to be a happy church, Jesus, and to pray often and rejoice often. And help us refrain from disregarding our preacher's inspired words and from dampening your spirit's influence in this, your congregation of faithful believers. In Christ's name. Amen.

Possible Metaphors And Stories

On Riverside Drive in Des Moines, there is a board suspended over the street just nine feet high. A little farther on is a railroad bridge nine feet above the road. So the board checks your clearance before you get to the bridge. The scripture and the church give us a clearance test for our Christian journey.

The Reverend James DeLange told at Sierra Pacific Synod the story of two office employees who for ten years kept turning off and on a fan in a ventilating shaft. They just couldn't agree. Then a remodeling project revealed the fan wasn't hooked up to the electricity all along. We may battle for years over things in the church and not be hooked up to the Christ as well.

Some jet engines on airlines have metal umbrellas on the back which the pilot can use like brakes. It changes the forward thrust to a reverse thrust with the same blast of air. God's *ruach* (or spirit wind) can be reversed to ugliness and hatefulness and dissension in a congregation as well.

Chim Pitch, one of my seminary students from Cambodia, wrote these *exact* words in describing his church and ministry: "We all help the poor, giving them sleeping net so that when they can escape from biting by mosquito, they can escape from many diseases ... As we break bread and drinking wine is in remember of Christ who died for us and as we are in His body. Therefore, let us love one another because we share in this same bread and drink in the same cup of wine."

Fourth Sunday In December

| 2 Samuel 7:1-11, 16 | Romans 16:25-27 | Luke 1:26-38 |

Seasonal Theme A time of expectation, anticipation, and preparation for the coming again of Jesus in Bethlehem and in our own hearts.

Theme For The Day Mary, the mother of Jesus, as our model of a trusting, faithful servant of God.

Old Testament Lesson 2 Samuel 7:1-11, 16 *God's Promise To David*

The promise is made by God that David would be given a great name and a people. Nathan tells David that God (the Ark) should have a permanent home instead of the portable tent and that David's name will be great and Israel will have its own country (v. 10). So here is the divine promise of a dynasty. The summary of God's care for David in verses 8 and 9 is nice. God has brought David from being a shepherd to making him a prince over the people. And God has been with him all the way. And now God will make his name great and provide a place for his people.

New Testament Lesson Romans 16:25-27 *Paul's Doxology*

This doxology is the ending of Paul's letter to the Romans and serves as a "homiletical frame" for the book in which the writer summarizes Paul's gospel. This is the gospel Paul preached and which Jesus brought to us all, counting on us to witness to others. It is one which strengthens us. It is a good news which was always there but brought to us by the Christ. It is gospel for us all and always has been for all humanity. And it is a gospel which calls for our obedience and deep faith. So this letter to the Romans ends with a grand song of praise.

The Gospel Luke 1:26-38 *The Birth Of Jesus Foretold*

This is no time to argue the doctrine of the virgin birth. Here are some things to notice. Mary and Joseph were engaged which, in that day, often included cohabitation. Jesus' lineage is also traced through Joseph (v. 27). Also, remember that when Mary was searching for Jesus at the Temple, she told him "your *father* and I have been searching ..." (Luke 2:48). Jesus is often referred to as Joseph's son (Matthew 13:35 and John 6:42). The important thing to note in this story is Mary's willingness to be used in a special way by God. The footnote to verse 28 says, "Blessed are you among women ..." from which we get the formulation of the "Ave Maria." And notice the Holy Spirit is a part of this special conception and birth. Mary calls herself "a servant of the Lord." Then there is a relative Elizabeth who, in her old age, is already six months pregnant (v. 36).

Preaching Possibilities

No matter how hard we try to save the "Christmas theme" until Christmas Eve, our people on this Sunday will be immersed in the Christmas story. So let's go with it.

The Old Testament may be a footnote about Jesus' being in the lineage of David and the promise God made with David. The New Testament Romans passage, I think, is more remote and difficult to use.

One could do a two-part sermon titled as "Today: God Begins The Process To Save Us" and, on Christmas Eve, "The Process Continues." One year I used the topical approach and preached on the theme: "Give my love to the family, Part I" and, on Christmas Eve, "Part II." In that case, we looked at the whole Christmas story as God's plan to give love to family (us) much like a person signs a letter or Christmas card or ends a phone call with the words, "Give my love to the family."

That love came through a willing servant, Mary.

That love came to people like us and to all the world through Jesus' birth, death, resurrection, and return in Spirit.

Possible Outline Of Sermon Moves

Title: Mary's Christmas *or* Pregnant With Whose Son?

A. Retell the Gospel story of the angel Gabriel coming to young, yet unwed Mary to tell her of God's plan to come into the world through her body.
   1. Mention how this was the fulfillment of what God had promised long ago in the Old Testament lesson: 2 Samuel 7:1-11, 16. Joseph was in the lineage of David.
   2. Tell how the advice of the angel in verse 30 is a big understatement! And how verse 28 is the basis for the familiar "Ave Maria." You may want to arrange to have it sung during this service.
   3. Call attention to Mary questioning how this could be done (v. 34) and then the answer that nothing is impossible with God (v. 37).
   4. Mention that the fact that Elizabeth was also pregnant fills in the story we have been looking at the last couple Sundays — for this is John the Baptist who announced Jesus' coming and also baptizes him.
B. Now move to what we can learn about God in this story.
   1. God is accustomed to using everyday people to accomplish God's will in the world. Here was an unwed teenager who would become God's instrument of Grace to the world.
   2. With God all things are possible if we will submit to God and seek to do God's will (v. 37).
   3. The point of Luke's account is not to prove Jesus' divinity because Mary was a virgin, but that the Holy Spirit was a part of the conception and gestation of this son who is and will be very special. "The child will be holy" (v. 37).
C. Discuss how there is a middle ground between the two extremes we see in the observance of Mary. Some worship her making a "holy quartet" and others give her no respect at all. We plead for a middle of the two extremes: a woman who calls for profound respect and devotion as Jesus' mother. And one who was willing to permit the will of God through the Holy Spirit to direct her life. A good example for us.
D. Now move to what we ought to do in our lives because of this lovely Gospel story.
   1. Pray that the same Holy Spirit might inspire us to more holy living, serving as God's instruments in the world.
   2. Work out ways to show profound respect for Jesus' mother as we observe Christmas this week. Perhaps a Madonna carving or picture predominantly displayed by our Christmas tree.
   3. Try to discern what our role might be to cause Jesus' birth again in our community.
E. Close with a prayer of thanking God for Mary and asking God to send the Holy Spirit upon us that we might be a willing servant like she was.
F. Arrange to have portions of the "Ave Maria" sung.

Prayer For The Day

We are thankful, dear Holy Parent, that you worked your glorious grace through Mary. Our prayer today is that you would help us to not only respect her, but also to become more like she was. In her son's name. Amen.

Possible Metaphors And Stories

I took my son and wife and grandson to the airport today. It's the day after Christmas and the place was jammed. The birth of the Christ Child still has the power to move people in great numbers all over the world!

A favorite story at St. John's, Des Moines, is about the Christmas Eve that Pastor Louis Valbracht wanted to let a doll down from the chancel ceiling and into a manger in front of the altar. He was preaching and gave the signal to Pastor Louis Piehl, who stood to the side with a fishing rod and reel to let the baby Jesus down. All went well until Piehl ran out of line about one foot short of the baby's being at rest in the manger. Finally Valbracht came out of the pulpit and pushed the doll into the manger, which pulled Piehl out into the chancel. He ran back to the wings, which pulled the baby back in the air, and so on! How many secular forces try to keep the baby from coming again this year?

One Christmas the movie *Back To The Future* was being promoted and shown. We often celebrate Christmas in a backward glance at what has been, without considering what this meant for our, and the congregation's, future.

In Sholem Asch's play, *Mary*, the author has Mary say to her other sons, "For as all rivers tend toward the sea, so every road to God must meet in him. He is the bread for those that hunger after it." In another passage she says to them, "Your qualities, however noble they may be, are the qualities of thirst. But your brother is the libation" (© 1949, G. P. Putnam's Sons).

Christmas Eve/Day

Isaiah 9:2-7 **Titus 2:11-14** **Luke 2:1-20**

Seasonal Theme God's putting on human flesh in the person of Jesus and coming into the world to demonstrate God's love for us.

Theme Tor The Day The birth of Jesus in Bethlehem means God will also come to us and understands how it is for us here.

Old Testament Lesson Isaiah 9:2-7 *A Promised Messiah Comes*

Matthew applied this scripture to Jesus who began his ministry up there in the northern part of Palestine (Matthew 4:15-16). Joy (mentioned 24 times in Isaiah) will be the result of this dawning new light. When the infant-Messiah comes, the tools of warfare will be decimated (v. 5). We won't need them because of Jesus' reign of peace. John A. Martin lists five things Isaiah tells us about the coming Messiah in his commentary titled *Bible Knowledge Commentary*.

1. He was born a child of one of the covenant people.
2. He will rule over God's people and the world.
3. He will have four descriptive names that will reveal his character: Wonderful, Counselor, Mighty God, and Everlasting Father. (This idiom is used to describe the Messiah's relationship to time, not to the other members of the Trinity.)
4. The Messiah seated on David's throne (Luke 1:32-33) will rule in peace and justice forever.
5. All this will be accomplished by the zeal of the Lord Almighty. The Messiah will rule because God promised it and wills zealously that the kingdom comes.

So it appears that Isaiah expected Jesus the Christ would begin his rule in one single event and then he would rule over all.

New Testament Lesson Titus 2:11-14 *God's Grace Arrives*

The grace of God has arrived and is training Christians a very different way to live from that of the enemies of the church. Verse 12 lists those new radical ways of behaving. Two things here are important to the Christmas message and are probably why this passage was chosen.

1. Jesus' birth means God's grace has appeared and brings salvation to all (v. 11) and,
2. He gave himself for us for our redemption and this makes us God's people (v. 14).

That's who this important Jesus is and what he will do.

The Gospel Luke 2:1-20 *A Close-To-The-Ground Story Of Birth*

The Roman occupying government took a census every fourteen years to find out who should be serving in the army and to know who should be paying taxes. The records from A.D. 20 to 270 are still in existence. It's an eighty-mile trip from Nazareth to Bethlehem. Places to stay were crude at best with only a fire for cooking and fodder for the animals. There were little stalls in a common courtyard where the couple would have stayed.

I like so much that the first announcement of Jesus' birth went to the often despised by the orthodox of the day: shepherds. They were, no doubt, simple men of the outdoors. These flocks may have belonged to the Temple authorities. There is a close-to-the-ground element in this tale which is appealing. So God's own son is born in common rough circumstances and goes on to live with the people, asking for no special accommodations. He thus knows us and our life circumstances.

The word "manger" meant where animals are fed, so it can mean either the trough that held the feed or the stable. Perhaps someone should tell the artist of Christmas cards these facts.

Preaching Possibilities

No matter how much we want to preach on the Old Testament description of the Messiah or the theology of God's grace arriving in the New Testament Reading, it's the birth narrative which our people have come to church to hear, read, and celebrate in all its simplicity and beauty. In my opinion, the reading of the scripture on this night or morning ought be the highlight of the service.

All three scripture readings can go together. The Isaiah reading describes the way the one promised might best be described. The Titus account tells us what the significance of Jesus' coming really is: 1) God's grace comes to us, 2) he comes to redeem us, and 3) this makes us God's own people.

Then the Gospel relates how it all began according to Luke. If we used all three, the major outline could look this way:
A. A wonderful counselor is promised (Isaiah).
B. The grace of God arrives to be our Savior (Titus).
C. A son is born to Mary and announced to the shepherds (Luke 2:1-20).

Possible Outline Of Sermon Moves
A. Retell the story. About the time Mary was due to have her son, she and Joseph had to travel eighty miles to Bethlehem for a census. This was for military conscription and taxes. Bethlehem was crowded and they had to stay where the poor without relatives often had to stay — an animal stable. So God's own son was born in the simplest of circumstances.

   The shepherds heard the good news first. It was lambing time for the temple flock so the shepherds were out at night watching the sheep. So they went into Bethlehem and saw the infant Jesus, the first ones to worship the Christ.
B. That event still affects us dramatically which happened 2,000 years ago, halfway around the world. We come to church at night, we bring families together, we buy many gifts and exchange them, we alter our schedules and take days off from work, we even sometimes embrace and speak words of endearment we haven't spoken for a long time. And many times we get panicky, are harsh with each other, feel tremendous pressure to match what others do for us, quarrel over who'll put up and take down the Christmas tree, and some of us preachers go night and day without sleeping and stretching our strength to the maximum to keep up with the frantic schedule at church and home. Then there are the Christmas cards. Our lives are changed even today by this event.
C. But what are the promises of the Christ's coming for us from the scripture?
   1. In Jesus, God brings the possibility of peace to the world of war. Talk about war at home and in other countries.
   2. There is a light for all those who live in darkness (Isaiah). List the dark now in our lives.
   3. God's grace arrives! Define it (Titus).
   4. This is the one who will save and forgive us (Titus).
   5. God knows what it is like to live like us (Luke).
   6. God celebrates God's birth with common people like us (Luke).
D. Now move to what our response ought to be because of this extraordinary event of Jesus' birth.
   1. We tell others about it and invite them to celebrate it with us like the shepherds.
   2. We could give an offering like the wise men to Jesus' church equal to what we spend on his birthday buying gifts for others and celebrating the birth.
   3. Like Joseph we ought to remain faithful to Jesus even when we are ridiculed by others for it.
   4. As Jesus was God's undeserved grace come to this world, we can be that grace to others who are searching for or resisting it.
E. Frame the sermon by returning to Luke's narrative. "It's a simple tale about simple people through whom God worked great things for all creation ... and for us. In that manger, something of God's strategy was beginning, which would bring us here tonight and change lives all over the world...." Luke knew it a wrote it down. We read it tonight.

Prayer Of The Day

We, too, have seen a great light in our world tonight and rejoice in it, O God. As the shepherds did, we pray we might be inspired to go from here and share this birth announcement with all who will listen. For coming into our world and living with and understanding us, we give you thanks. As you have promised, make us your people of light, grace, and peace. In the name of the one born in Bethlehem this night (day) we pray. Amen.

Possible Metaphors And Stories

Some years ago a submarine sank off the coast of Portsmouth, New Hampshire. When divers located it they heard a faint tapping from the inside. There were still some sailors alive inside the sub! In Morse code they communicated their crucial question: "Is there any hope?" The coming of the Christ at Christmas taps back: There is hope, for we have Emmanuel.

At the DeSoto Wildlife Preserve in Iowa, I observed a highway employee driving a pickup truck along the side of the road and, with a cloth, polishing the reflectors on posts marking the side ditch's edge. At Christmas we polish up again that light which came to us who live in darkness.

On an NBC news program, the director of the stage play *Annie* said, "I took a flat newspaper cartoon character named Annie and put flesh and blood on her." Martin Charnin was describing incarnation. The word became flesh. The word became flesh and blood in the person of Jesus.

On *CBS News* a man by the name of Al Copeland in New Orleans had millions of lights in his front yard for Christmas. One thinks first, how beautiful! Then it's reported the neighbors are suing him for disturbing the peace. I think the light of Christ is like that. When we really let it shine, those who prefer the darkness will always complain and try to extinguish the light.

Fifth Sunday In December

Isaiah 61:10—62:3   Galatians 4:4-7   Luke 2:22-40

Seasonal Theme   God putting on human flesh in the person of Jesus and coming unto the world to demonstrate God's love for us.

Theme For The Day Like Old Simeon and Anna, we, too, can see the Christ in our church and our faithfulness.

Old Testament Lesson   Isaiah 61:10—62:3   *The People Prepare For The Lord*

Because God had blessed them, the saved remnant will celebrate. Salvation and righteousness are mentioned as clothes which these saved wear. And as a bridegroom and bride wore special things to represent their joy, so these saved by God are decked out. As we begin chapter 62, we see an expanding of chapter 40 and the preparation being made for the coming of the Lord. The Lord announces he will work for the people of Jerusalem until her righteousness is recognized by the rest of the world. And those who live there will be like a crown of the Lord by the way they live (v. 3)

New Testament Lesson   Galatians 4:4-7   *The Spirit Of His Son*

Paul's proof we are God's children is the instinctive cry from our hearts when we are desperate. We call out to God as a child does to a parent. And Jesus' birth is God's action to adopt all of us as God's children. Even more beautiful is the fact that God has sent the spirit into our own hearts (v. 6). All this changes our status from slaves to children of God, which makes us God's own heirs.

The Gospel   Luke 2:22-40   *Simeon And Anna See Jesus*

Jesus' parents now take their firstborn son up to the temple in Jerusalem to do the things good Jewish parents were required to do, like offering a sacrifice. In the temple was one of those old deeply spiritual saints named Simeon. He had wished to see the Messiah before he died. His words of worship for this privilege are verses 29-32 from which we get our liturgical *Nunc Dimittis*. No doubt Simeon's words to them about their son, they remembered later (vv. 34-35). Next Anna appears and also recognizes Jesus as special. What beautiful, devout people hanging around there in their church to whom God reveals the special nature of Jesus. Then, it's back to Mary's hometown where Jesus grew into adulthood.

Note: There are several customs the Holy Family would have carried out during their trip to Jerusalem. On the eighth day, Jesus would be circumcised and then given the name announced by the angel Gabriel. The other Old Testament ritual carried out was the purification of Mary as put forth in Leviticus 12:2 ff. Forty days after childbirth, the mother is to offer a sacrifice and then is considered "clean" again. This was often called "the churching of women."

One might summarize the entire passage with the words, "... salvation has come," and that it is for all people. Simeon and Anna announced that the hope of salvation will be worked in this very special child. We can now add to the Christmas story and shepherds, inn keeper, Mary and Joseph — two old temple faithfuls: Simeon and Anna.

Preaching Possibilities

Depending on what you have done thus far in your preaching the Christmas story there are at least four ways to go this Sunday.
A. Use the Old Testament Lesson by itself as an exegetical sermon.
B. Use the New Testament Reading by itself as an exegetical sermon.

C. Use the two above with the following outline:
  1. The clothing of the saved (Isaiah)
  2. Living like a crown on the head of God (Isaiah)
  3. Being an adopted child of God (Galatians)
  4. No longer slaves, we are God's children
D. Simeon and Anna see their Savior.

If you have already covered the Christmas story well in narrative, consider simply going through the Galatians reading verse by verse. It is pregnant with gospel.

Galatians 4:4 — God's love is so great, he sent his son to us.

Verse 5 — This is God's plan begun at Christmas to save us and adopt us into God's family.

Verse 6 — God touches our hearts with God's spirit.

Verse 7 — We are freed from slavery and become heirs in God's family.

Possible Outline Of Sermon Moves

Title: Jesus Goes To Church *or* Simeon's Song

A. Begin by recounting the last few days of Christmas in your home. Then tell of Christmas in the lives of Mary and Joseph.
B. Now explain the story is not over yet. Luke tells us what happened next. Read Luke 2:22-32.
C. Tell about the temple requirements that Mary and Joseph had to carry out.
D. Then introduce Simeon — his hopes and faithfulness. He was so filled with joy he could now die content. Be sure to read his words of worship.
E. Introduce Anna as another character in the Christmas story.
F. Now tell what this beautiful story teaches us this Sunday in our own church.
  1. We, too, can see Jesus by being in his church.
  2. There is great joy in faithfulness and devotion to our church.
  3. This infant was destined to do great things on God's behalf in Jerusalem and in our town and church also.
  4. Our challenge is the same as Nazareth's.
     We must grow him up far beyond a baby in a stable to one filled with wisdom and with God's favor upon him (Galatians 2:40).
G. Now frame the sermon by returning to your opening sentences about the celebration of Christmas in your home and your church.

Prayer For The Day

Keep the spirit of Christmas alive in us and in our congregation, dear Holy Parent. Might we, like Simeon and Anna, know the joy of Jesus' presence in our church and our daily lives. And help us to grow him large here that he would be much more than a cute baby in a cow stall. Fill our hearts with your spirit that we might also worship the one who has come to save us. Amen.

Possible Metaphors And Stories

In the made-for-television show, *Inside The Third Reich*, a little boy saw soldiers at the train station coming back from the front. So he slept on the hard floor in order to sympathize with them. After this discovery, the father said, "Son, I hope I can always remember how much I love you right now." The God person comes incarnate to sympathize with the human existence.

Julie Walters, 34, an actress making the film *She'll Be Wearing Pink Pajamas*, announced during a nude scene that a new ruling by the Screen Actors Guild was that all technicians must also get nude during the filming. The naked truth was that it was a bluff; she told them after they had done it. Jesus came to earth to strip down just like us and share what it's like to be fully human — it's called the incarnation.

In Shakespeare's *Henry IV, Part One,* Falstaff claims he is still capable of changing his ways and says: "I have not forgotten what the inside of a church is made of."

John H. Blough writes: "The track of a three-toed dinosaur has been found on the top of a coal strata high up on the cliffs near Grand Junction, Colorado. People have never seen the animal itself, but they have seen its footprint. People have never seen God; but God has left his imprint, evidence of God's creatorship, upon the face of the world. The Babe of Bethlehem is the greatest evidence of the real character of God" *(Speakers' Illustrations for Special Days).*

First Sunday In January

Jeremiah 31:7-14　　　　　　　　**Ephesians 1:3-14**　　　　　　　　**John 1:1-18**

Seasonal Theme　　　God putting on human flesh in the person of Jesus and coming into the world to demonstrate God's love for us.

Theme For The Day　　God's word has put on human flesh and given to us grace upon grace.

Old Testament Lesson　　　　Jeremiah 31:7-14　　　　　　　　*The Return Home*

With great joy the Israelites return home from all over. I find great hope in the promise that no one will be too far away for God to restore him. And no one will be too insignificant either (v. 8b)! The trip God will make easy also (v. 9b). This is another exodus, this time into Israel. Then Jeremiah uses the father/son relationship to demonstrate God's great love for God's people. (See Hosea 11:1, 8.) And God will increase their material blessings. It will be like the abundance of a lush, well-watered garden (v. 12b). All this will produce their mourning into joy (v. 13).

New Testament Lesson　　　　Ephesians 1:3-14　　　　　　　　*A Song Of Praise*

This passage from verse 3 to 14 is all one sentence in the Greek! We ought consider it a lyrical hymn of praise. For preachers, perhaps it is most helpful to list the basic truths contained in Paul's long, run-on sentence.
1. We are blessed with spiritual gifts.
2. God chose us to be God's servants.
3. God chose us to be holy and blameless.
4. God adopted us as God's own children.
5. We are redeemed and forgiven through God's grace. (The word here for "redeemed" means to ransom us. It is the purchasing of a prisoner of war for his freedom.)
6. Jesus brought us also wisdom and common sense.
7. The experience of the Holy Spirit is a promise of the joys of heaven.

The Gospel　　　　　　John 1:1-18　　　　　　　　*The Word Became Flesh*

In the beginning of his Gospel, John states that only in Jesus is it made clear to us how God is and always will be. Jesus also reveals to us how God feels toward us. In Jesus is life for us which the world has not extinguished. Verses 6-9 are there because in Ephesus there were people who only knew John the Baptist's baptism. Verses 10-12 reminds us that the Christ was not recognized by many when he came in flesh. But for those who did recognize him, God gave great power to become God's own children. And we cannot make ourselves children of God; we must enter into the relationship God offers us.

Now the great verse of the fourth Gospel: verse 14. It's a new idea about God. God would become a human being. That this God would appear in creation in a form we could see God. This idea was fought by the Docetists who tried to teach that Jesus was just a shadow or ghost; God, but not real flesh and blood. There are three great theological words in this verse: glory, grace, and truth. Verse 16 seems to have an added punch of abundance of grace: "... grace upon grace"!

Preaching Possibilities

A lot depends on what you did Christmas Eve and the first Sunday after Christmas as to what will go well today.

With the John 1:14 verse, we have an excellent opportunity to speak of the theological truths of what it meant for God to put on the body of the human Jesus. If we have covered the "Christmas Message" well enough by now, you might want to do an exegetical sermon on the New Testament reading. Since, in its original form, it was all one sentence, we would do well to take it a phrase at a time and tell what that truth means to us. Or, you could do a sermon based on "Great 'verb words' of the Bible."

Old Testament: Proclaim, praise, save, ransomed, comfort

New Testament: Blessed, chose, adopted, redeemed, gather, destined, believed, and promised

Gospel: Witness, testify, the light shine, so all might believe, came to his own, gave power, became flesh, have received grace

Using all three readings we could take one thought from each: Old Testament — God gathers us too and invites us back home. New Testament — God has redeemed us and made us God's own children. Gospel — God has become a human and lived among us.

Possible Outline Of Sermon Moves

A. Introduction: We have survived another Christmas season. We have reveled again in the beautiful story of the birth of Jesus to Mary and Joseph. So, now that we have felt Jesus in our hearts, it's time to understand what God was trying to accomplish in all this.

B. Text: John, the Gospel writer, helps us understand just what Christmas is good for, anyway. Read John 1:14.

C. Main Moves:
  1. That which God had been promising, is put into action. Theory becomes reality.
  2. God's Word took on human flesh so God knows what it is like and we know what God is like.
  3. God lived with us humans on this earth, so is no longer detached and distanced.
  4. God in flesh helps us understand the grace and glory of God.

D. Our Response: Like John the Baptist, we are witnesses to this new light in our still dark world. We can now celebrate the power we have to become God's children. We have grace upon grace, too!

E. Frame it by returning to your opening comment about getting through another Christmas season and understanding why the first Christmas was (and is) so important to us.

Prayer For The Day

Dear God who became a human being like us, we pray today a prayer of thanksgiving that we've made it through another Christmas season again this year. And so have you. For that we really rejoice. You know what it's like to be human like us. We also rejoice that the boy Jesus will grow up and become a savior for all our sins. We pray in his name. Amen.

Possible Metaphors And Stories

A group of professional people posed the question to a group of four- to eight-year-olds: "What does love mean?" The answers they got were broader and deeper than anyone could have imagined: "Love is what's in the room with you at Christmas if you stop opening presents and listen." "God could have said magic words to make the nails fall off the cross, but he didn't. That's love." "There are two kinds of love. Our love. God's love. But God makes both kinds of them."

I was seated on a plane today, wearing a black suit and clerical collar. Ron Zalenski came to me and wanted to sit in the empty seat next to me. He had driven out from his home in Wisconsin to go hunting. His wife called to tell him their twenty-year-old son, Stephen, was in a car wreck, barely alive in hospital. They were Roman Catholics. Seeing me on the flight, he asked, "Please, let me sit next to you. I'm afraid."

There is often a ministry of presence called for when words are of little use. Just be there and stay close.

At the training camp for the Pittsburgh Pirates in Bradenton, Florida, there are four diamonds, a pitching machine, and a game going on with a junior college. And there are the old retired players who suit up and mingle with the young active players in the dugout and behind the home plate screen. They urge the younger ones on. So the incarnation when God suits up as Jesus, a human, and is with us.

In order to get a permit to teach in the People's Republic of China, I had to submit copies of my university degrees. And those copies had to be authenticated by a notary. Jesus is the authentication of God, how God is and what God wants for us. Now, can we be the authentication of Jesus? After seeing the original, can we be a copy?

Second Sunday In January

Genesis 1:1-5 **Acts 19:1-7** **Mark 1:4-11**

Seasonal Theme Jesus grows up and it begins to dawn on some who and what he is.

Theme For The Day Jesus' baptism and the beginning of his public ministry.

Old Testament Lesson Genesis 1:1-5 *The First Day*

God's first creative action is to produce light. Out of chaos and darkness is created light and it's the very first day. In our scripture, the dark and light are always symbolic of evil and good. Israel would think in these terms — that God is light. The Hebrew *bara*, which is translated as "created," is only used in the Old Testament to refer to God's activity. Questions about the origin of chaos, God's activity before creation, and whether creation was out of nothing, are really unimportant to this story. On the first Sunday of Epiphany it's the light and darkness that pertains, as does order out of chaos.

New Testament Lesson Acts 19:1-7 *Baptism In The Holy Spirit*

Here we have the story of Paul at Ephesus re-baptizing twelve disciples who had been baptized in John's name rather than that of Jesus. It's a good reminder for us that John's baptism was one of repentance (v. 4) and not of Jesus Christ. So we must be careful as we consider John's baptism of Jesus in the Jordan and remember that this was not Christian baptism. Jesus had not yet gone to the cross and worked the atonement for us. These twelve were likely members of a sect of John the Baptist. Paul now has the Apostolic power to give the Holy Spirit. And the proof of this is the speaking in tongues and prophesying (v. 6).

The Gospel Mark 1:4-11 *Jesus' Baptism By Cousin John*

The real beginning of the Gospel story is this event when cousin John baptizes Jesus in the Jordan. Mark doesn't seem to be interested in what Jesus did before this time. We ought not make too much out of John's apparel. It was simply that of an ascetic of the day. The same garb was used of Elijah in 2 Kings 1:8. Eating locusts and wild honey was the common diet of the poor Bedouins. The origins of Christian baptism are obscure. We really don't know whether Jesus practiced water baptism or not. John says in 3:22 and 4:1 that he did. But in 4:2 it is denied! We don't believe he needed it from John for forgiveness of sin. Matthew tries to deal with this problem in Matthew 3:14-15. Perhaps the best we can say is in this experience Jesus became aware of who he was and was convinced of his mission on earth.

Preaching Possibilities

The customary baptisms which take place on this day in many parishes will probably dictate that we go with the Gospel story. If not, both the Old Testament and the New Testament Readings can stand alone.

The Old Testament could go with the major theme that our God is able to make order out of chaos. God did in creation, God did in bringing Jesus into the world, and God still does by giving us God's presence through the Holy Spirit.

There is a novel approach to the New Testament Reading. We can tell the story of the twelve and then ask if the Holy Spirit is a part of our baptismal life — or how incomplete is our baptism if we have never taken it any further than an initiatory rite and cute name-giving ceremony. The whole idea of infant baptism being affirmed (confirmed) in the rite of "affirmation of baptism" may be addressed. Or, perhaps, it's an opportunity to talk about the Holy Spirit. We might even write a letter from Paul to twelve in our congregation asking them about their baptism and their discipleship afterward — as the sermon for the day.

Putting the three readings together would be tougher. It might outline this way:
A. Old Testament Lesson — God creates light out of darkness.
B. New Testament Reading — Paul conveys that light through the Holy Spirit.
C. The Gospel — Jesus becomes that light to the very dark world and to us.

Possible Outline Of Sermon Moves
A. Introduction: Retell the story of John's baptism of Jesus.
B. Text: Read Mark 1:11 to complete the retelling.
C. Moves:
   1. This was a time of resoluteness for Jesus and can be for us and our baptism as well.
   2. This was a time of recognition for Jesus and can be for us and our baptism as well.
   3. This was a time of benediction for Jesus and can be for us and our baptism as well.
D. This was a time of empowering for Jesus and can be for us and our baptism as well. Notice the Spirit is like a dove, the symbol of gentleness and peace. Oh, how we need be empowered with this Spirit for our ministries yet today.
E. A story or hymn between each of the above four moves will help drive home the truth.

Prayer For The Day
Creator of all the universe, who called order out of chaos and light from darkness, bring your Holy Spirit on us as Paul did in Ephesus and as you did at your son's baptism in the Jordan. And, as you did for him, affirm and empower us in our daily ministry where we work, live, and play. In Jesus' name. Amen.

Possible Metaphors And Stories
Former Bishop Blevins announced at the funeral of his 24-year-old son who had committed suicide: "Today we will claim Bob's baptism."
We do remain God's child regardless of our behavior.

On the road to Calmar, Iowa, a front yard had ice all over shrubs, grass, everything. This was April 19. Someone had left the lawn sprinkler on overnight and all had frozen into ice.
Could we scatter the water of Baptism like that? And let it plainly show and look beautiful?

When we moved from Des Moines to Berkeley, California, every single item had a tag fastened to it with its own number. It's Mayflower's system in case something gets lost along the way. There is a lot number and individual number for each item. As we moved into the President's mansion, every piece was checked off as received. Would that we could be so diligent in tracking and keeping from losing every one of the baptized!

Gregg Davidson of Trinity Lutheran Church, Marshalltown, Iowa, came to our observance of Jesus' Baptism. We all made name tags which gave our name and date and place of our baptism. Gregg forgot to remove it and went next to Vets Auditorium for a basketball game. He said everyone was so friendly and even called him by name! At our Baptism we are named and we join into a worldwide family of God.

Note: Today we begin using Corinthians for the Second Reading. It proceeds fairly in order of the two books. Here is a little background about these two letters of Paul written to a congregation with which he struggled:
Corinth, a wealthy trading center, is located in Southern Greece and was well known for its vice in the ancient world. According to the *New Revised Standard Version of the Bible*, "The letter revolves around a series of problems in Christian conduct permeating the church at Corinth. Thus it deals with progressive sanctification, the continuing development of holiness and character."

Third Sunday In January

1 Samuel 3:1-10 (11-20)　　　　1 Corinthians 6:12-20　　　　John 1:43-51

Seasonal Theme　　Jesus grows up and it begins to dawn on some who and what he is.

Theme For The Day　　God calls us to ministry and discipleship. That is a call to a certain kind of life as well.

Old Testament Lesson　　1 Samuel 3:1-10 (11-20)　　*The Call Of Samuel*

1. Verses 1-10 — Samuel had been serving in the Levitical ministry at Shilo. Now God was speaking to him directly. He was in the temple watching the burning lamp. At first he thought the voice was that of Eli. But Eli knew it was calling his successor so advised him to answer and obey.
2. Verses 11-20 — Eli's sons were wicked and he did not chastise them so God needed to remove Eli's family from the priesthood. In Samuel, God had found a man to whom he could entrust the ministry. The sign that he was a true prophet was that what he said came true (v. 19). Thus, a new era is underway. God's revelation through priest and Ephod was over and revelation through the prophets was beginning.

New Testament Lesson　　1 Corinthians 6:12-20　　*Christian Guidelines*

This passage by Paul to the Corinthians is packed full of guidance for Christian ethics, i.e., right and wrong for us disciples of Jesus.

1. Verse 12 — The Christian must not do some things even though it is perfectly legal to do so. We must be aware of any vice, habit, etc., that controls us rather than we control it.
2. Verses 13-15 — Our bodies are precious and we should be good stewards of their use.
3. Verse 17 — We are bodily united to Christ through the Spirit and must do all things which reflect well on his body, the church.
4. Verse 18 — To have sexual relations outside the marriage is to sin against our own bodies.
5. Verse 19 — We must treat our bodies as we treat a holy temple. It belongs to God and must be treated so.
6. Verse 20 — What we do physically should glorify God.

Paul meant these guidelines for the quarreling Corinthian Christians who lived in such an evil and tempting place. But, they will work for us today as well! In our American culture, verse 12 especially speaks to me. Often we Christians must refrain from a behavior, not because it is illegal or not our right to do so. We must refrain because of how it makes the Christian faith look to others. Now that will really preach!

The Gospel　　John 1:43-51　　*The Calling Of Phillip And Nathaniel*

This reading fits nicely with the Old Testament Lesson about yet another call. This time a brother's witnessing to his brother and his technique may still be the most effective witness in our day. Not a lecture but, rather, an invitation to "come and see."

1. Verse 46 — Phillip's emblem contains a basket because of his reply to Jesus.
2. John 6:7 — when he fed the multitude. His was a very close to the ground, practical approach. We meet Phillip at the last supper, also. He still wanted proof. See John 14:8-14. John speaks of Nathaniel here but the other evangelists call him Bartholomew, which means "son of Tolmai." We know almost nothing at all about him. After we are told how he became a disciple, we read nothing except that he came from Cana in Galilee. Perhaps he was present at Jesus' first miracle of changing water into wine at the wedding feast. His symbol is three flaying knives which indicate his martyrdom.

Preaching Possibilities

The New Testament Reading will easily stand alone as we preach on "Paul's Right or Wrong for Christians." You could use the principles laid out in the comments on the scripture above as an outline.

The Old Testament call of Samuel will also stand alone as we address the subject of "God's Call and Our Response."

But perhaps the best approach to today's readings is to use all three with the Old Testament and talk about what God's call really is and where and when God does call us. Then the Gospel can give us guidance about who God calls, like Phillip and Nathaniel, and into what kinds of discipleship God calls us today. Then use the letter by Paul to talk about the standards required from one called by God, like the following.

Possible Outline Of Sermon Moves

A. Introduction: Begin by telling about your call into the gospel ministry.
B. Now move to retelling Samuel's call from the Old Testament Lesson.
   1. Now relate how God usually calls us through other people, as Samuel was through Eli.
   2. Now explore the ways we might be the instrument through which God calls others into discipleship.
   3. Explore how a youth program in your parish might be effective in calling young people today as happened in church to Samuel.
C. Move to the Gospel and Nathaniel and Phillip.
   1. Talk about how "the call" is to average people like us and like them.
   2. Speak of why Phillip's answer was so inspired and effective: not a lecture but an invitation to come and see.
   3. Talk about how important it is when the ones invited do come and see — that they see something convincing!
D. Go to Paul's advice to the Corinthians and talk about into what kind of discipleship we are called. And what kind of behavior is expected. You might want to add some of Jesus' admonitions to Paul's list: turn the other cheek, love and pray for enemies, go the extra mile, and be kind to one another.
E. Now frame the sermon by returning to your story about your call. Finish by stating that God calls us all to ministry in the world — not just the preacher. Invite them to come and see and bring others to see, as well.

Prayer For The Day

Like Samuel, O God, help us to hear again and again your call. Like Nathaniel and Phillip, call us in our daily lives to be your disciples and follow you. And like Paul, show us the way to behave in this tempting world and culture, that others would want to accept our invitation to come and see. In Christ Jesus' name. Amen.

Possible Metaphors And Stories

Ruth, one of our older Hong Kong students and a recent Chinese Christian, won an award for writing the best Christian tract. In accepting the award, she told how she had opposed Christianity all her life and now that she had become a Christian, she wrote the gospel tract hoping that her husband would read it and believe. He was not there to see her receive the award.

In *Henry IV, Part Two*, Shakespeare has Henry say: "The oldest sins the newest kind of ways?" And in *Julius Caesar*, III, Caesar says, "The evil that men do lives after them." And in *Much Ado About Nothing*, III, "They that touch pitch will be defiled."

As I prepared to return to the People's Republic of China, I had to apply for a work visa again. On St. Martin's Day, I had to take my University diplomas to a notary and have her validate the copies to be submitted with the application. She first checked the original and then put her seal on the copy to show it was an authentic copy. Being in Christ and, as Luther called us, "Little Christ to our neighbor," how can we be authenticated as genuine disciples? Are we authentic copies of those early called disciples of Jesus?

After the lacing of Tylenol Extra Strength with poison in Chicago, there began to be what the police called "copycat" crimes. We ought to live out our call as copycats of the good ministry of others like Saint Francis, Joan of Arc, and Mother Teresa. And perhaps in the practice of our discipleship we might inspire others to "copy" us.

Fourth Sunday In January

Jonah 3:1-5, 10   1 Corinthians 7:29-31   Mark 1:14-20

Seasonal Theme   Jesus grows up and it begins to dawn on some who and what he is.

Theme For The Day   The call to discipleship and the strong desire to escape it as Jonah tried to do.

Note: This week we begin reading Mark's Gospel "in continuum" or in sequence for the next six Sundays. It would be good to tell today a little about this book of the Bible and its author. See the introduction to the book in the *New Revised Standard Version* (p. 41).

Old Testament Lesson   Jonah 3:1-5, 10   *Jonah's Story*

John D. Hannah tells the following about Jonah in *The Bible Knowledge Commentary* (p. 1461):
1. His name means "dove."
2. He was the only Old Testament prophet to attempt to run from God.
3. Jonah was one of the four Old Testament Prophets whose ministries were referred to by Christ (Cf. Matthew 12:41; Luke 11:32).
4. The events in the book of Jonah took place some time in Jeraboam's reign (793–753 B.C.).
5. He was a contemporary of Hosea and Amos (Cf. Hosea 1:1 and Amos 1:1).
6. Nineveh was located on the east bank of the Tigris River, about 550 miles from Samaria.
7. Before Jonah arrived, two plagues had erupted and a total eclipse of the sun occurred in 763. Perhaps this explains the Ninevites' response to Jonah's message around 759 B.C.

Hannah says that God's message in this book to Israel was:
1. God's concern for the Gentile peoples.
2. The book demonstrates the sovereignty of God in accomplishing God's purpose.
3. God's sinful nation Israel is rebuked by the response of the Gentiles.
4. Jonah was a symbol to Israel of her disobedience to God and indifference to the religious plight of other nations.

All this rich background ought make for rich "local color" in preaching on this fascinating Old Testament book.

New Testament Lesson   1 Corinthians 7:29-31   *Priorities For Christ's Coming*

We continue reading from Paul's letter to the Corinthian church in which he tries to give pastoral advice to a quarreling congregation. Paul's advice here seems to belittle marriage. But we know at least later he writes strong support for it in his letter to the Ephesians (5:22-26). We must read this passage, keenly aware that it is dominated by Paul's expectation of the Second Coming of Christ at any time. Everything must be set aside to prepare for that event. So he gives this advice.

The Gospel   Mark 1:14-20   *The Beginning Of Jesus' Ministry*
1. Verse 15 — often pointed out by scholars as the linchpin of the Gospel: The time is now, God's kingdom is here; we should repent and believe the news.
2. Verses 16-20 — the account of Jesus calling his first disciples. The story works in preaching because it shows a proper response to Jesus' call to us. When the call comes, we should drop everything and respond.
3. Verses 18 and 20 — Mark seems to want to emphasize that instantaneous response of these first disciples. I'm more impressed by the fact that they were average working men and Jesus called them at their work. Notice Jesus' call to them offered them a job to do: "... fish for people" (v. 17).

Preaching Possibilities

The Jonah account and the Gospel will work together today. It is about response. Jonah's response was to try to run away and escape the responsibility. Simeon, Andrew, James, and John's response was to follow. One might even include the 1 Corinthians reading with the idea that the response ought not be postponed by other considerations.

The Jonah story is a wonderful opportunity to use interesting narrative preaching telling Jonah's story. If last week you talked about "the call of God," then here is a great opportunity to dig into the Old Testament. Otherwise, you might want to go with the Gospel, which best fits the Epiphany theme of Jesus maturing, beginning his ministry, and it dawning on some who he is and the significance of his message.

We have in verse 15 the message and in verses 16-20 the call to discipleship to take it out to the world.

Possible Outline Of Sermon Moves

A. Begin with a story of a time when you or someone you know tried to get out of a responsibility. Then tell Jonah's story of God giving him a task and his trying to run away.
B. Now move to the fact that we also live in a Nineveh and tell how all the symptoms are here now: crime, unfaithfulness, greed, murder, corruption, hate, etc.
C. Then move to the truth that, like Jonah in Nineveh, we also have a responsibility to announce the need for repentance and the fact of God's grace and forgiveness.
D. Move again to say we are often just like Jonah and want to escape from being the one to bring the message. Perhaps not so much physically, but we certainly do mentally as we rationalize all the excuses for not being the one through whom God speaks to God's people.
E. Illustrate this by pointing to the Gospel and the call of those four disciples and how they didn't find excuses not to follow and bring the gospel to others. A second illustration might be Paul's advice in the New Testament Reading to put this above everything else.
F. Frame your sermon by returning to your opening story of trying to get out of something and urge the congregation to join you in accepting the call, taking out the message, and following the Christ.

Prayer For The Day

On this day, when you come especially close and call us to following and serving, help us to avoid giving excuses but, rather, to report for duty. Forgive us, Holy Parent, for the many times you were counting on us and we let you down. We pray to you today for new resolve to follow your lead and serve faithfully. In Jesus Christ's name. Amen.

Possible Metaphors And Stories

There used to be an ad on television for Lexus cars which began with the question: "Ever miss a great opportunity?" They then showed a young man suggesting that this water is so good it ought to be bottled and sold. His companion makes fun of the idea of bottling water and sneers, "Yeah, we could call it *Larry's Water*. Hey, man, water is free." The same idea is played out making a silicon chip and starting a chain of gourmet coffee shops. Then another car, Chrysler, tried using the same approach of missing a great opportunity when the person turned down the chance to purchase waterfront property, internet stock, etc.

We all miss great opportunities to witness to the faith and follow the Christ on God's behalf. So did Jonah, almost!

The Hartford Insurance Company shows pictures of natural disasters and how they've got us covered and then say the slogan: "Whatever life brings, bring it on!"

The Chaplain at PLTS, Ben Borson, once told of a man who hated his wife's cat so much that he took it out and drowned it. To soothe his wife's feelings he offered a reward for the "lost" cat. Those who knew he didn't like the cat ridiculed him for offering such a large reward. He replied, "If you know what you know, you can take some risk." Knowing of crucifixion and resurrection, we can risk a venturesome discipleship.

A motto for John Deere lawn tractors is "Some settle for second best." Then the following are compared: a rowboat and a yacht; a hose, a tub, and a swimming pool; a tiny camera and one with a telephoto lens; and finally a little power mower compared with a John Deere.

Wow! The second best in our discipleship often crowds out the possibility of the very best.

First Sunday In February

Deuteronomy 18:15-20   **1 Corinthians 8:1-13**   **Mark 1:21-28**

Seasonal Theme   Jesus grows up and it begins to dawn on some who and what he is.

Theme For The Day   Just as Jesus healed the possessed person in church, he will also heal us. And we must include all kinds in the congregation.

Old Testament Lesson   Deuteronomy 18:15-20   *A New Prophet Like Moses*

The people had asked at Horeb that there be a line of prophets after the greatest one, Moses. The ultimate one would be Jesus Christ, who was the mediator of the New Covenant. The leaders of Judaism were still looking for the completion of this promise of Moses (John 1:21). Peter preached that they no longer needed to look for it as Jesus had now come (Acts 3:22-23). Similar predictions may be found in Genesis 49:10-12 and Numbers 24:17-19.

New Testament Lesson   1 Corinthians 8:1-13   *Food Offered To Idols*

Here is what I like to call "Paul's stumble theory." The new Christians evidently wanted to know what to do about meat which their hosts served them which had been offered to idols. Paul establishes his great Christian ethic that even though it is quite often all right for a Christian to do something, we must refrain from doing that which causes another person to stumble. Drinking alcohol would be a prime example for our day. Another way of saying this ethic is that there are things we do and can handle okay; but we should refrain if they offend, or get into trouble, those much weaker than we are. And whatever we do, even if it's acceptable behavior, we must always consider how that behavior makes Christianity appear to others.

The Gospel   Mark 1:21-28   *The Man With The Unclean Spirit*

Our Gospel continues in Mark where we left off last week. As Mark tells it, this is the first event of Jesus' ministry. This happened in Capernaum on the northern shore of Galilee where it seems the disciples were headquartered. You can still see the ruins of this synagogue and, nearby, the round foundation of an ancient church that was built over the home of Simon Peter's mother-in-law, where it seems Jesus and the disciples often stayed. The scribes mentioned in verse 22 were experts in the law of the first five books of the Bible. The unclean spirit in verse 23 simply means a demon.

The scribes, who often taught, would quote what the Pentateuch said. When Jesus taught, he would say, "... This is what I say." It astounded everyone for him to claim such authority. It was personal authority and they just were not used to that. It was like a breeze of fresh air — and it caught their ear. The Greek word translated as "authority," literally means "out from himself."

The Jews and all the ancient world believed in demons, who got the blame for almost all that was wrong with a person. Most people connected these demons with Genesis 6:1-8 and 2 Peter 2:4, 5. The word for demons is *mazzikin* which means one who does harm. In my younger years of theological study I was sure this phenomenon of demon possession could be explained through the science of mental health. After seeing for myself demon-possessed people in Liberia, West Africa, Suriname, South America, and on the Island of Sumatra, Indonesia — I have no answer to it. I have laid my hands on their heads and prayed and they have been relieved. In Buji church, Shenzhen, People's Republic of China, nearly fifty witnessed such an exorcism and also "... were all amazed" (Mark 1:27).

Preaching Possibilities

If you have not done so yet, the New Testament Reading is an excellent opportunity to preach on the ethics of Paul. A sermon titled "Right and Wrong for Christians" using the passage from a week ago and this one will provide close to the ground rules of behavior for Christians.

A. Two weeks ago (1 Corinthians 6:12-20), we learned that we must guard against any vice which controls us rather than we control it. We ought to treat our bodies as temples of the Holy Spirit. And we must do all things which reflect well on the body of Christ, the church.
B. Last week (1 Corinthians 7:29-31), we learned that above everything else that is in our lives, we must put Christ first, just as if he were coming again tomorrow.
C. Today (1 Corinthians 8:1-13) even though something is okay for us to do, we must refrain if it will cause someone else to stumble. We must always look at how our ethics make Christianity look. Your people will love this kind of close to the ground advice.

I don't see a very strong connection with the Old Testament Lesson to either the New Testament Reading or the Gospel.

Possible Outline Of Sermon Moves

For a complete manuscript on this miracle, see my "When Demons Come to Church" in the book, *The Miracles Of Jesus And Their Flip Side* published by CSS Publishing, 2000.

The outline goes like this:

A. Retell the story from Mark in your own words. Tell of the ancient belief of demon possession and how Jesus accepted the teaching of the day and accepted what the man believed. As he stilled Galilee's storm, he stilled this troubled man. We all need that kind of calming down from time to time.
B. Speak of demons in our contemporary lives today and how Jesus can rid us of all those as well. Assure your people that Jesus is interested in our mental health as well as our physical health.
C. Now look at the flip side of this miracle. When someone raised a ruckus, they were not removed from the congregation.
D. Then talk about the demonic power which still works against God — and often in church! Often the role of our faith is to cope with that which we may someday, but do not yet, understand.
E. Now frame the sermon by returning to the Mark account and the way you began. Perhaps here you can imagine what the man did the rest of that Sabbath in Capernaum once the demons were gone.

Prayer For The Day

Rid us, O God, of those distortions and powers that ruin our lives and others' lives, also. Help us to be a congregation that accepts all those who are deemed "possessed" in our day. Show us our behavior that works against your will here and at home. And accept our thanks for the way Jesus, the Christ, still comes into our lives, willing to drive out the evil and restore sanity to our being. In Jesus' name. Amen.

Possible Metaphors And Stories

I witnessed demon possession several times in Liberia, West Africa, as I was preaching through an interpreter into the Loma language. Wozi, in the interior, is a center of animism. They had laid a vine around the village to keep me out. During my preaching the "lion" came to town to try to scare my young listeners away from hearing the gospel. They also played drums and danced outside the building to drown out the gospel proclamation. But through all the fear and superstition, we were heard and the Holy Spirit moved some to believe. Still, there is the demonic, which tries to drown out the gospel in our communities.

In Lloyd C. Douglas' play about the Passion, there is a character who claims the crucifixion did more than demonstrate God's love, did more than save and forgive us. He said, "There was something about the man that made us into a tight little band of blood brothers and sisters." Someone has said, when asked, "Am I my brother's keeper?" that the answer is, "No, you are more than that. You are your brothers' brother and sisters' sister." Now, that will preach.

We still have help when evil grips us and demands
to raise a ruckus in God's holy sanctuary
there is a freeing which empowers us once again.
We invite with welcome all sorts and kinds of humanity.   — JLS

Clarence E. Macartney writes in his *Macartney's Illustrations*, "The people in the time of Jesus — in their ignorance — thought an insane man was demon-possessed by the devil. I'm not so sure that they were not right. When I read the morning paper and see what men and women, made in the image of God, have done, I am not certain that people today are not possessed of the devil. When I see what people do under the bondage of drink, and lust, and hatred, and anger, and jealousy, I am not at all certain that the evil spirits no longer take hold of a person's soul."

Second Sunday In February

Isaiah 40:21-31 **1 Corinthians 9:16-23** **Mark 1:29-39**

Seasonal Theme   Jesus grows up and it begins to dawn on some who and what he is.

Theme For The Day   Jesus will heal us and give us strength for the day. We can be the channel through which others are healed.

Old Testament Lesson   Isaiah 40:21-31   *Strength For Our Weak Times*

We have, in this passage, the incomparable power of God as Creator. We are assured that God knows all about our struggles and most trying experiences and appoints the time when God will help us. We have available to us that same creative power used by God in calling the universe into existence. I have quoted verse 31 often in the hospital. To "... wait for the Lord ..." is much more than patience. It is complete trust which is fueled by our hope. To know this is to be strengthened depending on God's power. I like the idea of "... mounting up with wings like eagles," for it promises we can rise above our troubles. We can overcome our fatigue, we can regain our strength ... and not faint. If Christ is real to us, we can actually experience this delightful strengthening and overcoming.

New Testament Lesson   1 Corinthians 9:16-23   *Ministry Method And Responsibility*

If we are preaching to clergy we could list here advice Paul gives to preachers. The preacher is under compulsion to preach the gospel. Our reward for doing so is that we might make it free to all and live under it ourselves. We are to be servants to others. We must be many things to many people in order to relate the gospel to them that they might have salvation. And we get to have a part in the blessings as well. So here is the ministry presented by Paul as a privilege, a responsibility with a great pay back which calls for a clever methodology in order to reach all we can with our very good news.

The Gospel   Mark 1:29-39   *Healings At Peter's Home*

The story continues as we read from Mark following last week's reading. This time we learn of Jesus' healing of Simon Peter's mother-in-law and many others at her home in Capernaum. Then in verse 35 we see Jesus embarking on a preaching tour of Galilee. Verses 29-31 tell of the healing of this mother-in-law, whose response to the healing was to get up and serve. Then we learn there were many demons cast out and many people cured who had diseases. Notice in verses 35-37 the press of the crowd caused Jesus to need "quiet time" for himself. There seemed to be a rhythm to his life which we could also emulate: into the real world to help and then retreat into a quiet place for prayer and reflection. Notice, too, that Jesus did not need a large audience to do his miracles. Here is a private one in this nearby home after synagogue.

These are nice stories by Mark, for they portray Jesus not only as a person of wise, inspired words, but also as a person of action. I do think it wrong to try to prove Jesus' divinity by telling of these miracles. What they prove is that our God is one of compassion, willing to act in response to our need.

Preaching Possibilities

The Old Testament Lesson will stand alone in bringing a message of encouragement and hope using the healings at Capernaum as proof and examples of how much God cares and wants to help.

The New Testament Reading could be used by itself by first talking about the characteristics of ministry and minister and then move to the truth that all the baptized are called to be ministers out in the world all week long.

The Gospel might best be divided into two sermons. The first would be verses 29-31 on this private healing. The second could be verses 32-39 with an outline as follows:
A. The compassion of Jesus for us when we are possessed and/or ill. Use the Old Testament premise to "fly like an eagle."
B. The prayer life of Jesus as an example for us. If God's own son needed quiet time and prayer, think of how much more we need it.
C. As Jesus proclaimed the message, so must we. We all have "neighboring towns" where we proclaim the Good News and are blessed in the proclaiming of it.
D. Jesus began in the synagogues (v. 39). Are there messages that need to be proclaimed in our churches as a starting point? And what are the demons that want to haunt our congregation?

It's a bit of a stretch, but one might use all three readings for today, collecting their inspiration under a theme of "What God does":
A. God gives us strength and wings of eagles (Isaiah 40:31).
B. God blesses us as we share the gospel (1 Corinthians 9:23).
C. God heals and has compassion (Mark 1:31 and 34).

Possible Outline Of Sermon Moves

A manuscript of a sermon based on this Gospel, titled "Blessed Are The Mothers-In-Law," is in my book *The Miracles Of Jesus And Their Flip Side*, published by CSS.
A. Begin by telling of the setting of Capernaum and Galilee, the Synagogue and the mother-in-law's home nearby.
B. Tell the story again of the exhausting morning in the Synagogue. Then retell today's story of the healing from possible malaria of Peter's mother-in-law.
C. Make the point that it's just like us men not to even know her name.
D. Make the point that her response to being healed was to *serve*. We often ask for help but forget the proper response when we get it.
E. Talk about what a congregation would be like made up of folks like this mother-in-law. And notice that Jesus didn't need an audience to praise him for doing the healing. We shouldn't either.
F. Call attention to the fact that Peter was married. You can't get a mother-in-law any other way!
G. Another lesson here might be to emphasize there is strength for tired Christians. Quote Isaiah 40:28, 29, 31. And probably the one most blessed that day was the mother-in-law, not as much for her healing but for the joy of serving!
H. Now close by reading again Mark 1:29-31.

Prayer For The Day

You have blessed us and healed us and saved us in so many ways, O God. Help us to get up and serve all this next week, that others would know your compassion through us and that we would be mindful of our need for quiet time and prayer that we might always gently celebrate your presence in our hectic lives. In Jesus' name. Amen.

Possible Metaphors And Stories

We, too, have been saved that we might also serve
the Christ who comes into our humble homes.
There he has compassion for our present fevers.
Ours is a ministry of witness to take into the world.   — JLS

I recall living in a mobile home park while attending a seminary in Springfield, Ohio, years ago. Our neighbor was quite poor and lived in a small, rundown home. He had asked me to pray that he and his wife might, one day, have a more comfortable, long, double-wide model. One day when I came home from classes they were backing in a beautiful new unit on his lot. I was so happy for him as he explained he had received an unexpected inheritance from a distant aunt — so the new trailer. I remarked that we should have a time that evening to thank God for this wonderful gift. He replied that it would not be necessary as they had their mobile home free and clear now!

"Three years after this miracle, I can picture a bent over, faithful, old Capernaum woman with scoured hands from years of hard kitchen work, who was unlike most Galileans, malaria-free, and from her humble home made her way each day to the nearby synagogue to do what she could as a woman back then to help with the ministry. On the Passover Friday, about 3 o'clock, she wailed a mournful cry as she had earlier that morning at cockcrow. On the first day of the next week, early in the morning, there was a different sound, which also came from her. As it echoed through the wadies and skipped across the mirror-like lake's surface, it sounded almost like a disguised hallelujah. This early matriarch and saint of the little synagogue moved again more quickly than she had for several years. There would be fish to catch and fry ..." (*The Miracles Of Jesus And Their Flip Side,* Jerry L. Schmalenberger, CSS Publishing Company, 2000).

Third Sunday In February

2 Kings 5:1-14   1 Corinthians 9:24-27   Mark 1:40-45

Seasonal Theme   Jesus grows up and it begins to dawn on some who and what he is.

Theme For The Day   The compassion of Jesus and the trust and confidence necessary for him to do miracles in our day.

Old Testament Lesson   2 Kings 5:1-14   *Naaman Healed By Elisha*

Now the story of the prophet Elisha healing the Aramean commander of dreaded leprosy: a disease which degenerated one's body and eventually meant death. There was no known cure. Naaman could continue his duties as long as he could do them. An Israelite slave girl served Naaman's wife and was concerned about Naaman's welfare. She told him of the prophet Elisha who could heal leprosy. So the Arimean king sent his general to the King of Jordan with lots of gifts and a letter asking that Naaman be healed.

The Israelite king did not even think of the prophet as one who was always opposing him. Elisha told him to send the leper to him and he would heal him. Naaman was angry because of the off-handed way he was treated. And he didn't like to bathe in a river inferior to his own hometown river. Naaman eventually humbled himself and carried out the prescription of Elisha. Not only was he healed, but his skin was made like when he was a young lad! That's a story begging to be told with all the local color.

New Testament Lesson   1 Corinthians 9:24-27   *Running The Race*

Paul uses the metaphor of an athlete who trains and then runs a race. He advises to train and then run in such a way that you not only run but win. And that takes a lot of discipline and self-control. In our "training" for the Christian life, he claims we, like the athlete, must use discipline and training and give it everything we've got. His point is that as an athlete will punish himself for a winner's wreath, we ought be willing to do even more for the prize of eternal life with God. And notice verse 27b warns against telling others to train and forgetting to do it ourselves.

The Gospel   Mark 1:40-45   *Jesus Heals Another Leper*

Because leprosy is dealt with in the Old Testament Lesson and the Gospel today, let's take a further look at it. E. W. G. Masterman in the *Dictionary of Christ and the Gospels* writes, "No other disease reduces a human being for so many years to so hideous a wreck." The name comes from the Hebrew word *Zara'ath*, which could be translated "scourge." Oftimes in the Bible, it could be seen as psoriasis. A description is found in Leviticus 13. Treatments for the patient are specified in Leviticus 14. Often victims were cured: Moses, Exodus 4:7; Miriam, his sister, Numbers 12:10; four lepers in 2 Kings 7:3-11. In the Gospels, we have Jesus curing leprosy in Matthew 8:2-4 and Luke 5:12-15 and also the ten in Luke 17:11-15. The Old Testament often claims the disease is a result of sin. Three things to notice about Jesus in this story:
1. He *touched* the leper and helped one in tremendous need.
2. He *had compassion* on one who had no right to ever speak to him; and
3. Jesus had him *follow the prescribed ritual* of his religion.

Preaching Possibilities

The Old Testament Lesson and the Gospel are stories which will work well together, although each one could stand alone as well. The New Testament Reading seems far removed from the other two and, if used, is best used on its own. It does say a lot and is worth considering. Perhaps it can be dealt with in the following manner:

Title: Training for Discipleship
A. Begin by telling how athletes, both women and men, train to be at their best for their participation. If you did so in college or somewhere, share that with your listeners.
B. Announce that today's passage from 1 Corinthians 9:24-27 is Paul's advice on how to train to follow Jesus and live a life of discipleship.
C. Explain how the Corinthians would know all about races and training for them as the Isthmian games were held there and these were second only to the famous Olympic games.
D. Move to what Paul is trying to say by using this familiar metaphor of athletes and races.
   1. These athletes use a lot of self-discipline and energy just to win a temporary crown of laurel leaves. Shouldn't we be willing to do even a lot more to win the award of eternal life? This is the main point of this paragraph.
   2. William Barclay, in his *Daily Study Bible*, says that we have here Paul's philosophy of life:
      a. Life is a battle.
      b. To win the battle demands discipline.
      c. In life, we need have a goal and focus on it.
      d. We need be convinced of the worth of that goal.
      e. And we cannot save others unless we are in control of ourselves.
E. Witness to what the above advice for discipleship means for you to change and set as a goal in your own life.
F. Frame your sermon by returning to your opening comments about training for an athletic endeavor and how that also is important in a disciplined disciple's lifestyle.
G. A note: *I'm a little uneasy about this passage and Paul's advice and hope you, too, will be careful about this becoming a sermon advocating works-righteousness and gung-ho driving of oneself beyond reason.*

Possible Outline Of Sermon Moves
A. Begin by telling in the first person the Old Testament account of Naaman's healing through the eyes of his wife's servant who was from Samaria and knew of the prophet Elisha.
B. Explain how this story teaches us about what God will do for us if we trust and believe in the Almighty. Explain that a certain humbleness is required in order for our healing to take place.
C. Move to the Gospel and the healing of the leper by Jesus, telling the story in the first person through the eyes of Peter, relating it to his mother-in-law, (or through the eyes of the leper).
D. Reinforce from the Old Testament story that trust and humility were important in this man — he knelt and was sure Jesus could do it (v. 40).
E. Return to Peter's words as to what this teaches us about Jesus.
   1. He has compassion (v. 40).
   2. He reaches out to all sorts of people (v. 41).
   3. He was no grandstander (v. 43).
   4. He respected all the liturgical prescriptions of his day (v. 44).
F. Sum it all up by telling what these two stories speak to you, and what you challenge the congregation to join you in doing this week at home, work, and play.
G. Frame the sermon by taking on the little servant girl's voice, again imagining the celebration of Naaman's new skin. Then the voice of Peter telling how the one he saw healed just couldn't keep quiet about such a great thing in his life. It will preach.

Prayer For The Day
Dear Holy Parent, give to us the trust and humility necessary for you to do great things *to* and *through* us. Help us to bathe in the water of our baptism each day so we also might be cleansed. And make us bold to witness to your mighty healing power just like that little servant girl and the leper Jesus healed who couldn't keep quiet about it. Amen.

Possible Metaphors And Stories

(For the New Testament Reading) In the California Gold Rush, they often claimed, "I have seen the elephant." The saying comes from the story of a man driving produce to market and seeing, for the first time in his life, an elephant. It was a circus parade. It was the first time for the horse, also, causing it to bolt and overturn the wagon. The man lost his produce. The owner said it was worth it for he had "seen the elephant." It became a metaphor for paying the price for a worthwhile goal (from Joann Levy, author of *Women in the California Gold Rush*).

We tried playing the sound of a crow in trouble to keep thousands of crows out of our trees around the church. It worked for a few weeks; then they came back and just ignored it. Steve Gunson explained how crows have strong tendencies to form habits like where they roost, and so forth. So they get used to about anything, even the cry of their own for help. And could it be of us as well?

Del Monico told on radio: A man seated in a wheelchair at the Vatican suddenly got up and walked away. Everyone was amazed and shouted and praised God for a miracle. But the man hadn't been ill. He was just resting for a little but in a vacant chair.

God is accustomed to doing miracles every day and they appear quite commonplace. On the other hand, some things which seem miraculous just aren't explainable yet. God most often works within God's own natural law.

In a small discussion group on miracles, some questioned whether there really were any. A wife of a recovering alcoholic responded: "I don't know why you find these miracles so hard to believe. I saw beer turned into furniture in my own home."

Fourth Sunday In February

Isaiah 43:18-25   2 Corinthians 1:18-22   Mark 2:1-12

Seasonal Theme   Jesus grows up and it begins to dawn on some who and what he is.

Theme For The Day   Jesus wants to forgive us our sins and un-paralyze us so we might bring others to him and overcome the barriers which prevent it.

Old Testament Lesson   Isaiah 43:18-25   *God Forgives That Which Is Undeserved*

This passage begins with the advice to not just dwell in the past (v. 18) and then announces something new God is about to begin in verse 19. The literal translation is "even now it sprouts up." God's future mercies are already beginning. The former president of the Lutheran Theological Seminary in Hong Kong tells how, when he came across this very verse (v. 19), he decided he was to build a new seven million dollar seminary on Tau Fong Shan mountain. And he did!

Verses 22-24 list the many acts of devotion which the people had neglected to do. Then, verse 25 announces that even though they had neglected to worship God or deserve God's mercy, God would forgive them and "... not remember their sins" (v. 25). Whew! That's a relief!

New Testament Lesson   2 Corinthians 1:18-22   *The Down-Payment*

A little background is necessary to understand what Paul is writing here. Paul had promised to revisit them. But things got so bad that he postponed it so as not to cause them more pain (v. 23). Then his enemies charged him with not being able to count on him and that his "yes"es were sometimes "no"s. In addition, they said that if they couldn't rely on Paul's little promises everyday, they could not trust what he had told them about God. This passage is Paul's answer. He states simply that we can trust God's promises. And that the Son of God, Jesus Christ, proclaimed to them by himself, Timothy, and Sylvanus was a "yes" (vv. 19b-20). Great! "Amen" means "it shall be so" and we finish our prayers with it, confident that because of what Jesus did, we can count on God's promises — Jesus is our guarantee (v. 20b). Verse 22 tells us of Paul's belief that he was commissioned as an apostle by the Holy Spirit's seal. The Greek word is *arrabon* which is a down-payment, the first installment of a contract. So the kind of life we have in the spirit is the first installment of our life in heaven. How about that "yes" promise, folks? Our life in the Spirit now promises and pledges greater things to come.

The Gospel   Mark 2:1-12   *Jesus Heals A Paralytic*

The background is worthwhile. Jesus was back at Simon Peter's mother-in-law's home in Capernaum, which served as his headquarters when he was in Galilee. It was the same house that is, perhaps, 100 yards from the synagogue where he drove the demons out of the possessed man. And it is the home in which Jesus healed Peter's mother-in-law of malaria. So now the people crowded in to see this wonder-worker. This house was flat-roofed with a side stairs outside to the roof. The roof was made of sticks and mud: easily removed.

We don't know if this paralytic even wanted to be there. And we don't know on whose faith he was healed, if any. Verse 5 seems to indicate that it was the mat bearers' faith. It would be an interesting happening if Mark means that this man was healed on the basis of someone else's faith and not his own. In my book, *The Miracles Of Jesus And Their Flip Side*, I have dealt with this story at length. The fact that Jesus connects sin and illness and forgives the man's sins is an interesting thought.

The scribes must be considered here. The paralyzed man is healed and all they can do, instead of celebrating the miracle, is criticize Jesus, that he had the audacity to forgive sins (v. 7)! See my first metaphor listed after the Prayer For The Day. What a sight it must have been in Capernaum after one of their own would get up and walk again. Then I wonder who had to patch up the roof that evening on the little house? Perhaps Peter and Andrew, supervised by their mother-in-law.

Preaching Possibilities

Isaiah 43:18-25: Perhaps we look back too much rather than look forward. What new things is God doing in our lives and in our congregational life together? We also neglect to worship God as those did back then. Still, God removes our sins and will not hold them against us. Selah!

2 Corinthians 1:18-22: If you want to use the New Testament Reading, consider the following points: God's "yes" is always stronger then the world's "no." Jesus is the great "Amen" to God's promise to forgive us. God's Holy Spirit in our hearts is the first payment to us as to how it will be for us in heaven. To what things and promises does Jesus say Amen for us?
1. We have forgiveness for our sins.
2. God knows our struggles and wants to help.
3. We can start over again and again.
4. We are part of His body, the church.
5. We are secure right into eternal life.

Possible Outline Of Sermon Moves

A. Begin by picturing brothers Peter and Andrew patching a hole in their mother-in-law's roof, supervised by Peter's wife.
B. Review the events leading up to this miracle of healing of someone let down by his neighbors through a hole in the roof:
1. John baptized his cousin, Jesus, in the Jordan.
2. Jesus was tempted and decided on his style of ministry.
3. The disciples were enlisted.
4. Demons were driven out in the synagogue.
5. Peter's mother-in-law was healed of malaria.
6. Sick and demon-possessed people were brought to Jesus.
7. The crowds got bigger and bigger.
8. A man with a skin disease was cured and told everyone.
9. Now this story of guilt, forgiveness, overcoming obstacles and severe criticism while doing the right thing.
C. Retell the story of the four bringing this man to Jesus and letting him down through the roof.
D. Now ask — "What can we learn from this event?"
1. It pays not to give up, like these four mat bearers.
2. Jesus will forgive our sins, which can paralyze us, too.
E. Refer to Old Testament Lesson — Isaiah 43:19-25
F. Now consider the flip side of the story. There is the misery of those scribes who came to criticize rather than celebrate. And there is the presence of Jesus in our homes. Jesus teaching in the synagogue down the street is one thing — taking him home where the forgiveness and healing can take place is another!
G. Then imagine what the celebration was like in Capernaum that night and finish by returning to Peter and Andrew finishing patching the roof and the appearance of their mother-in-law making the final inspection.

Prayer For The Day

God of compassion and forgiveness, help us to overcome the barriers which keep others from Jesus. Show us those whom we might be able to bring to Jesus, and who need his compassion and forgiveness. And God, forgive and remove the sins which now paralyze us as a congregation and as your individual daughters and sons. We pray in Jesus Christ who is our Amen.

Possible Metaphors And Stories

The Germans have a very strong word, *schadenfreude*, which means "gloating" or "the human impulse to take pleasure in the misfortune of others," according to an article in *Newsweek*. *Schaden* means to do harm or damage. *Freude* means pleasure of joy. I have been looking for this word which seems to me to describe well a tendency in our sinful human nature. It instructs and warns me — *schadenfreuden*!

At the Cathedral of the Virgin of Guadeloupe in Mexico, there is a long narthex hall full of hand-painted plaques representing the miracles occurring in individual lives. An example is a picture of a boat on fire, or a car hitting a pedestrian, or a person getting out of a hospital bed.

What miracles of our members could we paint on the walls of our church narthexes?

A hole-patched Capernaum roof reminded many who saw
one paralyzed with guilt and near bitterness of life,
whom friends willingly transported on invalid's stretcher.
We, too, must give up fault finding and celebrate healing.   — JLS

I went to the optometrist. I learned a blind spot in my vision is where the optic nerve is. So I took a Humphrey peripheral vision test, punching a button when a dot appears. We certainly all have our own blind spots, recognized or not, about ourselves or others or certain circumstances.

First Sunday In March

| 2 Kings 2:1-12 | 2 Corinthians 4:3-6 | Mark 9:2-9 |

Seasonal Theme Jesus grows up and it begins to dawn on some who and what he is.

Theme For The Day Jesus and discipleship appears in a whole new light. The Spirit also waits to change us.

Old Testament Lesson   2 Kings 2:1-12   *Elijah Ascends*

Elisha, here, is acknowledged as Elijah's successor. He inherits both his mentor's mantle and spirit. As Elijah parts the water of the Jordan, we are reminded of Moses and Joshua. This story of his death connects us to the Transfiguration story when the disciples claimed a vision of Elijah who was taken up to heaven in a special way. Because of this special way to die and go to heaven, we do not have an earthly grave to point to (Mark 9:4-5). Perhaps the best way to approach this translation to heaven and parting of Jordan's waters is to try to discern why it's in the Book of Kings and what its author is trying to convey in its preserving, rather than prove or explain anything by the magic performed there on the river bank. You decide.

New Testament Lesson   2 Corinthians 4:3-6   *Light For Transfiguration*

I'm sure this reading was selected because of its reference in verse 4 to the "... light of Christ," which connects with the Gospel's description of the religious experience for Jesus and his disciples up on a "high mountain," which describes Jesus' attire as "... dazzling white" (Mark 9:3), and as seeing the "... glory of Christ." There is a verse here, however, that really jumps out at me. Verse 5 gives us a great focus for our ministry and our preaching: Not to call attention to ourselves — but to Christ. And we proclaim ourselves not in some grandiose role, but as "... your slaves for Jesus' sake." After saying that, let us return to the quotation of Genesis 1:3 in verse 6 and bask in even more light for preaching on the Transfiguration: Light in our hearts and light of the knowledge of the Glory of God in the face of Jesus Christ. There's the Transfiguration.

The Gospel   Mark 9:2-9   *The Transfiguration Of Jesus*

It's a familiar story of a deeply religious experience recorded in Matthew, Mark, and Luke's Gospels and referred to in 2 Peter 1:17-18 by the eyewitnesses. *The Interpreter's One-Volume Commentary* says of this experience: "The Transfiguration represents a special attempt of God to cure the spiritual blindness of the chief disciples, Peter, James, and John." Scholar Lindsay P. Pherigo then adds, "To regard (this) as a misplaced resurrection account, as others do, adds problems, though this is a possibility."

To add to the Corinthians connection, notice that the word for transfigured is exactly the same word used in 2 Corinthians 3:18 for "being changed." Look at 1 John 3:2-3 and Romans 12:2 for additional back up of this passage.

While it is not named specifically in the Gospels, Mount Tabor, an isolated hill in the Valley of Jezreel, six miles southeast of Nazareth and Jesus' home, is the traditional site of this event.

Jesus is first called "Rabbi" (Master) here. For me, that is the key for opening up the event. Jesus took his three best disciples on a spiritual retreat upon Mount Tabor and he taught them from Elijah and Moses, the great spiritual fathers who had not died a natural death. Upon learning these truths, these three saw Jesus in a whole new light. It must have been an educational *and* spiritual experience, which they tried their best to describe in human terms. The light and white almost always represents heavenly things in the scripture. Now they began to understand. This Jesus, their teacher, was none other than the promised Messiah, God's son. With that understanding, he took on a whole different appearance.

Look at Peter. He didn't know what to say (v. 6)! But he soon recovered and wanted to build a church there. No way! They had to get down the hill and serve. A young boy needed their help (v. 17). That would be their monument to this new revelation from God. It must change the disciples' appearance as well as Jesus'.

Preaching Possibilities

Obviously, all three scripture readings will go together today. But one could just use the Old Testament Lesson to talk about why the author of Kings wanted the story of Elijah and Elisha told: to establish the passing from one generation to another the mantle of prophecy; to establish the fact that the prophets were more than right preachers, etc.

Let me outline various homiletical approaches to these passages:
1. Use each one by itself.
2. Use the Gospel, backing it up with passages from the Old Testament Lesson and the New Testament Reading.
3. Use all three readings approaching it from why the author of each wrote it down to be shared down through the ages.
4. Use all three, sharing with your listeners what each passage means to you and your spiritual faith.
5. Preach an exegetical sermon on: 2 Kings 2:9, 2 Corinthians 4:5 or 6, or Mark 9:7.

Possible Outline Of Sermon Moves

A. Begin with a story about you (or someone else) going through a dramatic change in your (his/her) life. Or use a story about a person or a place changing in physical appearance.
B. Now re-tell the Gospel story in Mark 9 in your own words, not yet revealing the response of Peter or the going back down the hill.
C. Relate what we learn from this experience:
   1. When we study the prophets and scripture, there is power in them to change how we appear to others and how we live our lives.
   2. As we come to worship and pray and study the scripture, who and what and how Jesus is can change for us, too: More than a good, kind person; he is God's son — a Savior.
   3. We, too, need spiritual retreats and up close religious experiences to inspire and instruct us for our discipleship.
D. Return to the story with Peter's response. Point out that it is still our temptation to remain on the hilltop of life and refrain from going into the valley to help others and do our ministry.
E. Ask the congregation to define its "valleys" where we should all go to minister. Name examples you think of like the hungry to feed, AIDS victims to be comforted, homeless and battered to be sheltered, marriages struggling, etc.
F. Now frame your sermon by returning to the person or thing you saw change dramatically and finish up with a prayer that you and these listeners might also be changed as dramatically in the days ahead.

Prayer For The Day

Change us, too, O God, that we might see Jesus in a whole new light and be different because of the experience. And because we have been on this spiritual mountain today, now show us the dark valleys of our day and neighborhood, that we might go into them bringing the light of your loving concern. In Jesus' name. Amen.

Possible Metaphors And Stories

On United Airlines Flight 527, from Chicago to Oakland, we had to stop in Las Vegas to get more fuel. The high, strong jet stream we were bucking all the way across the country had used more fuel than usual.

We, too, often need refueling because of bucking the forces that work against us. It's a good reason for regular worship and personal devotions. It's not wise to gamble running on empty.

Way back in the Liberian bush of West Africa, "Mama Ganna" (Amanda Gardner) wanted me to see the church she had built. It was made of mud packed between bamboo sticks and would seat about twelve. I thought it was the ugliest little hovel I had ever seen! Then she confessed that she had built the whole thing by herself with her ninety-year-old hands because, she said, "Where I live there will be a church." Suddenly that little mud hut with a crude cross protruding out of the tin roof took on the appearance of a great cathedral.

We recognized a police officer, Gary Cowger, of Des Moines, Iowa, who saved a little boy by diving in and pulling him out of a lake. A police officer who was a member of the congregation, Dan Dusenbery, was asked to read the scripture. He was very frightened to do so, but did because I asked him. After the service at the door I overheard Dan telling Gary, "The next time, you read the Bible and I'll jump in the lake." There are times which call for reading the word and there are times just to jump in.

A memorial to firefighter Don Mackey, who died fighting forest fires in Montana, was left untouched when the fire roared through the surrounding forest. CNN showed pictures of the black charred ground and trees all around the memorial. It burned up to it and stopped. It's as if God said, "That's far enough; this is sacred ground." There are places like that, aren't there?

Second Sunday In March

Genesis 9:8-17 **1 Peter 3:18-22** **Mark 1:9-15**

Seasonal Theme   Jesus makes his way toward Jerusalem and the cross that we might have undeserved forgiveness for our sins.

Theme For The Day   The baptism, temptation, and beginning ministry of Jesus.

Old Testament Lesson   Genesis 9:8-17   *Noah's Covenant*

So, after the flood, God makes some promises to the survivors. The Hebrew word for rainbow is *qeset,* which is also the word for a battle bow. So the rainbow is like a battle bow hung against the clouds and standing for peace. And in verses 15 and 16 this symbol will remind God of the covenant God has made with the people. And the covenant is universal (see v. 17). So the rainbow becomes an important symbol that our grace-full God remains faithful to us. Signs like this are to remind those who have a covenant with another to keep the promise of the agreement and all the stipulations.

It was often the custom in the Near East to make a covenant after a war as a treaty toward striving for peace. God judged sin in the flood and now makes a covenant of peace.

New Testament Lesson   1 Peter 3:18-22   *The Suffering Savior*

In verse 19 we have the "seat of the doctrine" for the phrase in the Apostles' Creed "... he descended into hell." This passage put together gives us the significance of Jesus death on the cross. Verse 18 tells us it was for everyone and need not ever be repeated (Romans 6:10; Hebrews 7:27; 9:28; 10:10). And notice it was for sins that he suffered — to restore a broken relationship between us and our God (1 Corinthians 15:3).

It was also vicarious, i.e., "... the righteous for the unrighteous." I really like verse 18b, which is a new discovery for me. Jesus' human body killed but new life in the spirit. The incarnation body done and now alive with us in spirit. Then verses 20-22 tell us that the resurrection leads to a priestly role for Jesus in heaven. So the covenant symbolized by the rainbow and made with Noah now extends into heaven to a final rule there.

The Gospel   Mark 1:9-15   *The Temptation Of Jesus*

Typical of Mark's Gospel, we have in rapid-fire narration Jesus' baptism, his time in the wilderness, and the beginning of his Galilean ministry. I will not spend much time on this baptism account by Mark, except to say for Jesus it was a time to begin his mission, to receive from God the power for that mission, to make public his approval from his God, and to identify with the cause of God's people.

It is interesting that the forty days of temptation come right after the marvelous experience at the Jordan River. Satan can simply be defined as that power which works against God. It became representative of all which is opposed to God. So Jesus had to decide between God's way and the adversary's way.

Because the beast in the golden age of the Messiah were no longer to be humans' enemies, we have this comment that "... he was with the wild beast."

These words in verse 14b summarize Jesus' beginning ministry: *repent, believe,* and *good news* — that will be his message and where these are taken seriously, there is the Kingdom.

Repent — Greek, *metanoia* = change of mind
Believe — we believe what Jesus tells us about God
Good news — Greek, *euangelion* = we are saved and forgiven

Preaching Possibilities

You may want to announce a series for the weeks before Easter. Titles and texts could be:

Mark 1:9-15 — The message and ministry begins.
Mark 8:31-38 — The service is defined.
John 2:13-22 — The battle lines are drawn.
John 3:14-21 — The promise is certain.
John 12:20-33 — The results are predictable.
Mark 14:1—15:47 — The supper is prepared.

If you also need to prepare mid-week sermons, you might try a series on "Second Reading Assurances":

1 Peter 3:18-22 — The crucifixion was for everyone (v. 18).
Romans 4:13-25 — Faith will give us God's grace (v. 16).
1 Corinthians 1:18-25 — Christ crucified is our message (v. 23).
Ephesians 2:1-10 — God's graceful gift is salvation (v. 8).
Hebrews 5:5-10 — Reverent submission (v. 7).

The Old Testament will preach this Sunday with a natural symbol: the rainbow. We could talk about the covenant of peace. Relating this symbol to our storms in life and God's covenant to be with us and see us through could help our people see the rainbow in a new light and be reminded of God's promises each time they see it.

Possible Outline Of Sermon Moves

Title: Out Of Baptism Comes Ministry
Text: Mark 1:9-15

A. Introduction: Tell how Mark begins his life of Jesus omitting the birth narrative of Matthew and Luke. Bring the listeners up to date in the early life of Jesus and now these three big events take place.
B. As Jesus was baptized so were we. And as this confirmed God's love for Jesus his son, so our baptism confirms God's love for us, his child.
   1. Use an example from below in "Possible Metaphors And Stories."
   2. Pray a prayer of thanksgiving for our baptisms and for being a member of God's family.
C. Even as Jesus was tempted, so we are also tempted (v. 13). And as angels waited on him they will wait on us also.
   1. Use an example from below in "Possible Metaphors And Stories."
   2. Pray a prayer for help in temptations and one of thanks for God's protection from evil.
D. Even as Jesus had a ministry and a message, so do we have one (vv. 14 and 15).
   1. Use an example from below "Possible Metaphors And Stories."
   2. Pray a prayer for guidance and motivation in doing our ministry into which we were also commissioned at Baptism.

Prayer For The Day

We pray you will show us, and equip us, for our ministry. Make us mindful of the many temptations which surround us and keep us ever reminded of our baptism into your family. In Jesus Christ's name. Amen.

Possible Metaphors And Stories

In response to a course on Discipling that I taught in Hong Kong, student Han Kum Ju from Korea wrote the following: "I was baptized from the Pastor in autumn, he sprinkle water three times on my head. My tears come down from my eyes. I felt something special."

There is washing and there is washing. At a car wash today an elaborate sign described the prices for various wash jobs:

    Outside rinse only
    Outside double wash
    Outside with wax
    Outside with drying
    Outside and inside
    Add perfume to make it smell like a new car.

How much we permit Baptism to wash us is also to be considered — outside only, inside with forgiveness toward others.

Don Strong, in explaining preventive maintenance, said: "We should be pro-active rather than re-active. You don't wait till something breaks before you replace it." So, too, with our spiritual faith. We must work at it before the crises of life threaten to break it.

Clarence E. Macartney writes about temptation: "If the thought of a Godly father or a praying mother, or a faithful spouse, or an innocent child will sometimes hold a person back from sin, how much more will the thought of the presence of Christ deliver the soul in the time of temptation."

When Bishop Wayne Weissenbuehler of Denver spoke to the *Invitation to Service* event at California Lutheran University, he told this story:

"An Episcopal Bishop signaled for the acolyte to bring a pitcher of water and pour over his hands before communion. 'Wait a minute,' the Bishop said. 'This isn't water; this is wine.' The acolyte promptly replied, 'It was water when I put it in there.' " May the water of our baptism turn into wine of our ministry (vocation).

Third Sunday In March

Genesis 17:1-7, 15-16   Romans 4:13-25   Mark 8:31-38

Seasonal Theme   Jesus makes his way toward Jerusalem and the cross that we might have undeserved forgiveness for our sins.

Theme For The Day   Resisting temptation, taking up the cross, following Jesus, and living the abundant life of living for others.

Old Testament Lesson   Genesis 17:1-7, 15-16   *Sign Of The Covenant*

The change in name here is crucial. Abram means an exalted father. He was out of a royal lineage. The name Abraham in Hebrew sounds like the father of a multitude. This name anticipates descendants and the founder of a nation. Sarai to Sarah, which means princess, was correct, as her seed would produce kings. So here is a covenant with 99-year-old Abraham — he will be the father of the Jewish nation. First Abraham laughed at such an impossible promise and prediction. Then along came Isaac.

New Testament Lesson   Romans 4:13-25   *Abraham And Jesus*

This passage begins by harkening back to the Old Testament Lesson of Abraham and Sarah's covenant with God. This is a tough passage to understand because the logic is so flexuous. On the human side we have trust in God. Abraham and Sarah exemplify this. Verses 14-15 are parenthetical. Verses 18-25 tell us the root of faith is the belief that God is able to put righteousness where there is none in us humans ... a righteousness which can overcome death. This was foreshadowed in the birth of Isaac to his near dead parents. Wouldn't it have worked better for Paul to have used the sacrifice of Isaac here to make his point? To sum up Paul's theology, we can state that God creates righteousness where our faith will receive it. The example of this is not only Abraham, but also the death and resurrection of Jesus (vv. 24-25).

The Gospel   Mark 8:31-38   *Jesus Foretells His Death And Resurrection*

To disciples who had always pictured the promised Messiah as a victor and conqueror, these words seemed incomprehensible! Jesus connected, instead, the Messiah with great suffering and even death. Then Peter had to tempt Jesus again just as satan had in the wilderness after Jesus' baptism. So often it is our close friends who can bring the most persuasive temptation. In verses 34 and 35 Jesus is very honest with the disciples. Discipleship will not be easy. But, of course, Jesus was not asking them to do what he was not willing to do.

To our American culture, there is an important message in verse 34. Disciples deny themselves. This means we do not "do it if it feels good." We must say no to many of our desires and wants and drives. Verse 35 says we give ourselves away as disciples. And in the doing, we discover real life. If we are always thinking of what is safe and practical, our lives will become less and less abundant. Verse 37 asks us to locate our life-values and 38 demonstrates Jesus' confidence in his rejoining God his father.

Preaching Possibilities

Under the theme that, indeed, God makes promises, we can join all three of these readings together.
From: Genesis 17: God keeps his promises to us.
    Romans 4: Faith makes the difference. Abraham's faith and our faith in Jesus' resurrection.
    Mark 8: Jesus promises suffering and sacrifice and a saved life.

The Gospel could easily be a three part sermon given over three weeks:
> Verse 31: Jesus will go to the cross and come out of the grave.
> Verse 34: There is a cross to carry for us also.
> Verse 35: Abundant life is giving one's life away for others.

Now let's consider the easiest and most powerful approach for this week.

Possible Outline Of Sermon Moves

A. Begin by telling a story of bad advice or a tempting proposal given to you by a friend and why having the friend give it made it so tempting.
B. Continue by telling how Jesus had a similar experience given to him by one of his favorite disciples, Peter. Read verses 31-33.
C. Explain how often Jesus was tempted to not go to the cross but rather claim power and glory on earth.
D. Then tell how in the weeks ahead we will see him go to the cross as he predicted he would have to do. That was the first big shock to the disciples. The second one was denial and sacrifice.
E. Read verse 34. Discipleship involves denial of self and taking up a cross (sacrifice) and following Jesus.
F. Make two points:
  1. Taking up a cross means a willingness to sacrifice for our faith. That may mean giving up certain things and doing extra things. We must be careful lest we trivialize this idea of "cross bearing."
  2. Following Jesus means living out the priorities and truths he taught us, like: loving enemies, going the extra mile, turning the other cheek, praying for those who hate you and being God's instrument of love in this world.
G. Move to verse 35. We have a great teaching of Jesus here. The abundant life for us disciples of Jesus is in giving ourselves away and not in living to one's self. Jesus would still question a friend who advised us to get what's coming to us, stake out our turf, assert ourselves, demand our rights. Hoarding for ourselves is not joy-filled discipleship. Giving away for others is.
H. Give an example — see the "Possible Metaphors And Stories" below.
I. Frame your sermon by returning to your opening story of a friend's advice or temptation and tell how it all came out. Tell how Jesus handled Peter's advice and how it came out, too.

Prayer For The Day

Holy God, sometimes it's really hard to accept any discomfort for our religion. Sometimes we are tempted by ourselves and our friends. Sometimes we want to keep everything for ourselves. In these times, give us the will to resist temptation, take up our cross, and live our lives for others. In Jesus' name. Amen.

Possible Metaphors And Stories

When we checked in at the Denver airport, I noticed the tag put on the luggage starts with the ultimate destination. It may get lost or even go a different route — but ultimately it ends up at the final destination. And how about us? Are we marked for the ultimate destination? Perhaps the sign of the cross at our baptism tags us, too.

Because he was born so close to where we live and because there are many Dimaggios still living here, I took great interest in the book titled *Joe Dimaggio, the Hero's Life* by Richard Ben Cramer. It's a sad story. He was a man who died alone with all his money piled around him. In 1989 he was commanding forty to fifty thousand dollars a day for autograph and memorabilia sales. From the book this sad sentence: "... for the most part he'd stopped doing anything for free." He never spent a penny of his big pension he got from baseball. After the '89 earthquake he rushed home from Candlestick Stadium, went up into his partially destroyed San Francisco home, and brought out of his room, in a black garbage bag, $600,000 in cash! And he would not let his sister, who lived with him, make long distance calls because of the expense. He fought with his brother Dom and his only son, Joey, Jr., and died alone. Jesus told the disciples, "Those who want to save their life will lose it ..." (Mark 8:35a).

Marvin Kalb on NBC interviewed an old man who had the grazing rights for his cows on the land where the Pope would preside at a mass. Kalb asked, "Would the cows mind not having this grass to graze on tomorrow?" "No," was the answer, "and their milk will be all the sweeter because the Pope was here." Sacrifice makes life richer and more worthwhile.

Fourth Sunday In March

Exodus 20:1-17   1 Corinthians 1:18-25   John 2:13-22

Seasonal Theme   Jesus makes his way toward Jerusalem and the cross that we might have undeserved forgiveness for our sins.

Theme For The Day   Jesus teaches us a valuable lesson about our place of worship and the fact that he sacrificed himself for us.

Old Testament Lesson   Exodus 20:1-17   *The Ten Commandments*

What shall we say about these commandments? These are the very core of Israel's civil and religious rules. They have two parts. The first have to do with the relationship to God and the second six have to do with the relationship with each other in the covenant community. Verse 2 first sets out for the people what God has done for them. They have reached Mount Sinai and now need some guidelines by which to travel and relate to their God and each other. Paul claims in Romans 3:19-20b and 7:7 that these laws serve to show the sinfulness contrasted with the holiness of God. Martin Luther called them "schoolmasters," which taught us our need for God's grace and forgiveness. John D. Hannah in *The Bible Knowledge Commentary* writes: "The Ten Commandments are an excellent summary of ten divine rules for human conduct. They might be called rules of 1) religion, 2) worship, 3) reverence, 4) time, 5) authority, 6) life, 7) priority, 8) property, 9) tongue, and 10) contentment."

New Testament Lesson   1 Corinthians 1:18-25   *Christ The Power Of God*

We must be careful in our interpretation of this passage, lest we give way to a false sense of anti-intellectualism. It seems to me that Paul is warning against a sort of dependence on human wisdom without religious faith in Christ. As he often does, he says here "how much more" worthwhile is our spiritual faith in Christ. The wisdom of God is even more powerful than the wisdom of humans.

The Christian message didn't seem to have much promise of success in the Jewish or Greek setting, Paul claims (v. 25). All the world's wisdom had not found God; but the Christ points God out and provides us a presence which is powerful.

The Gospel   John 2:13-22   *Jesus Cleanses The Temple*

This incident in Mark, Matthew, and Luke is placed during the week of Jesus' trial and crucifixion. John puts it at the beginning of Jesus' ministry but still at Passover. The Synoptic Gospels give it as a protest against the desecration of the Temple. John's account gives it even more meaning. It is provided as a sign of what will happen because of Jesus' death and resurrection. Notice that he not only drives out the evil money changers but also the animals there to be used for sacrifice: sacrifice no longer called for because of his sacrifice on the cross for all of us and for all time to come. So temple worship is changed — the end of the old ways of animal sacrifice has come.

Jesus' words recorded in verse 19 were used against him in his trial before the Sanhedrin (Mark 14:57-59). This temple was started in 20 B.C. and completed in A.D. 64. It was destroyed by the Romans in A.D. 70, which had been predicted by Jesus in Mark 13:2 and Luke 19:43-44.

Does not this event bring into question many of the commercial practices and fund-raising in our church building today? Can we really justify the selling of stuff, new and used, and events merely to raise money for a cause, no matter how good the cause might be? And how wise is it to do such things while trying to teach radical financial stewardship? Several previous churches I have served in, like the ULCA and the LCA, forbade such activities by constitution and yet seemed to survive quite well.

Preaching Possibilities

Each of these readings will stand alone. The Old Testament gives us the opportunity to speak of "Rules for living," developing the theme that these were first for the people to use in traveling through the wilderness. They also can be used by us as we travel through life.

The New Testament Reading will also work by itself as we talk about the power of God in Jesus the Christ. Power can be the focus talking about the power of: our message (v. 18), God (v. 18), Jesus' crucifixion (v. 24), those called (v. 26), and the source of our life (v. 30). If we use all three readings, an outline might look like this:

A. Rules to live by — Old Testament
B. Power to live on — New Testament
C. Worship to live with — Gospel

The first three metaphors listed below are in this order. After exploring the above possibilities, I would like to develop the Gospel reading as a sermon outline.

Possible Outline Of Sermon Moves

A. Give the lead-up to this event according to John's Gospel. Jesus is baptized in the Jordan, is tempted in the wilderness, recruits his disciples, works his first miracles at Cana's wedding feast, and now sets out to observe the Passover Feast in Jerusalem.
B. Describe the existing situation when Jesus got there. Several million Jews were there — the barefaced extortion of those pilgrims coming to the obligatory worship; the exorbitant rate charged by the money changers; the social injustice of it all.
C. Tell why Jesus acted this way. He loved God and, thus, God's children. He just could not bear to see those he loved taken advantage of and especially right in God's temple. Some additional reasons:
   1. God's house was being desecrated.
   2. There was racial and gender-based discrimination as it was the court of the Gentiles where all this took place, making it impossible for them to pray (see v. 11 in Mark 7).
   3. Animal sacrifice was no longer needed since his arrival.
D. Now move to what this teaches us today: God doesn't want God's temple desecrated by secular commercialism — take this as far as you dare. A sacrifice has been offered for all of us and sacrifice is no longer necessary.
E. Add some humor and also creative imagination by describing an emergency meeting of the congregational council that night. The property committee would have to clean up and repair the courtyard. The elders would have to discuss excommunication for this unruly member. The stewardship committee would have to write new guidelines for who uses the temple and for what purpose, etc. This can give relief for what could be a very threatening sermon on "Temple Abuse."

Prayer For The Day

Dear Heavenly Parent, our prayer today is that you would give us open and critical minds to decide what is appropriate to do in our church. Help us to practice a financial stewardship that does not anger you but in which you celebrate. We are thankful that you have made the supreme, once-and-for-all sacrifice for our sins, even though we fall far short from deserving it. In Jesus' name. Amen.

Possible Metaphors And Stories

Stella Min is from Myanmar (formerly Burma) and a member of the Keren tribe, which took over a Thai hospital demanding medical help for their families. Twelve were slaughtered after surrendering and were pictured on the cover of *Newsweek*. She will return to her country to teach in a new school of theology there. During my class on "teaching the catechism," she became very quiet, almost panicky, and kept watching the window and door. After class I asked what was wrong and she explained that as we were considering the first commandment and Luther's meaning of it she could not teach such a thing back home. Stella said the military had asked the Buddhist monks to go through the Bible and announce why it was all wrong. Since that time, it has been very dangerous to make the claim that only our God is the true God and that we should "have no other gods." If she did so, it might mean her arrest and the closing of the seminary there (which does not use the word seminary).

It was the first time I have witnessed such fear of saying out loud that God is our God (except for the times as a parish pastor I have asked Lutherans to witness to their faith!). She forgot for a time she was not under her home military government and looked as if they would come to get her at any moment. The words whispered in her home country but openly spoken by these students were so scary for her to hear.

I later held a learning group session in which Stella Min was in attendance. I learned more: she revealed that her brother-in-law was taken from their home one evening for speaking against the military and admitting he was a Christian. They didn't know where he was or if he were alive or dead for two years. Then he was found by her sister in a prison where he has been for seven years. No wonder she is afraid when people around here speak about "no God but our God"!

Pastor Joe Allison of Saint Peters, Monrovia, Liberia, tells that after 600 were slaughtered in the sanctuary of his church, the group decided to worship in the Lutheran Church in Liberia guest house area. Just as Pastor Allison was about to pronounce the benediction, armed troops broke through the wall's gate and headed toward their little congregation. Allison said, "Everyone, hold your Bible in front of your head, shout the word 'Jesus,' and follow me." They marched out of there with Bibles and "Jesus." The soldiers parted to let them through, not one raising his gun against them. There is still power in the name of Jesus.

At the Berkeley, California, BART train station, there is no change available at the toll booth. But there is one vendor outside who sells sandwiches and soda. He demands a very large "take" to provide change for you to use in the machines to purchase a ticket. It must have been similar for the pilgrims who came to give their annual required offering in Jerusalem's temple.

Fifth Sunday In March

Numbers 21:4-9 **Ephesians 2:1-10** **John 3:14-21**

Seasonal Theme Jesus makes his way toward Jerusalem and the cross that we might have undeserved forgiveness for our sins.

Theme For The Day Jesus being raised up on a cross is our example of how much we are loved and is our light in a dark world.

Old Testament Lesson Numbers 21:4-9 *Snakes In The Wilderness*

Apparently, Moses changed the planned route into Canaan and instead took a circuitous way around Edom. The people following became frustrated by this chance and complained about the desert's harshness with lack of water and food. They hit a snake-infested area and were sure it was their complaining for which they were being punished. So they asked their spiritual leader to intercede to God for them. Moses was told to erect the bronze snake high on a pole and tell the people who had been bitten to look on in and be healed. And they were! Here is a look of faith (see John 3:14-15). Many of the stories in Numbers talk of the people's complaints, God's punishment of them, and Moses' intercession on their behalf. This story is probably here to account for the bronze serpent in Solomon's Temple (see 2 Kings 18:4). This is also the origin of the American Medical Association logo in the U.S.

New Testament Lesson Ephesians 2:1-10 *From Death To Life*

Paul probably wrote this letter to the most important city in Asia and to be read in his other congregations. He was in jail in Rome at the time of its writing. Its purpose was to convey, on Paul's behalf, the eternal purpose and grace of God. This portion says simply because of our sins we were, and are, dead and that a merciful God who loves us made us alive in Christ (v. 5). The moral decadence of life without Christ is described as, "... following the desires of flesh and senses." When we were hopelessly captured by this decadent life, still God entered our history to redeem us. All this because of God's mercy and great love for us. Our new life, then, according to Paul, is in and with Christ. And this is a corporate matter, not private. We believers are together in Christ. What Jesus does is to reconcile us not only to God, but also to each other. It will preach!

The Gospel John 3:14-21 *The Little Gospel*

John quotes Jesus as saying in verse 14 that what Moses did as told in the Old Testament Lesson, God would do with him because he would be crucified.

Of course, verse 16 is the core of it all and is often called "the little Gospel." It's just the facts: God loves us, God sacrificed Jesus for us, we will have eternal life. But so many miss verse 17, which, in my opinion, should always be quoted with 16. Jesus came to save and not condemn us.

Then we have the often used Old Testament and New Testament metaphor of light and darkness (vv. 19-21). Jesus is the Old Testament light promised to the dark world. Still, many refuse to see it and prefer to live in the dark of evil.

William Barclay, in his *The Daily Study Bible*, provides an outline for 3:16, which he calls "Everybody's Text."
A. The origin and initiative in all salvation lies with God.
B. The mainspring of the being of God is love.
C. The width of the love of God is the world.
Then Barclay quotes Augustine: "God loves each one of us as if there was only one of us to love."

Preaching Possibilities

There is an obvious connection which can be made between the Old Testament's account of Moses lifting up a serpent on a staff to save the people from snakebite, and God lifting up the cross on which Jesus was crucified to save the people living in darkness. Paul's words in the New Testament Reading will also connect as he talks about death to life in 2:4 and 6. All three of the readings talk of raising up: Moses the serpent on his staff; God raises us up with him in the heavenly places (v. 6); and the son of man being lifted up in John 3:14.

Of course, John 3:16 will stand on its own as has been carried out by many preachers over many years. (See Comments on the scripture for a three-point outline in the Gospel portion.) I recommend you also include 3:17 in this kind of exegetical sermon so that the picture gotten by our hearers is not seeing God as one out to punish all those who ignore what God has done on the cross because of his love, but rather, see God as one who loves "the world" and wants to save everyone.

The Ephesians passage is also filled with possibilities if we make it stand alone. It's all there:
A. We are dead through our sinfulness (v. 1).
B. God is merciful and loves us and brings new life (v. 4).
C. All that God does for us is a gift of grace (v. 8).

If you use these three moves for your outline, put an illustration after each one, close with a hymn poem, and you'll have an old-fashioned sermon presentation.

Possible Outline Of Sermon Moves

A. Introduction: With today's Bible readings, we have a strong and clear message of what our Christian faith is all about. If I were choosing one Sunday out of the whole church year to bring someone who knew nothing about our faith, it would be today.
B. Three great personalities of the faith bring us the message: *Moses*, who was a murderer with a stutter in his speech and with blood on his hands; *Paul*, in jail, whose behavior he could not control and who persecuted the early Christians; and the *disciple John*, a young boy who wrote down for us what Jesus told and taught the disciples.
C. First, let's look at Moses (Numbers 21:4-9). God gives help and new life in time of suffering and death. Faith in God enabled the snake-bitten people to be healed when they looked upon the serpent on a staff. We also have help in our suffering and we must have God-given faith.
D. Now, look at Paul and what he explained to his congregations (Ephesians 2:1-10). We receive new life from God who loves us and saves us by God's grace as a gift. This God raised up Jesus on a Jerusalem cross and when we look upon it with faith, we see the "... immeasurable riches of his grace in kindness" (v. 7b). What a gift!
As the Ephesians had new life possible through God's gift, so do we.
E. Then look at what John recorded Jesus as saying. It's the heart and center of the Gospel (John 3:16). God gave his son for us, too.
F. Read John 3:17 and tell how John claimed that God didn't come to judge and condemn as often pictured by preachers and television evangelists. God came to save and not judge us, also.
G. Tell a story which illustrates the message of today and pray. Meaningful preaching to you.

Prayer For The Day

We marvel today, Holy God, how much you love us and pray for your continued help to gain new life from our sinful existence. We thank you for the symbols of your grace and great gift to us, which surround us even yet today. When we stray back into the darkness, point us again and again toward your light, in whose name we pray. Amen.

Possible Metaphors And Stories

St. Paul Insurance Company used to have a wonderful ad on television when they said, "Trust is knowing you are safe in any environment." Then there was a little girl pictured being charged by a big ugly rhino. It stops just short of her and she pets it. The announcer says, "Trust is knowing you are safe when you are most vulnerable." (For "trust," read "faith.")

On my early morning walk I saw an unusual sight. The fountain at the foot of Black Diamond Street was overflowing with soap suds. There were tons of suds running all over the sidewalk and into the street. It was beautiful! Someone, as a prank, had put detergent in the fountain. How God's grace overflows into our lives and into our church sanctuaries out of the baptismal fount. As John writes in the Gospel of John: "... the immeasurable riches of his grace in his kindness toward us in Christ Jesus" (2:7).

A group of professional people posed this questions to a group of four- to eight-year-olds, "What does love mean?" The answers they got were broader and deeper than anyone could have imagined. From the internet we read, "During my piano recital, I was on stage and scared. I looked at all the people watching me and saw my daddy waving and smiling. He was the only one doing that. I wasn't scared anymore." "Love is when Mommy sees Daddy smelly and sweaty and still says he is handsomer than Robert Redford." "Love is when your puppy licks your face even after you left him home all day." "My mommy loves me more than anybody. You don't see anyone else kissing me to sleep at night." "Love is when Mommy gives Daddy the best piece of chicken."

First Sunday In April

Jeremiah 31:31-34   **Hebrews 5:5-10**   **John 12:20-33**

Seasonal Theme   Jesus makes his way toward Jerusalem and the cross that we might have undeserved forgiveness for our sins.

Theme For The Day   Jesus presents paradoxes of the Christian life and makes important promises for our discipleship.

Old Testament Lesson   Jeremiah 31:31-34   *A Covenant Of The Heart*

The theme of this text is the new covenant God promises between God and the people of the northern and southern kingdoms. Jesus used this phrase of "new covenant" at the last supper. This covenant is with every person, not just with Israel. Here is promised that, when the time comes, people will do the right thing from inner conviction and desire so the covenant will be renewed. Ezekiel claims it also (Ezekiel 36:24-28).

Three elements are exciting and preachable in this new "deal."

A. This was a new covenant unlike the one based on the Mosaic law at the time of the Exodus.
B. This covenant will be internalized. They will not need exhort people to know the Lord, for they will already know him in their hearts (vv. 33-34). So we have here the inspiration of the Holy Spirit in all believers (see Joel 2:28-32).
C. A third new element in this new covenant is how sin will be handled. In the old one, God would curse the people for their sin (Leviticus 26), but in this new one, God forgives and "remembers their sin no more" (v. 34).

New Testament Lesson   Hebrews 5:5-10   *Jesus, Our High Priest*

A priest was thought of as the mediator or link between us humans and God. In Israel they offered the sacrifice for people's sins. So they worked to restore the relationship between God and humans. This was to open the way back to God for us sinners. All this Jesus does, so he becomes our high priest. Verse 9 says Jesus was "... made perfect." To the Greeks this meant that a thing was made perfect when it perfectly carried out its purpose. So the writer is claiming that Jesus was made perfect by all he did: crucifixion, resurrection, etc.

Melchizedek was a symbol of the ideal king-priest. In Genesis 14:17-20, we read of his ministry to Abraham. Verse 10 is a quotation of Psalm 110:4.

The Gospel   John 12:20-33   *Paradoxes And Promises*

The other three Gospels do not mention this story. It is probably a solid hint that John wrote his Gospel to appeal to the Greeks. It was Passover, so Greeks would be in Jerusalem. I have a hunch that some Greeks had seen that day when Jesus drove the money changers out of the temple courtyard and now wanted to ask him more about what he taught. Phillip is a Greek name, so they come to him first. Andrew seemed more certain that Jesus would want to talk with them. The Title, "Son of Man," which Jesus calls himself in verse 23, has its origin in Daniel 7:13. For the Jews, "Son of Man" meant the God-sent world conqueror. No doubt they all gasped when they heard Jesus apply this concept to himself.

William Barclay, in his *Daily Study Bible,* says Jesus was teaching three things in verses 25 and 26. 1) Only by death comes life. 2) Only by spending life do we retain life, and 3) only by service comes greatness. He goes on to close with this comment: "And the extraordinary thing is that when we come to think of it, the paradox of Christ (above 3) is nothing other than the truth of common sense."

Then comes the great promise that has been proven correct down through the generations. When Jesus is lifted up on that cross, there will be a drawing power to all people (v. 32).

Preaching Possibilities

Since this is the Sunday before "Palm Sunday" or the "Sunday of the Passion," we could use all three passages talking about what Jesus did for us.

A. Old Testament, Jeremiah — He touches our heart.
B. New Testament, Hebrews — He opens our way to God.
C. The Gospel, John — He promises us new life and love.

I believe the Hebrews passage is also pregnant with preaching possibilities. One can take the metaphor of High Priest and extend it all the way through the sermon comparing the function of a priest to what Jesus does for us. (Homiletically, this is called an extended metaphor sermon.)

A. The Priest offers sacrifice for sin to God for us.
B. The Priest opens the way to God for us.
C. The Priest demonstrates God's love for all God's children.
D. The Priest shows us the way to salvation.

One more approach this week would be to take just one verse, John 12:32, and speak about how that has proven so over the 2,000 years since the crucifixion and how we lift up the cross and *take down the cross* in our lives. Be sure to apply that as a congregation as well as an individual. Some try to hit others over the head with the cross, others profess to lift it up but live in such a way as to kill its drawing power of love, while still others, without even trying to hold it up, live in such a manner that it is obviously there with all its drawing power.

Possible Outline Of Sermon Moves

Title: Three Great Truths/Promises To Live By

A. Use the first illustration below in "Possible Metaphors And Stories."
B. Now relate a promise made to you or one you made to someone which was (is) extremely important to you.
C. Explain that Jesus made certain promises or truths which we can always count on as his disciples.
   1. John 12:25 — To love and conserve one's life is to lose real life — but to give it away will give us abundant life here and in eternity.
   2. John 12:26 — To serve Jesus is to follow him and his teachings. And God will not leave us by ourselves.
   3. John 12:32 — When we lift Jesus up on the cross, people will be attracted to him.
   In verses 21 and 22, the Phillip and Andrew story with the Greeks will work here. (Who are the Greeks in our day and parish?)
D. Now talk about what these promises mean for us as individuals and as a congregation together.
   1. The disciple life is one of risk and not always playing it safe.
   2. There is an apostolic radical to follow and teach as a congregation. We are servant and not demanding being served in our congregational life.
   3. There are ways of facing suffering and of sacrificing ourselves for others, which will hold Jesus' cross up in our community.
E. Frame your sermon by returning to the promise(s) mentioned in "B" above.
F. Read the 3 verses: 25, 26, and 32.

Prayer For The Day

We give thanks today, Jesus, for these days before Easter, which make us especially mindful of your cross and its rich meaning in our own lives and the life of our congregation. We are thankful that you lead us to a real, abundant life and show us how to follow you. Now we pray we might be the instrument through which the cross of Jerusalem might be lifted up here in *(your town)* so that its power would once again draw all to you. In Christ's name. Amen.

Possible Metaphors And Stories

Gerald Kennedy writes in *Who Speaks for God*, "A member of the House of Commons who had listened to the war-time speeches of Neville Chamberlain and Winston Churchill made this comment: 'When Mr. Chamberlain said the fine, true thing it was like a faint air played on a pipe and lost in the wind at once. When Mr. Churchill said it, it was like an organ filling the church, and we all went out refreshed and resolute to do or die.' And this is the difference between the promises of people and the promises of God ... when God gives us a promise, it comes with the fullness of the organ in the cathedral, filling us with courage and determination. Resting on his promises, folks through the years have been made strong again."

In an old movie *Beyond Rangoon,* about an American doctor who becomes caught up in the violent upheavals of the '80s in the Burmese (now called Myanmar) capital of Rangoon, Laura says to the former Buddhist professor: "I was taught that if I worked hard that I would have happiness. I was a fool, wasn't I?" The old professor answers: "We are taught that suffering is one of the promises life always keeps, so that if happiness comes, we know it is a precious gift which is ours only for a brief time."

My friend Joel Teigland showed me a copy of a letter of recommendation written by a professor of medicine in South Carolina, which stated, "His value system rests soundly on his Christian beliefs which are secure, not requiring any public show." A good description of the Christian disciple.

With the neighbor's financial help, we were able to cut down two huge eucalyptus trees which had died and stood near the seminary chapel. The surprise was that now the cross could be seen from way down the hill. I wonder what other things and schemes need be cleared away to let the cross shine in our own lives.

Palm Sunday/Passion Sunday

| Isaiah 50:4-9a | Philippians 2:5-11 | Mark 14:1—15:47 or Mark 15:1-39 (40-47) |

Seasonal Theme — Jesus makes his way toward Jerusalem and the cross that we might have undeserved forgiveness for our sins.

Theme For The Day — There is an extravagance of love in Jesus' anointing at Bethany as he prepares to enter Jerusalem.

Old Testament Lesson   Isaiah 50:4-9a   *Humiliation Of The Servant*

We can see in this passage in Isaiah a description of Jesus' sufferings. *Vine's Expository Commentary on Isaiah* calls this "a joyous lowliness ... taken from discipleship." Jesus knew what lie ahead and headed toward the cross anyway (v. 5). In verse 7 he repeats his comfort in that God helps him. In this, which is often called a "servant song," the description is metaphorical. The prophet is vindicated. Jeremiah and Job share the same conviction as Isaiah — he will be protected and his opponents overthrown. These are not God's sons complaining. These are ones sure of God's care no matter how bad the suffering that comes is.

New Testament Lesson   Philippians 2:5-11   *The Mind Of Christ*

Here Paul advises in not very clear language that the common mind of the church ought be on what one thinks of Christ. *The Interpreter's One-Volume Commentary* tries to paraphrase for clearer understanding: "Think among yourselves what you think in Christ — i.e., think of each other the way you think about Christ; regard each other from the same perspective." This agrees with 2 Corinthians 5:16-17. It is still confusing as to nuance, but I think we get the main emphasis: We are to act consistent to what we believe about Christ. Verses 6-11 further describe this way of regarding Christ. If this were not the Sunday before Easter, I would love to develop this into a text perhaps rarely developed. If we are to have Christ's mind, from the text we learn it would be: He did not try to pull rank like we might do and exploit our privileged relationship with God; he gave up his prestige and became a servant as we ought do; he was obedient to God even if it meant his death; so God exalted him so that we would kneel in respect for him and admit our love for him and glorify God by worshiping him.

The Gospel   Mark 14:1—15:47   *The Holy Week Narrative;*
                    Mark 15:1-39   *The Trial And Crucifixion;*
                    Mark 15:40-47   *The Burial Of Jesus*

The portions of these Gospel Readings you use will depend on whether you will also have Thursday, Good Friday, and, perhaps, Easter Vigil services. If you do hold these services, you will want to use only Mark 14:1-11 on this Sunday.

To understand this week, we ought know a little about the Passover, which had brought Jesus, his disciples, and the crowds to the Holy City. All male Jews living within fifteen miles of Jerusalem were required to be there for the observance of the deliverance of the Israelites from their slavery in Egypt. (See Exodus 12.) When the angel of death passed over the houses marked with the blood of a lamb, it began an historical observance each year near the 14 of Nisan (about April 14). This was also an observance, like our Thanksgiving, when the barley harvest had been gathered. Rules for this part of the observance are found in Leviticus 23:10-11. Every male Jew wanted to observe Passover in Jerusalem before he died. So pilgrims came from all over the known world. (The historian Josephus put the number one year at 256,500.) And because of that enormous crowd, the occupying Romans were very nervous and tried their best to keep a lid on things. This reading will cover the plot to kill Jesus, the anointing at

Bethany, the betrayal by Judas, Passover with the disciples, the Lord's Supper, Peter's denial predicted, arrest of Jesus, Jesus before the council, Jesus before Pilate, soldiers mock Jesus, the actual crucifixion, the death of Jesus, the burial (42-47).

Preaching Possibilities

This may not be the Sunday to preach a full-blown sermon. Keeping with ancient tradition and respecting this portion of the scripture to stand by itself, you may just want to read the whole story without your own comments. I suggest you select readers carefully ahead of time so it is not all one voice but several. You can have readers represent: a narrator, Jesus, the crowd, the disciples, Peter, Judas, and Pilate. You might also consider singing a hymn in between reading portions of the story. Since the characters call for male voices, you could use a female voice to offer short prayers every so often dividing up the story as it's divided by topic headings in the *New Revised Standard Version Bible*.

Possible Outline Of Sermon Moves

If you must preach this day, the anointing at Bethany is a marvelous story of stewardship and reverence for the Christ (Mark 14:3-9).

Like an antiphon in the psalms, verse 9 can be repeated over and over during the brief homily.
Things we can learn from this story:
A. There is an extravagance of love expressed here, which can serve as an example for us.
B. It is in giving oneself away that the great things in life are accomplished. This was one of the last acts of kindness to Jesus before his crucifixion and death.
C. We must beware lest in our cautiousness we miss the opportunity to express our (and God's) love for one another.
D. When we do the "good service" there will always be criticism.
E. There is something promised here which will happen this week. She is anointing his body for burial.
Use verse 9 between each of the above sermon moves.

Prayer For The Day

Holy God, who went to the cross for our forgiveness, show us the way to do acts of kindness like this woman did in a home in Bethany. And, God, give us a sense of reverence all this week when your only Son went to the cross after suffering at the hands of cruel people. Show us the way to respect him too like that unnamed woman whose act of love *has* been remembered wherever the Gospel is preached in all the world. In Jesus' name. Amen.

Possible Metaphors And Stories

In the movie *Starman*, an alien crash-lands right into the life of a widow. He hears her use the word "love" and asks her to define it. She replies, "Love is when you care more for someone else than you do for yourself." Jenny came very close to defining God's love which we have for another.

A scene from television's *Night Court* which really moved me: Bull has fallen in love with a hooker who is milking him for his money. When he finally realizes it, he says, "I feel sorry for you. I see many like you. They take and take but they can't give because they are empty in there and they can't get filled." I wonder what the writer of the show had in mind as he or she wrote this great message of stewardship.

In the days of old, when a king converted to Christianity and ordered his knights to be baptized, many of them held their right arms out of the water. As they were submerged into the baptismal water, they kept their weapons dry so they could continue to use them in ways of killing and war. I sometimes have a picture of us modern Christians undergoing our baptisms while trying to hold our wallets and purses out of the converting waters.

A group of professional people posed this question to a group of four- to eight-year-olds: "What does love mean?" The answers they got were broader and deeper than anyone could have imagined.

"Love is when a girl puts on perfume and a boy puts on shaving cologne and they go out and smell each other."

"When you love somebody, your eyelashes go up and down and little stars come out of you."

"You really shouldn't say, 'I love you' unless you mean it. But if you mean it, you should say it a lot. People forget."

Thursday In Holy Week

Exodus 12:1-4 (5-10) 11-14   1 Corinthians 11:23-26   John 13:1-17, 31b-35

Seasonal Theme   Jesus makes his way toward Jerusalem and the cross that we might have undeserved forgiveness for our sins.

Theme For The Day   A banquet of love is prepared for us.

Old Testament Lesson   Exodus 12:1-4 (5-10) 11-14   *The Passover Instituted*

In the first four verses we have laid out for us how the Passover shall be observed. Optional verses 5-10 further detail the rules for preparation of the sacrificial lamb. Verses 11-14 tell more about the people's conduct in carrying out the observance. Then comes the announcement of the striking of all the firstborn except those who have an exemption and whose blood-marked door post shall be a signal for the angel of death to pass over them. And no plagues will reach them either! Verses 11b and 14 put together give us the theme for this day of passover.

In verse 6 the words "the whole assembled congregation of Israel" is used for the first time in the Old Testament. This gives us a sense of newness and beginnings. Notice the Passover was to be celebrated in homes.

We can connect this passage with Jesus and Holy Week through the symbol of blood. The blood of the lamb (or goat) was the salvation of the people there in Egypt, so the blood of Christ in Jerusalem will be (is) our redemption for all believers (see Romans 5:9 and Ephesians 1:7).

New Testament Lesson   1 Corinthians 11:23-26   *The Lord's Supper*

We read the earliest account of the Eucharist in the upper room on Mount Zion with Jesus and his disciples. It is our warrant for observing Holy Communion.

Let's remember that when Jesus said these "words of institution" while celebrating the Jewish Passover, he was still alive and in the body. So the words cannot be taken as literally as we sometimes try to interpret them. "This is my body," then, could not have meant literally as he in his body was handing out that same bread. These words of William Barclay in his *Daily Study Bible* I find very helpful: "The broken bread of the sacrament does stand for the body of Christ; but it does more; to him (or her) who takes it into his (or her) hands and upon his (or her) lips with faith and love and warm devotion, it means not only a memory but of living contact with Jesus Christ."

The words, "This cup is the new covenant in my blood," can be translated, "This cup is the new covenant and it cost my blood." The Greek here can mean "in" but it can also be translated "at the cost of." This particular week that will preach. So here is a new relationship between God and the people. This time, instead of being dependent on keeping the law, now it is based on God's grace of love. This changes everything. A new covenant indeed!

The Gospel   John 13:1-17, 31b-35   *Humbleness And Love*

First we have the washing of the disciples' feet by Jesus. There is a marvelous humbleness exhibited and modeled by Jesus that night. It took some explaining for Peter to understand (see v. 15). Perhaps we can find a reference to Christian baptism in the way the Gospel writer John wrote verse 8. Since foot washing was the way into the household, we have washing of baptism as the way into the household of faith. And, like Peter, we must not be too proud to submit to it.

In verses 34 and 35 we have not only the farewell command of Jesus to his disciples, but also the way others would judge if they were real disciples of Jesus. Like Jesus loved them, they are to love one another. Perhaps that best explains the humble service Jesus demonstrates in his foot washing also.

Preaching Possibilities

It's an easy assignment to preach on this day (night) in Holy Week. If not foot washing for everyone, at least consider yourself as preacher washing someone's feet in front of the whole congregation before the service begins. To demonstrate the humbleness of Jesus, make it a homeless person off the street, a very old saint of the congregation, or a youth. Let the congregation sing during the footwashing, "Lord, Whose Love In Humble Service" (text by Albert F. Boyly; tune: BEACH SPRING).

Consider doing this congregational activity instead of preaching. Have everyone get in groups of three. Ask them to tell each other the following about themselves, giving topics one at a time and allowing time between each to do it:

A. Your earliest memory of your kitchen table while growing up.
B. The happiest memory you have of being around that table.
C. The saddest memory you have of being around that table.
D. Describe the altar or communion table in your home church as a child — or in a church you love.
E. Now explain that the altar is the "Lord's Table."
F. Now have them tell each other the happiest and saddest time around the "table of the Lord."
G. Close by asking each group to separately hold hands and, in turn, pray for each other in light of what each has shared.

I have done this exercise for a congregation as large as 1,000 in attendance to one with 27 in attendance.

Possible Outline Of Sermon Moves

A. Begin by telling of your memories of your first communion experience.
B. Now move to re-tell the story of the disciples' first communion in the upper room on Mount Zion.
C. Explain the background of Passover from the Exodus 12:1-4 (5-10) 11-14 Old Testament Lesson, especially quoting verses 11b and 14a.
D. Give the teachings to be learned.
   1. As the blood on the doorpost saved the Israelites, so Jesus' blood will save us from our sins.
   2. Paul explains that this is a *new* relationship with God (1 Corinthians 11:25).
   3. It all begins and plays out with baptism in the humble washing of feet and disciple service (John 13). We still have washing possible through baptism.
   4. This night we learn that Jesus' wish for us in God's family is to love one another.
   5. How we carry out this command will show to others our true discipleship ... or not.
E. Now list some areas where you think you can improve on keeping this new commandment. Then some areas where those hearing you can do so as well.
F. Frame your sermon by returning to your memory of your first communion and your hopes for living that out a lot better just like Jesus asked the disciples to do.

Prayer For The Day

Show us true discipleship tonight, dear Holy Parent, even as you demonstrated to your other Mount Zion disciples on this very night 2,000 years ago. Help us to be humble servants and to love each other here in your family called *(congregational name)*. And as we take the bread and wine tonight, which cost you your life, help us to do so with heart-felt love for you and for each other. In Jesus' name. Amen.

Possible Metaphors And Stories

A while back, the national restaurant chain Olive Garden had a slogan which might be claimed for us in our congregations: "When you are here, you are family."

The saintly old Andrew Hsiao, many years president of LTS, Hong Kong, told of his first return in 1979 to the little mainland town where he grew up. Just before China began to open up and after thirty years' absence, he returned and secretly took private communion to the ninety-year-old widow of the former pastor. She had no Bible, hymnal, or chance to worship all these years; but long ago she had memorized the psalms and could still recite them. And, like many Chinese Christians, she could pray. She insisted on receiving the sacrament on her knees. As he was giving her the bread, they heard someone coming up the stairs. Terror struck their hearts for fear they had been discovered. Then a seventy-year-old woman appeared who wanted communion also. It was the little girl Andrew's father had baptized sixty years before! Andrew said the widow prayed a prayer of thanksgiving like he has never heard before or after. They cried tears of joy and real presence.

Pastor Carlos Schneider tells of Ted and Tom, who sat in the balcony at Saint John's, Sacramento. Ted has died. Tom sits in the same place and keeps a place open for his deceased brother even when the balcony is crowded. "The communion of the Saints" lived out by Tom of Saint John's, Sacramento.

During the Gulf War, Peter Jennings told of an Iraqi family in Texas who named their first son Saddam Hussein and the second son born during the war George Bush. They told Jennings it was their prayer that they, too, one day should be brothers.

Good Friday

Isaiah 52:13—53:12   Hebrews 10:16-25   John 18:1—19:42

Seasonal Theme   Jesus makes his way toward Jerusalem and the cross that we might have undeserved forgiveness for our sins.

Theme For The Day   Calvary's cross works for us an atonement with God.

Old Testament Lesson   Isaiah 52:13—53:12   *Suffering Servant*

This "suffering servant" passage is read on God's Friday. Here is a great theme of the servant of God who suffers, is rejected, and atones for the people's sins. It is a marvelous example of the work of Jesus on the cross today. The translation "startle" in verse 15 is fascinating. After the way this servant is degraded, he astonishes all that one so humiliated could be exalted as described in verse 13. In this regard, also note verse 53:3, which describes his rejection.

Verses 10-12 describe the results on the servant because of his obedience to God.
A. "He shall see his offspring."
B. "He shall prolong his life."
C. "... the will of the Lord shall prosper" through him.
D. "Out of his anguish he shall see light."
E. "... he shall find satisfaction through his knowledge."

One more benefit of the suffering servant's sacrificial death: He will be given a great portion because he gave himself in death. These last three verses crescendo in the prophecy of the suffering servant who we can connect toward the Christ crucified today.

New Testament Lesson   Hebrews 10:16-25   *Because Jesus Sacrificed, We Must Act*

There seems to be a cause and effect in this reading. Verses 16-18 say that God is establishing a new covenant with God's people by forgiving them their sins. The result is that no longer are offerings for sins required (v. 18). We can enter the sanctuary which Jesus opened for us. We can approach God with a "true heart" (v. 22). And we can persevere with hope because God is faithful and keeps God's promises (v. 23). We must encourage each other to do good deeds and come together regularly giving encouragement to each other. The above is the practical implication for the writer's claims about the work of Christ. We are encouraged to apply our faith in all out concern for others. And the writer says this is even more important because of the shortness of time (v. 25b).

The Gospel   John 18:1—19:42   *The Betrayal, Trial, Crucifixion, And Burial Of Jesus*

It's God's Friday and we now move to John's account of the terrible acts by the religious and political powers of the day, which led to his crucifixion and death. I think a simple listing of the story according to the *New Revised Standard Edition* paragraph headers will be helpful:

The events
    The betrayal and arrest (18:1-11)
    Jesus before the High Priest (18:12-13)
    Peter denies him (18:15-18 and again 25:27)
    High priest questions Jesus (18:19-24)
    Jesus before Pilate (18:28—19:16)
    Jesus is crucified (19:17-37)
    The burial of Jesus (19:38-42)

A teaching
> We can betray him, also.
> Our religion can persecute, also.
> We disciples deny, too.
> Religion can be cruel, too.
> Power can corrupt us, as well.
> The crucifixion was for us, also.
> Like Nicodemus, we, too, can bury Jesus.

I have used the above seven as a seven-part sermon for a three-hour Good Friday service instead of the traditional words from the cross.

Preaching Possibilities

There are many possibilities for this day. One good one would be to take the Old Testament description of the suffering servant and relate it to the crucifixion of Jesus:

Verse 52:13 — Jesus is "lifted up" on the cross.
Verse 52:15 — Jesus "startles many nations" still. He was exalted in spite of the degradation of crucifixion.
Verse 53:3 — Jesus was "despised" and beaten by soldiers and Annas.
Verse 53:4 — Jesus "has born our infirmities" (our sins) on the cross.
Verse 53:7 — Jesus "did not open his mouth" at the trial or on the cross.
Verse 53:11b — Jesus, God's servant, by his crucifixion "made us righteous."
Verse 53:12 — God has made Jesus "great" because he "poured himself out to death."
Verse 53:12b — Jesus "bore the sin of many" and continues to make "intercession for us transgressors."

It's almost as if John wrote his account of the crucifixion to fit the well-known Jewish image of the suffering servant.

Another approach is to use the Hebrews reading and the outline provided in *Comments on the Scripture*, New Testament Reading. The sermon can be titled "Cause and Effect."

There are many ways to approach the crucifixion narrative of John's Gospel. One might be to look at the sign that Pilate had placed on the cross (v. 19:19) and imagine what sign we think ought to have been placed there.

A. Our Suffering Servant
B. The Prince of Peace
C. The one who is present in our communion meal
D. An innocent man dying for our sins
E. God's gift to God's family

Possible Outline Of Sermon Moves

Title: People Around The Cross
Text: John 18:1—19:42
Moves:
A. Peter who denied him. How do we deny him in our discipleship?
B. Annas who was threatened by him. How can the religious threaten us?
C. Mary Magdalene who stuck with him to the end. How might we stick with Jesus to the end?
D. Joseph of Arimathea who was a secret disciple.
E. Nicodemus, also a secret disciple. How might our discipleship be more than secret?

Prayer For The Day

Let us not take part in your crucifixion again, dear God, by the language we use or the things we do and think that pain you. We give you thanks this day for working our forgiveness from your cross and pray we might live a life worthy of such a sacrificial love. In Jesus' name. Amen.

Possible Metaphors And Stories

At the funeral of James Simmons I attended, the Reverend Parish said, "I did not come today to preach a funeral — for we all preach our own funerals by the lives we live here. I came to share these few moments of tragedy with this family."

What a sobering idea that we prepare our own funeral sermons by the lives we live! But we also have a cross and Easter grace and a returned spirit to be with us now to get us through.

I remember the hearings for U.S. Supreme Court Justice nominee Clarence Thomas. I wonder what a hearing for a Christian would be like who was nominated to be a disciple.

Joel and I were out to "bless the fields" with a little pheasant hunting. We came to an electric fence. Joel commented that it wasn't "hot." But I insisted he go across first. Throwing one leg over the fence, he came astraddle it, and he discovered it *was* "hot." So he jumped first on one leg then the other trying to get over or back. It's painful to straddle the fence and yet we often encourage it with a halfhearted following of the Christ and living in the world.

A university student who vandalized St. Mark's Lutheran Church in Bowling Green, Ohio, is now a member of the congregation. According to the pastor, my friend, the Reverend Dale Schaefer, Bowling Green State University student Gerard Guhde was found in the church after a day of drinking. He has helped to restore the sanctuary and has been forgiven by the congregation and has joined the church.

Easter Sunday

Acts 10:34-43   1 Corinthians 15:1-11   John 20:1-18 or Mark 16:1-8

Seasonal Theme   Alive and out of the grave, the risen Christ is witnessed in the real world.

Theme For The Day   Jesus out of the grave and in our church alive.

First Lesson   Acts 10:34-43   *Inclusive Preaching*

For the next eight Sundays the First Lessons will come from the book of Acts. These passages can be seen as the alive body of Christ out in the world and among God's people. Not only are these recorded events testimony to the resurrection, but they are examples of his disciples being about his real presence ministry in their real world. In this Acts 10 account we have Peter preaching to the Gentiles, as well as Jews, the gospel. First a summary of what God did in the flesh of Jesus the Christ (vv. 38-41). Then comes Peter's mission to witness to what he actually saw and experiences as an eyewitness and disciple (vv. 42-43). If it were not Easter Day, I would go immediately to the Acts 10:34 and talk about God being race and color and nationality blind. But today the expectation of the resurrection story is so great that we must center our proclamation there. Let's come back to those verses a little later in the Easter season.

In this particular passage, we have the core of early Christian preaching. The listeners are Gentile Cornelius, his relatives, and close friends (v. 24). The message was: The one God had sent to them, Jesus, as a gift, the people killed on the cross. That same Jesus came out of the grave and the preacher is a witness to that. The aftereffect of this all is the forgiveness of sins. We now have a different relationship with God.

Second Lesson   1 Corinthians 15:1-11   *Resurrection And Apostleship*

This is a summary, by Paul, to the Corinthian congregation, of what he had proclaimed to them about Jesus' life, death, resurrection, and appearances the weeks after Easter. Paul sees these appearances of Jesus after Easter the basic evidence of Jesus resurrection. The 500 mentioned in verse 6 is perhaps referring to Pentecost.

The last of these appearances was to Paul (v. 8) and because of this, Paul considers himself an apostle, which is defined as one who saw Jesus eye to eye. Because his reason for claiming to also be an apostle is quite different than the rest, he goes on to stress how hard he has worked and that it was God's gift of grace (v. 10b). In preaching this text perhaps we could claim, as Paul has done here, that we are also apostles if the Christ has appeared to us in religious experience.

The Gospel   John 20:1-18   *The Resurrection Of Jesus*

It is a breathtaking story well told, which I hope we can read well in a style which is narrative and rings with conviction. You might consider reading it in two different portions. First read 20:1-10 and then preach on that. Then move to verses 11-18 as the "rest of the story," as Paul Harvey used to say. There are some delicious characters we can talk about and use as examples:

A. Mary Magdalene who had sinned much and who loved Jesus much.
B. Simon Peter who was the natural leader of the disciples.
C. The "other disciple, the one whom Jesus loved" (v. 2). Perhaps this was the author John, or perhaps it was Lazarus, whom Jesus had brought out of the grave just a week or so before this Easter. Or could we be the "other disciple"?
D. Mary, mother of Jesus, who loved her son even though she just couldn't understand what was going on. They went out to the grave somewhere between 3 and 6 a.m. to finish the embalming, which had to be postponed because of the keeping of the Jewish Sabbath. We get the idea from the Greek language that the body of Jesus had just disappeared from the cloths and they were there still in

place. There is a lot of love in this story. Mary's love for her son, Peter's love for his leader, and the love of "the one Jesus loved" for his savior. They really took their hearts to the tomb that early morning.

Mary could not recognize Jesus because of her tears clouding her sight and she had her back to him as she looked into the tomb. William Barclay writes about this: "... we must never fasten our eyes upon the grave and forget the heavens."

It could be that a better translation of verse 17 would be "Do not be afraid." Or, perhaps Jesus is telling her not to tarry there touching him — but go tell the others. Verse 18 is the heart of a Christian's experience. We can say with Mary, "I have seen the Lord." Not just know about the Lord, but we have seen him, also.

Preaching Possibilities

Unlike almost any other Sunday's scripture readings, we can use all three, use any one of the three, or even any two of the three. It's a slam dunk this week.
A. The Acts account — Easter is for *all* people and the message is still the same for us today.
B. The Corinthian account — We are also "Easter People" because we have seen the Lord.
C. The John account — As Mary, Mary Magdalene, Peter, and the "disciple Jesus loved" lives were forever changed, so are our lives.
D. I also like the account of Mary looking for Jesus in the tomb rather than in the world. That's our temptation in our day as well. We might not recognize him either!

Yet another possibility: that of apostleship or discipleship. In the three accounts there is a theme of witness. It just wasn't enough to believe and witness the resurrection. One must also go and tell the good news to others. We ought to be more than a witness *of* the resurrection — instead be a witness *to* the resurrection. That's how Easter becomes real to us today. When we take it and its message to others. Acts 10:39, "We are witnesses." 1 Corinthians 15:11 Paul was a witness. "So we proclaim...." John 10:17b "... go to my brothers" and verse 18b "... I have seen the Lord."

Possible Outline Of Sermon Moves

Let's try an extended metaphor sermon on this Easter morning. That means we will begin by telling a metaphor like the first one under "Possible Metaphors And Stories" and then weave it all through the sermon.
A. Begin by telling the story of the Chinese at Buji church in mainland China during the Communist and cultural revolution. See the first one listed below.
B. Now tell how the disciples of Jesus had been shattered by the events of Good Friday. How, like the Buji Christians, they first wanted to be near the tomb and perhaps touch it out of their love for Christ.
C. Then move to telling how the Buji Christians were probably looking for the Christ in the wrong place (the building) rather than in the risen Christ within them in Spirit whenever they got together. So Mary was looking in the wrong place (or reverse the order of these two thoughts).
D. Move to the present situation at Buji. Since the Chinese government has relaxed a little their regulations on religion — more than 600 have come to worship and believe. It was true of the disciples also. Out of the witness to this pivotal event of resurrection when it seemed all was lost — now millions around the world join us in worshiping the Christ on this Easter Day.
E. Tell how the Buji Christians still must struggle under the Communist rule to practice, contrasting that with how easy it is for us in America to gather today.
F. Move to the laws forbidding Christians to witness and yet how they quietly bring more and more to Christ. Look at your own congregation and their witness to Easter Resurrection. Tell how all three of the texts today call for witnesses to this Easter event. Explain how that helped the early Christians believe, helped the Buji Christians believe, and will surely help us believe in this community.

G. Frame the sermon by very briefly telling the Easter story according to John. Then move to the Buji Christians and their resurrection from a few old, old secret Christians to the many today who gather for worship in their old precious building, which used to be a horse stable. Then pray for the Buji Christians and then your own Christians.

Prayer For The Day

We give thanks today, dear God, for faithful Christians who still must take risks and know oppression for the practice of the faith. Bless the new resurrected congregation in Shenzehn, China, that they might continue to be powerful witnesses to the resurrection. And bless us here that we might also be faithful witnesses in a place where it is much easier to do so. Along with Mary, Mary Magdalene, Peter, and the disciple Jesus loved, help us also to see you alive and out of the grave. And then send us out to witness. In Christ's name. Amen.

Possible Metaphors And Stories

Missionary Ted Zimmerman of Hong Kong told me of the church in Buji, Shenzhen, China. The building was built by the Basel mission over a hundred years ago. The Communists took it away from them and turned it into a horse stable. When they were not allowed to worship, Ted says, they would walk up the alley on Easter just to be close, and sometimes when no one was looking they would risk reaching out to touch the brick wall. They did this to acknowledge that they were still Christians and worshiping in their hearts.

They got their building back a couple of years ago. Only six very old original members were still alive. From them, the congregation of mostly young people has begun to thrive. I traveled there several times to preach in 1999-2000 and 2001 and there are over 600 to hear the gospel and receive the sacraments! Truly a resurrection of a body of Christ, again.

In candidate for President of the United States Al Gore's concession speech, he told one of his father's favorite sayings during adversity: "Shake the soul and get the glory out."

A story from Margaret in Forest City, Iowa:
A woman died and went to heaven, which was more beautiful than she'd ever expected. She couldn't wait to show it to her husband when he arrived, because he was an eternal pessimist.
A year later her husband joined her, and she took him on a tour. "The sky, the flowers, the music, the people — heaven is truly heaven, isn't it?" she exclaimed. He surveyed Paradise briefly, then said, "Sure. And if it weren't for you and your darned oat bran, we'd have been here five years sooner!"
Could it be we avoid death too much? If paradise is really paradise, what is it we so fear?

On August 7, 1994, Dean and Ruth Fardahl dropped off their lunch partners at Lord of Life Lutheran Church in Sun City West and headed home. A few blocks from home, Dean's heart stopped and he ran the car across the boulevard, into a yard, and into the side of a garage. Ruth was all right with some bruises. They rushed Dean to the hospital where the doctor told me that the airbag had opened and slammed into Dean's chest and started his heart again. I visited him the next day in Boswell Hospital in Sun City, where he was sitting up on the side of the bed dangling his feet. Oh, to start the dead hearts again — inside and outside our congregations. It's an Easter story.

Fourth Sunday In April

Acts 4:32-35 1 John 1:1—2:2 John 20:19-31

Seasonal Theme   Alive and out of the grave, the risen Christ is witnessed in the real world.

Theme For The Day   Because of Easter we are changed people just like those first Easter disciples were.

First Lesson   Acts 4:32-35   *Charity*

Luke gives us a description of life in the early church. It is similar to Acts 2:42-47. The "heart and soul" in verse 32 describes a faithfulness (see Deuteronomy 6:5). The sharing of goods described here was required at Qumran but here it seemed to be only if wanted. Notice that the main function of the apostles was to give testimony to Jesus' resurrection. Laying things at the apostles' feet is like the ancient custom of laying offerings to the gods.

These early members of the church had a deep feeling of stewardship for each other and they wanted to share with others what they had. So we have an early example of charity and loving concern for each other.

Second Lesson   1 John 1:1—2:2   *Jesus And Real Being*

During these next weeks after Easter the New Testament Reading will be from 1 John. A brief introduction in your comments or printed in the worship bulletin will enrich the use of this little letter. From the introduction to the letter in the *New Revised Standard Version* (Reference Edition) of the Bible we learn that "false teachers were trying to mislead first-century Christians by denying, among other things, the true humanity of Christ. This view ... is the background of much of 1 John. The author had two basic purposes in mind in this letter: 1) to expose false teachers, and 2) to give believers assurances of salvation. The author is John, son of Zebedee — the apostle and the author of the Gospel of John. He was a first cousin to Jesus."

The message is quite clear in this first part of the letter. John says Jesus was a real human and he knows because Jesus lived with him. He saw him, heard him, and touched him. Then in verse 3 he claims he tells them this so that they might join their fellowship. Verse 4 can be translated either way: they make this witness about Jesus so their joy will be complete or they make it so that the ones hearing it might have their joy complete.

Verses 8 and 9 have been used for centuries in the liturgy of the confession. One might translate "my little children" in 2:1 as children or beginners in the faith or literally a term of endearment. Verses 2:1b-2 describe what the work of Christ was in Holy Week and Easter: he becomes our advocate and he atones for our sins and all people's sins.

The Gospel   John 20:19-31   *Doubting Thomas*

Jesus' first appearance to the disciples is recorded. The disciples are hiding in a locked room. He offers the grace of his after-Easter life which brings a sense of safety and, above all else, peace. In verse 21 he tells them to take up his work with a new power he is giving them. Now they can forgive sins (vv. 22-23).

Thomas wasn't there but returned the next week. This time he no longer doubted Jesus' resurrection. Thomas thus becomes the representative of all who followed Jesus and had doubts, like us. The Thomist Church of south India, where, legend has it, Thomas went to be a witness to the resurrection, does trace its origin to Thomas.

Verses 30-31 seem to read like the natural end of this Gospel. Perhaps chapter 21 is a postscript. Verses 30 and 31 serve to remind us that the Gospels only give us a brief sample of what Jesus taught and what he did. And we discover in these verses that the Gospels are to give us life rather than provide a biography or history of the time of Jesus.

Preaching Possibilities

All three readings provide a solid foundation for preaching again the Easter message.
A. The First Lesson. To be Easter people is to be deeply faithful and to have love and concern for others. And a desire to share.
B. The Second Lesson from 1 John tells us that Jesus was a real person and we share the good news about what he did for us that we might have joy and those we tell might also have joy.
C. The Gospel lets us know that the gift that the resurrected Jesus has to give us is grace and peace. He unlocks the doors of fear in our lives by his presence with us and out presence with each other. If we did a "Doubting Thomas" sermon last year, perhaps we could consider a more topical sermon today by looking at what it means to be an Easter people.

Possible Outline Of Sermon Moves

Title: Easter People After the Resurrection
A. Text: Use all three readings for Easter 2.
B. Tell the story of the disciples in the locked upper room and how they were afraid.
C. Move to asking your hearers if they ever wondered how different those disciples were *after* Easter from *before* Easter. For example:
   1. Impulsive Peter who denied Jesus.
   2. James and John worried about their place in the Kingdom.
   3. Judas who cheated as treasurer of the group.
   4. Timid Andrew, afraid to witness to the gospel and who lived in the shadow of his brother Peter.
   5. Above all, Thomas who had to be convinced.
D. Move to talking about how we are after Easter people and we, too, can be changed because of that empty tomb and risen Christ with us. We can be changed:
   1. From people who used to be shallow in our faith to people who believe deeply (Acts 4:32).
   2. From selfish people all wrapped up in getting and keeping our possessions to folk who practice charity and sharing (Acts 4:34-35).
   3. From people who never really felt the real presence of Jesus with us nor ever shared him with others to folks who sensed a closeness and shared the joy with others (1 John 1:2-4).
   4. From people who are afraid and not sure to people who believe and experience through God's Holy Spirit God's grace and peace (John 20:21-22).
E. Move to what are the implications for our congregation.
   1. We ought to be sure our services are spirit-filled.
   2. We ought to be certain we are bringers of peace on God's behalf in our marriages, homes, congregations, and communities.
   3. We ought to learn how, and actually find places and ways, to share the Easter news. We will be changed by sharing this good news as well as those who hear it.
F. Conclude by telling your people how you are changed because of Easter this year.
G. Frame the sermon by returning to the Easter Gospel for today and the locked doors now standing open with a welcome sign reading: "Welcome to our fellowship, come on in and celebrate with us, the Easter people."

Prayer For The Day

Help us to be changed because of Easter again this year. And give us the courage to live out our Easter faith where we live and work and play. Make us giving people who want to share rather than hoard. You came out of the grave; now enter our church that we might know your grace and peace. In your risen name. Amen.

Possible Metaphors And Stories

From *Harper's Bible Dictionary* about Thomas: "... he is further identified as Didymus (twin). No incident is recorded about him in the Synoptics or in Acts, but in the Fourth Gospel he becomes prominent in the closing scenes. Thomas displayed courage and loyalty when Jesus proposed to return to Judea in spite of Jewish hostility (John 11:8, 16) ... Thomas made the most forthright and all-inclusive confession of faith to be found in the Gospels (John 20:26-29). Tradition declares that he was a missionary to Parthia or to India."

Stella Min, a member of the Karen tribe in Myanmar (Burma) whom I was advising on her Master's thesis, writes that the word "steward" in her language is now used for people who are responsible for hosting and the safety of the people of a gathering of any kind. They serve as host, helpers of people in distress, and crowd control. They represent the institution. Easter people are stewards of God's peace and of God's kingdom and even stewards of God's worship service. God grant us the need for crowd control there, too!

On the television program *60 Minutes*: Laurence Olivier at the age of 59 said that he still got stage fright and always had someone stand in a certain place in the wings so he could see the person. He told him, "If you are not there, I shall run."
We have the Christ and his people always standing in the wings for us. We never need to run.

At a Bishop's conference at Livermore Laboratory with theologians and scientists, the Bishop said, "After all, the fact is we are all determined to protect our things and hang on to them with our nuclear weapons, even if we destroy ourselves in the meantime."
"Blessed are the peacemakers," said Jesus.

First Sunday In May

Acts 3:12-19 1 John 3:1-7 Luke 24:36b-48

Seasonal Theme   Alive and out of the grave, the risen Christ is witnessed in the real world.

Theme For The Day   Jesus is alive and with us still equipping us to be powerful witnesses.

First Lesson   Acts 3:12-19   *An Early Sermon*

Peter was preaching to the crowd that saw him heal a crippled beggar who was now clinging to him. Here is a sample of Peter's, and no doubt early Christian, preaching. Notice the basic elements:
A. Jesus was out of the great Jewish heritage.
B. They killed Jesus on the cross.
C. The disciples are witnesses to the fact that Jesus came out of the grave.
D. The healing was by Jesus' name.
E. An invitation to repent and turn to God.

The place of this teaching was in the Temple courts as Peter and John were on their way to prayer. Beggars sat in these courts because they knew people were more apt to give after they had been to worship. (They still sit there today.)

Second Lesson   1 John 3:1-7   *God's Children*

Again the author of 1 John addresses his message to "little children" and makes again the comment we are "children of God" (v. 2). He also assures us that we will become even more than a child. Because we are his children, one day we will be like him and see him as he is (v. 2b). Verse 4 condemns sin. Then a tough verse to interpret and understand. Verse 6 does not mean we who are "in Christ" are sinless! Rather, the person who is God's child is pointed in the right direction. We know and try to do the right thing and love our fellow people.

The Gospel   Luke 24:36b-48   *Another Experience Of The Alive Jesus*

Again we have the image of Easter people being witnesses. And again we have the witness of the Gospel writers that Jesus not only came out of the tomb but also was very much alive and with them. In this particular passage we learn he had them look at his hands and feet and touch him. Then he ate broiled fish with them. All this to prove he was real and there.

Then he taught them what this meant by quoting the scripture that promised one who would "suffer and rise from the dead on the third day" (v. 46). And "repentance and forgiveness of sins" is to be proclaimed to all the nations (v. 47). Now the strong kicker, verse 48 — they are to be witnesses to all this. And that they don't witness alone — they will receive power from God to do it. And so they did! We could be also.

Preaching Possibilities

The theme in these post-Easter passages is often that the disciples (and so us) are *witnesses* to the crucifixion and resurrection of Jesus (Luke 36:48; Acts 3:15b). A good approach would be to focus on "Easter witnesses" first looking at the scripture's admonition to witness and then looking at our potential and possibilities together as a congregation and individually in our daily lifestyle. Remember when the disciples had to choose a person to replace Judas, they made the criteria: "a witness to the resurrection."

One could also go with the Acts reading for today, which pleads with the people to "repent and turn to God." In this passage also there is something very lovely in the picture. According to 3:11, the crippled beggar just healed was clinging to Peter and John. Picture it. They are proclaiming the gospel and one healed by it is standing there with them. Who would cling to us because they experienced God's healing power through us?

A textual exegetical sermon could develop from 1 John 3:2. We are God's children, we will one day be like him, we can have hope to become better as we experience him.

Possible Outline Of Sermon Moves

Let's use my homiletical formula based on how listeners listen to a sermon.[1]
A. Build a fire: Describe how it would be having a dead corpse appear alive at a family meeting a couple of days later.
B. Bridge: Tell how we all wonder about the mechanics of Jesus returning in body to be with the disciples after his death. And we wonder how it will be for us, too.
C. Points: These things can be learned from Luke's account of Jesus appearing to the disciples after Easter day.
   1. He is recognizable and has real flesh and bones (v. 39).
   2. We may still have some okay doubts (v. 41).
   3. His death and resurrection was promised by the prophets (v. 44).
   4. The disciples' (and our) task is to proclaim the result, which is forgiveness of sins (v. 47).
D. Examples: See below in "Possible Metaphors and Stories."
E. Witness: Now give your own personal witness. You are reminded today that not only do we disciples have a Savior who overcame death and the grave; but we also have an alive Christ with us, who gives us a job to do. We are to be witnesses to the resurrection. Tell what that means in your own life.
F. So what?: We are to be witnesses (v. 48) and that means we must know how and where and with whom to do so. And we have been promised a certain spiritual power to do it.
G. Frame it: Return to your contemporary story of a dead body returning and how frightening that would be. Then read verses 24:36b-49.

Prayer For The Day

Give us the power to witness, too, O God, as you promised you would give all disciples after Easter. Calm our fear and administer to us a big dose of your holy peace. Show us again today your alive after Easter presence that we, like those early disciples, would be "in-joy" as they were. In the Easter Christ's name. Amen.

Possible Metaphors And Stories

William Barclay tells how W. H. Davis, the tramp poet, relates how one of his vagrant friends told him that, whenever he came into a new town, he looked for a church spire with a cross on the top, and began to beg in that area because there, from experience, he found people most generous.

In a *60 Minutes* television segment, Archbishop Desmond Tutu of South Africa was being interviewed. They asked Tutu about how the Council of Reconciliation was being run by him. He explained that if those who committed atrocities during the time of apartheid would confess their sins, they would be granted amnesty from the council and the present government. The reporter asked, "Archbishop, isn't this carrying your Christianity too far?" That is Christianity — we carry radical forgiveness way too far. It's what Jesus taught us from the cross and after the resurrection. Carrying it that far makes us unique in our discipleship.

There was an ad on television for *Monday Night Football*. An old man is near death and in a coma in the hospital. The doctor puts earphones on the patient and plays the theme song for *Monday Night Football*. The man revives. There is power there. And God gives us power to witness also.

Sam Donaldson on the ABC news told of Yellowstone Park, which burned in the summer. It is now covered with a foot of snow. Underneath grass is starting to take root and seventy percent of the trees will survive. The heat of fire provides a gum which protects the pinecones. Two weeks later there is a shower of seeds that will start new pine trees. This is called "nature's fire insurance." It's new life out of destruction. A lived-out resurrection!

In the Batak language of Sumatra there is no word for "surrender." It is also very difficult to say, "I'm sorry" in Batak. But in the language of the cross we can surrender to the one who sacrificed his son in order that we might use the words often: "I'm sorry."

---

1. For further explanation of this style of homiletic, see the author's book, *The Preacher's Edge*, CSS Publishing Company, Lima, Ohio, 1996.

Second Sunday In May

| Acts 4:5-12 | 1 John 3:16-24 | John 10:11-18 |

Seasonal Theme Alive and out of the grave, the risen Christ is witnessed in the real world.

Theme For The Day Our security and unity in the Christ whom we follow as our Good Shepherd.

First Lesson Acts 4:5-12 *Peter And John Before The Council*

The Easter readings continue the same pattern again today. The First Lesson is an example of the early church live as the body of Christ; the Second Reading some theology about what this resurrection means for us; and then another story from the Gospels about Jesus alive and with the disciples after Easter and before the Ascension.

After healing a cripple in Solomon's portico, Peter and John were arrested by the temple police and taken before the council. Notice how in verse 9 Peter ("filled with the Spirit") stated in his answer the obvious that they had done a wonderful thing for this cripple and because of this act of mercy were hauled before the council. His answer is threefold: the healing was in Jesus Christ's name; God had raised from the grave the same Jesus they had killed on the cross; and this Jesus was none other than the Messiah promised by their hero Isaiah (see Isaiah 28:16).

Then comes the no doubt shocker to those very pious Jews (v. 12). It was only through this same Jesus that they could be saved. And no one else, either!

Second Reading 1 John 3:16-24 *Loving God's Children*

The theme of this passage is repeated over and over in several different ways. Jesus loved us so much that he gave us his life for us and that means we ought love each other. Again the phrase "little children" is used, which probably is an address of love similar to "dear ones."

John claims that certain signs ought to flow from loving God and each other:
1. If we have the world's goods we will share them with others who have need.
2. Our love ought to show in action as well as in words.
3. We will receive from God whatever we ask and we will do whatever pleases God (v. 22).
4. God will give to us the Holy Spirit and God will live in us (v. 24).

The Gospel John 10:11-18 *The Good Shepherd*

It's a familiar passage of the New Testament, Jesus as the Good Shepherd. It is based on Ezekiel 34 and addressed the contemporary time of the evangelist when the religious were more "for hire" than faithful. The main emphasis is on the love of the shepherd contrasted with someone who is translated as "the hired hand." This person probably represented the false teachers with the wolf in verse 8 representing the persecutor occupying the country from Rome. The contrast is between Jesus who lays down his life for the sheep and the "hired hand" who deserts them in time of danger.

Verse 16 deserves our attention. It claims universal parenthood of God and calls for unity. There were earlier translations that mistakenly called for one fold. Here the *New Revised Standard Version* corrects earlier mistakes. Our unity is not in placing everyone in one fold; but rather is following one Shepherd. The unity is not in ecclesiastical unity but in loyalty to Christ.

Verses 17 and 18 let us know that Jesus' death on the cross was voluntary and not forced upon him. He chose it and there was glory connected with it. God's own son paid the ultimate price because of his love for the sheep (us) and because of his obedience to God.

Preaching Possibilities

The Acts reading will easily preach by itself using the outline above in the First Lesson. We could take the approach of "our defense on trial" for being Christian. See the first illustration in that section as a powerful metaphor that could be extended throughout the sermon.

We could also continue using "the Easter people" theme, combining all three readings:
A. Acts: Our sure defense as Easter people.
B. 1 John: Easter people love in truth and action.
C. John: Easter people have one shepherd.

There is a close emphasis in the Second Reading and the Gospel. Both tell us that Jesus laid down his life for us (1 John 3:16 and John 10:11 and, more remotely, Acts 4:10b).

Yet one other way all these readings might be used:

Theme: Our unity in Christ

Scripture: Through Christ we are all saved (Acts 4:12); we are united in loving each other (1 John 3:23); we are united by having one shepherd (John 10:16b).

Possible Outline Of Sermon Moves

Focus on the Good Shepherd image as the sermon theme.
A. Begin by paraphrasing the Gospel in contemporary imagery and language. Perhaps the shepherd could be female and the "good nurse" or the "good police officer" or the "good doctor" — you get the idea.
B. Move to the imagery of the shepherd and compare it with the contemporary one above.
C. Move again to what Jesus was trying to teach as he told this only parable in the Gospel of John.
   1. Jesus loves us and will not desert us.
   2. We have protection for scary times.
   3. Jesus knows us as individuals just like God knows him and he knows God.
   4. We have a unity in being in this flock.
   5. Jesus went to the cross on purpose for us, his flock.
D. Return to your imagery of a contemporary Good Shepherd like a "good foreman" and point out the difference between the good and bad one, using the above five teachings. For instance, a good doctor will not desert his/her patient to play golf when the patient needs him/her (see 1 above).
E. Conclude with prayer.

Prayer For The Day

Holy God, Good Shepherd, we rejoice today in our protection and unity in following you. Help us to be your sheep and follow your direction. Bless us in this fold that we would share and love each other. In the name of the Christ. Amen.

Possible Metaphors And Stories

Andrew Hsiao, former president of LTS, told me of his mother in Hunan Province of China during the cultural revolution. As an old woman she was called into their Lutheran Church building and put on trial for being a Christian, forced to renounce her faith in the sanctuary of her own church! She never recovered from it. I am not sure he has either.

One of my Chinese students wrote these words for me in a class I was teaching on discipleship in Hong Kong: "I've given materials to my husband as well as in-law's family but the response is, OK, Jesus is another deity that I can go to ask a blessing. So they will come once in a while to a church and go to the Buddhist temple at the same time."

In *My Fair Lady*, Eliza Doolittle sings to her suitor, Freddie, about being "sick of words." "If you are in love, show me!" she demands. Jesus shows us from the cross.

The church of the New Testament is no longer a territorial church but a church of all people, a church which has its children in all lands and gathers them from every nation. It is the one flock of the one shepherd, called out of many folds (John 10:16), the universal church which flows through all time and into which all people pour.

Third Sunday In May

Acts 8:26-40   1 John 4:7-21   John 15:1-8

Seasonal Theme   Alive and out of the grave, the risen Christ is witnessed in the real world.

Theme For The Day   Easter people take the good news of Jesus' resurrection out into the world and love others as God loved us.

First Lesson   Acts 8:26-40   *Philip And The Eunuch*

Here is a beautiful conversion story that took place in a part of the Holy Land with which we are very familiar — Gaza. This particular intersection would be a route of many international travelers. The Ethiopian Eunuch was head of the treasury of the Queen of Ethiopia. He must have been in Jerusalem to worship either as a "God lover," which was a non-Jew who carried out the Jewish practices, or what was called a Jewish proselyte, who were people who took on the Jewish law. He was reading from Isaiah 53 and did not understand it. Philip explained that Jesus was the fulfillment of this prophecy he was reading. Philip's witness must have been mighty powerful for the Ethiopian asked to be baptized. Water for adult immersion baptism isn't available in that area so it's a mystery as to verse 36 and the water. I personally doubt it was by immersion. I have a hunch it was by pouring. However, see Romans 6:1-4 for the symbolism. There were three things baptism symbolized in that day: 1) the beginning of a new life; 2) water meant cleaning or washing away sins; and 3) it was a time when the baptized became one with Jesus.

Tradition has it that this convert from Ethiopia returned to his home country and brought the Christian faith there. Let's not worry about Philip's baptism with very little instruction. I won't even go there. It's a grace gift anyway and not the reward for passing an exam on its theological meaning. Philip probably included in his witness the demand to repent and be baptized. (See v. 2:38.)

Remember this is the same retiring personality who introduced Nathaniel to Jesus and who may have been the one who, when called by Jesus, wanted first to bury his father (Luke 9:57-60). He was instrumental for bringing the faith to Northeast Africa. The *Harper's Bible Dictionary* states about Philip: "He took up residence at Caesarea on the Mediterranean, where he was host to Paul, who stopped there on his last journey to Jerusalem (Acts 21:8-15). Philip had four unmarried daughters who were Christian prophetesses" (v. 9). What meat for an interesting biography sermon!

Second Lesson   1 John 4:7-21   *A Commandment Of Love*

The author has finished his words about light in the first part of this letter. God is light and he has said that we must live in that light obedient to God. Now he says God is love and we must live in that love out in the world. So this whole letter is one that makes the claim that Christian belief and life are inseparably connected. *What* we believe is *how* we live. In this very focused passage, God makes the first move and loves us. Some of the claims about that love are:

1. Love is from God (v. 7).
2. If we don't love we really don't know God (v. 8).
3. God's love for us was revealed by Jesus coming into the world (v. 9).
4. God's love was so great that it became a sacrifice for us (v. 10).
5. Because God loved us, we should love each other (v. 11).
6. When we love each other, God's love is perfected in us (v. 12).
7. God has given us God's spirit (v. 13).
8. We witness that God sent God's son because of love (v. 14).
9. God is love and those who abide in love abide in God (v. 16b).

10. Love gets rid of fear (v. 18).
11. We love because first God loved us (v. 19).
12. We cannot love God if we hate others (v. 20).
13. We are commanded by God to love others (v. 21).

The Gospel   John 15:1-8   *Jesus, The True Vine*

There is a cause and effect here similar to the second reading. There it was: if you love God, you will love others. Here it is: if you abide in God you will produce good works. Many times in the Old Testament Israel is pictured as the vine or the vineyard of God (see Isaiah 5:1-7). The vine was on their coins and in the temple representing the state. Here Jesus' claim is that *he* is the true vine. Israel has grown wild, he is the real one. Not Jewish blood but faith in Jesus was the true way.

Each year the everywhere present grape vine is drastically pruned back so it will develop correctly. Those branches that are not productive are the ones cut way back. Jesus uses this picture as an analogy of the Jews and also of his followers whose deeds did not match their words. We could extend that out to say those who won't listen, listen but don't act, or listen and abandon.

The passage is about abiding in Jesus. It is a mystical thing we ought do, which is difficult to describe. It means keeping in constant contact — in our worship life, our prayer life, our Bible study, our social fellowship — we are always in constant contact like a branch is always connected to the vine. And the source of life for the branch comes from the vine. "Abide" is defined in the dictionary as "remain, last, or reside, endure, agree to."

Then we have the claim that God is glorified by what we followers do while abiding in God. If we are in him, we can ask whatever one would ask (while in him) and it will be given (v. 7).

Preaching Possibilities

The choices today will be to focus on the witness of Philip in the First Reading or use the theme, which is cause and effect, in the Second Reading and Gospel. Of course, the analogy of a vine and its branches is a strong and understandable one, which will preach by itself. The 1 John account of loving each other also is full of potential. Down through the ages, followers of the Christ who professed a love for God have often been very hateful toward each other. It happened in many of our congregations where this message needs proclamation. A possible outline might be:
A. Theme: To love God is to love each other.
B. The reason: We love God because God first loved us from the cross (1 John 4:10-11).
C. Our response to God's love is to reach out in love to each other. There are many ways we can do this in our home, congregation, community, and world.
D. Our dare is to love more than the lovely — to love those no one else loves and who will never love us in return.
E. Our method is to have God's *love* for the other even when we do not *like* them (John 15:9).
F. An example can be found in the section "Possible Metaphors And Stories."
G. Some possible targets of God's love through us would be the misfit in the community, the abrasive in the congregation, the unruly child in our home, the person of a different culture and skin color and language, the person of a different sexual preference, or the one who personally hurt you.
H. Conclude by reading 1 John 4:16b and 21 again.

Possible Outline Of Sermon Moves

This is a good Sunday to do a dialogue sermon. Pretend we are able to overhear the conversation between the Ethiopian Eunuch and Philip on that road through Gaza. The Acts 8:26-40 can be read by three people. One can be Philip, one the Eunuch, and one the narrator. Prepare a discussion you can imagine the two had that day before baptism. I suggest you call in the two who will read and have them help you prepare the manuscript. This will make it more meaningful to them and keep the language and theology close to the ground. Some ideas follow:

Eunuch:	"I can't make any sense out of this Bible."
Philip:	"I can help you."
Eunuch:	"Who are you and why should I listen to what you have to say?"
Philip:	Gives his witness about being a disciple of Jesus and what he saw with his own eyes.
Eunuch:	"This may be what I'm looking for! How do I become a part of this movement?"
Philip:	Tells about what it means to follow Jesus.
Eunuch:	Asks about baptism.
Philip:	Baptizes him.
Eunuch:	"Come back to Ethiopia with me."
Philip:	"You will need to be Jesus' witness there."

Of course, you'll need to expand this. But you can end it by having the narrator challenge the congregation to respond to this dialogue:
1. Like Philip, they, too, can be witnesses.
2. Like the Eunuch, they, too, can take their faith back home with them. Elaborate.

To carry the idea just a little further, you might have Philip and the Eunuch offer a prayer to end the sermon.

Prayer For The Day
Make us bold in our witness as Easter people, O God, and show us how to make it in an effective and powerful way. And, like the Ethiopian on the Gaza road, help us to repent, believe, and take the faith to our homes. In Jesus' risen name. Amen.

Possible Metaphors And Stories
There is a powerful video titled *Enslavement: The True Story of Fanny Kemble*. She was an English actress who came to the U.S. and married a slave owner. There is a scene where he is whipping a slave tied to a stake and his wife Fannie embraces the slave so as to take the lashes for him. She wrote the famous *Georgia Journals* telling about the horrors of slavery, which helped abolish it.

W. H. Davis, the "tramp poet," tells how one of his vagrant friends, whenever he came into a town, looked for a church spire with a cross on top and began to beg in that area because there, from experience, he found people to be most generous.

I have many allergies and so when we built a new home in Arizona we paid extra to have an electronic air filter installed with our furnace. After three years we discovered that the electrician never hooked up the device! For three years I suffered with my allergies, but the air cleaner was not connected to the power. The branches *are* connected to the vine!

In Shakespeare's *The Two Gentlemen of Verona*, Julia says, "They do not love that do not show their love." And Lucetta later claims, "O, they love least that let men know their love." Then in Act Four, we have the phrase, "Love will creep in service where it cannot go" (meaning where it cannot go upright).

Fourth Sunday In May

Acts 10:44-48   1 John 5:1-6   John 15:9-17

Seasonal Theme   Alive and out of the grave, the risen Christ is witnessed in the real world.

Theme For The Day   We are chosen to be God's friends and intimate companions, which gives us a mission to carry out.

First Lesson   Acts 10:44-48   *Gentiles Receive The Holy Spirit*

The story continues from last week and the announcement made by Peter at the home of Cornelius, a Gentile, that "... God shows no partiality" (v. 24). Peter has preached another powerful sermon and included the Gentiles in God's plan of salvation for all the people. A marvelous thing happened there in Caesarea, the Holy Spirit came upon all who heard Peter, including the uncircumcised Gentiles being baptized in the spirit *before* baptism: this is a sign that God accepts the Gentiles, also. In verse 46 we have the proof that the Holy Spirit had come upon them: they spoke in tongues. The formula does not seem to be as commanded in Matthew 28:19 and as Trinitarian; but, rather, it is just in Jesus' name.

Second Lesson   1 John 5:1-6   *Faith Conquers The World*

An interesting analogy John uses: "... everyone who loves the parent loves the child" (v. 1b). Verse 3 claims that to love God is to obey God's commands. And these commands are not burdensome (even though they are often presented that way by us preachers!). The word "faith" is used in verse 4 but is rarely used in John's writing. Here it is presented as a victory that conquers the world. That is unusual to me to think of victory and faith together.

The Gospel   John 15:9-17   *Abiding In The Love Of Christ*

There are a number of strong theological teachings here:
1. We are to abide in the love of Christ.
2. To abide in God's love is to fulfill our joy and bring joy to the Christ.
3. We are to love each other as Jesus loved us.
4. We are friends of God and not just servants.
5. God chose us; we did not choose God.
6. God sends us out to do good things on God's behalf.

"Friends of God" is a very meaningful phrase that John uses to describe us and our relationship to God. The Eastern kings had a small intimate group called "Friends of the King" who could enter at any time without a security check. They had immediate and complete access to the king. So Jesus says we are "friends of God" who have immediate access to God through him, anytime, anywhere! It's so much more than just a constituent or servant or even neighbor. It's as much as, or even more than, a daughter or son.

Preaching Possibilities

The reading from Acts is an opportunity to preach about inclusiveness. The 1 John reading gives us opportunity to address the concept of *faith* in our lives and the Gospel can be the basis for what it means for Easter people to be "chosen by God" and to be "friends of God." All this can come under the theme of "abiding in Christ." If we preached last week on the Cornelius story, we can make this week part 2 and do a "The rest of the story" sermon. If we continue on the idea of "Easter discipleship" we can add that using all three readings for today we discover:

A. Easter disciples are inclusive and spirit filled (Acts 10:47).
B. Easter people love God's family and have deep victorious faith (1 John 5:4).
C. Easter people are no longer servants but friends of God (John 15:15).
D. God has chosen us to be Easter disciples (John 15:16).

Possible Outline Of Sermon Moves

This is an excellent Sunday to try an extended metaphor sermon. The metaphor comes from what we know about the Eastern kings in the days prior to Jesus and how they had a close circle of "Friends of the King." This can be used throughout the sermon to illustrate our relationship between us and God.

A. Begin by telling about a time when you wanted to see an important celebrity and how difficult it was (is) to see him and communicate with him.
B. Move to telling about the friends of the King in the time of Jesus.
C. Read the text in John 15:15 calling attention to the word "friends."
D. Relate what this means to us as "Easter people" today which we learn from the 3 readings:
   1. Our fellowship is inclusive and spirit-filled (Acts 10:47).
   2. Being friends of the King we love each other and have a deep victorious faith (1 John 5:4).
   3. We have direct and continuous access to God.
   4. We are treated like family and not like servants (John 15:15).
   5. We are appointed to go and do (John 15:17).
E. Now give your own witness what this all means to you referring again to the "Friends of the King" idea.
F. Then tell your listeners what you believe this "Friends of God" means for your congregation like: we work for an inclusive fellowship; we ought see the spirit in our worship; we ought work at our love for each other being obvious; our prayer life is done in direct connection with God; we develop what our mission is outside our church walls.
G. Return to the metaphor of "Friends of the King" and explain that if the King came to our town we would have direct access to him like a very big contributor has to a dignitary who comes to town. It would be like our standing on tip-toe to see the President in his motorcade and he would pick us up off the curb and place us in his limousine.
H. Frame your sermon by reading the text again (John 15:15) and returning to your story about seeing an important celebrity.

Prayer For The Day

We rejoice today that we are your friends, dear God, and not just your servants. We rejoice that you have chosen us for this special, intimate relationship with you (and with each other). Teach us to love each other and to have victorious faith, which propels us out into the world to be inclusive and an effective witness to the Easter resurrection. In Christ's name. Amen.

Possible Metaphors And Stories

Race is skin deep. A *New York Times* article by Natalie Angier (August 26, 2000) was headlined "Race Is Only Skin Deep." She wrote that scientists say it may be easy to tell at a glance whether a person is African or Caucasian or Asian but the differences dissolve at the DNA level. (May they dissolve at our church's level, as well!)

Dr. Craig Venters is quoted as saying, "We all evolved in the last 100,000 years from the same small number of tribes that migrated out of Africa and colonized the world." Venter and scientists at the National Institutes of Health have unanimously declared *there is only one race.*

So equatorial populations evolved dark skin, presumably to protect against ultraviolet radiation, while people in Northern latitudes evolved pale skin, the better to produce vitamin D from pale sunlight.

"All the races of men have sprung from the same blood and thus have the same bloodline ... as I in my age am a drop of the great river, a member of the church, so am I a brother of the fathers who came before me and the children who came after me" (Wilhelm Loehe).

For the lonely man, all the treasures of the world are no substitute for companionship. Narrower than a prison is the wide earth to an abandoned and lonely man ...

"Behold the Church! It is the very opposite of loneliness — blessed fellowship! There are millions of saints and believers who are blessed in it. No longer lonely, but filled, satisfied, yes blessed ..." (Wilhelm Loehe, *Three Books about the Church*, translated by James L. Schlaf).

Most of us have learned to live with "voice mail" as a now-necessary part of our daily lives. But have you ever wondered what it would be like if God decided to install voice mail?

Imagine praying and hearing this:

> *Thank you for calling Heaven. Please select one of the following options: Press 1 for Requests; Press 2 for Thanksgiving; Press 3 for Complaints; Press 4 for All Other Inquiries.*
>
> *I am sorry, all of our angels are busy helping others right now.*
>
> *However, your prayer is important to us and will be answered in the order in which it was received, so please stay on the line.*
>
> *If you would like to speak to God — press 1, to Jesus — press 2, to The Holy Spirit — press 3.*
>
> *If you would like to hear King David sing a Psalm while you are holding, please press 4.*
>
> *To find out if a loved one has been assigned to Heaven: press 5. Enter his or her Social Security number, then press the pound key. If you get a negative response, try area code 666.*
>
> *For nagging questions about dinosaurs, the age of the earth, and where Noah's Ark is, please wait until you arrive here.*
>
> *For reservations in Heaven, please enter J-O-H-N, followed by the numbers 3-1-6.*
>
> *Our computers show that you have already prayed once today. Please hang up and try again tomorrow.*
>
> *This office is closed for the weekend to observe a religious holiday. Please pray again Monday after 9:30 a.m.*
>
> *If you are calling after hours and need emergency assistance, please contact your local pastor or rabbi.*

First Sunday In June

| Acts 1:1-11 | Ephesians 1:15-23 | Luke 24:44-53 |

Seasonal Theme   Alive and out of the grave, the risen Christ is witnessed in the real world.

Theme For The Day   The time of Jesus' physical presence comes to a close and a new age of witnessing discipleship begins.

First Lesson   Acts 1:1-11   *The Ascension Of Jesus*

Addressing it to the same non-Jew "God lover," Dr. Luke had written his *Life and teachings of Jesus*; now he begins to write about life in the early church among the Apostles in Jerusalem. In his Gospel, Luke had described Jesus' life from the birth in Bethlehem until the Ascension, which we celebrate today. It is that ending of his physical presence by the Ascension Luke uses to begin this new book about life in the early church.

Perhaps the greatest thing Luke says in the second volume is that the life of Jesus is continued in the church. A couple of things to notice here. The disciples were to wait for the spirit (v. 4). They were not to go off "half-cocked." Wait for the power and the equipping of God's spirit, then go.

Verse 8 has been quoted by missionaries for centuries. We receive power, we are witnesses, and the church goes out into ever-widening circles.

These two men in white robes hearken us back to those same angels who were at the Easter empty tomb. They were messengers of God announcing for God the instructions. And as at the transfiguration, the instructions were that it was now time to get busy. There was witnessing to be done. A kingdom had to be organized and workers recruited.

Second Lesson   Ephesians 1:15-23   *Paul's Prayer And God's Power*

Paul is giving thanks to God for the faithfulness of his readers. Verse 17 assures us that to have God is to have wisdom and revelation. Verse 18 uses an old Hebrew thought. The "eyes of your heart," the heart is the seat and center of our deepest knowledge and experience. It conveys the change in the whole person as they are opened up to God's grace.

In the Christ, God's power was at work in the resurrection and the Ascension.

The great thought of this passage is that the Christ is the head of the church. And that the church is the alive body of Christ in the world (vv. 22-23). Second to that verse is verse 19 which talks about God's "immeasurable greatness of his power for us who believe." That will preach.

The Gospel   Luke 24:44-53   *The Ascension Of Jesus*

All that the Old Testament had promised, Jesus had now done. It was time to end this part of our salvation history and begin the mission of the church. Verse 47 lets us know that proclamation of repentance and forgiveness must now go to all nations. Disciples are witnesses and as such are clothed with God's power.

While I wouldn't present it to the congregation, it is odd that Luke dates the Ascension forty days after Easter in his book of Acts account, but here he puts it Easter night. Perhaps it's the emphasis each book was making. Luke's Gospel seems most likely as the promise to the thief on the cross seems to indicate (Luke 23:43). The Acts account was most interested in the significance of the risen Christ founding the church. And there needed to be those post-Easter appearances to prove the resurrection before the Ascension.

Notice that the Gospel ends where it began — in the temple. And with great joy.

Preaching Possibilities

The best approach to preaching on the Ascension may be to speak of why the writers wanted this story preserved and what it teaches us for our discipleship today. For instance, Gospel writer Luke tells it twice to Theophilus, the "God-lover" to whom he was writing, once in the Gospel and once in Acts. We read both accounts today. Combining these two readings lets us speak of the nature and mission of the church then and now. No longer with us in physical body, the Christian church now becomes his alive body in the world. There is power available to us to equip us for mission in the world. We have done enough looking into the heavens; it's time to go out as witnesses. Joy is to be found in witnessing and in the temple.

So we can easily use all three readings or any one of the three. I'll do a topical sermon based on "God's Immeasurable Greatness" in Ephesians 1:19.

Possible Outline Of Sermon Moves

Title: God's Immeasurable Greatness
Text: Ephesians 1:19

A. Introduction: Paul was writing a letter to be circulated among the Christian congregations he had begun. He told them that he prayed for them and that he was so thankful for them. Then he spoke of God's immeasurable greatness. Listen as I read his words to you (read the text).
B. Ask the question: What do you think Paul had in mind when he spoke of God's greatness?
   1. We have great power from him if we believe.
   2. God's power to raise Jesus from the grave and to do the same for us is promised.
   3. God's power, as manifest in God's worldwide church, is available to us.
   4. Throughout that church and in us, God's power to witness, heal, forgive, love, comfort, and teach us disciples. Is this complete?
C. State what you believe: My life can be dramatically changed because of God's power:
   1. Anger into kindness
   2. Jealousy into joy
   3. Slavery of sin into freedom in the Christ
   4. Greed into spirit of sharing
   5. Frantic worry into peace of mind
   6. Fearful of witnessing to bold in our reaching out
D. Go to the other readings: Tell of the power in Acts 1:8 and in Luke 24:49b.
E. Use Paul as an illustration: Tell how God took a bitter little Jew persecuting the Christians and changed him into the world's first and greatest Christian missionary.
F. Sing a verse of the famous hymn, "How Great Thou Art."
G. Conclude by reading again the text Ephesians 1:19

Prayer For The Day

Clothe us with your great power, O God, as you promised your disciples you would do. Give us the boldness to be effective witnesses out in the world where we live and work and play. We celebrate today your ascension that we might now be your presence in the world. You are great and we would do great things on your behalf here. In the risen and ascended Jesus' name. Amen.

Possible Metaphors And Stories

I once had an intern nicknamed "Crash Adrian." She drove church vans. She once crashed one into the other in our church lot. (We do hurt our own.)

Also, a van developed a power steering leak and began to turn only right, not left. She had to figure out her route from Walgreen's back to the church while turning only right. She did it by backing up a couple of times. There are times when we ought back up and go the other way. Perhaps we should examine our "power steering" also. What powers it and how reliable is it for us?

We almost always underestimate the power of the wind. I followed a truck today with its canvas flapping in the wind. You see it whenever humans try to tie down a cover on anything and then move it — or when the wind comes up. We almost always underestimate the Spirit's power as well. Let Pentecost blow!

In a promo for a television show, Class of '96, someone says: "Your true birthplace is the place where you find out who you are. Havenhurst — I have come home to the place of my birth." In my relationship with the Christ I have found out who I am and how I am. In the Christian church I have come home to the place of my birth.

In Iowa the highway snowplow trucks have two mirrors on top. One is on each side of the rotating blue light so you get the effect of three emergency lights rather than the one it really is. We can be the mirror of the light of Christ in the dark world in which we live. We are not the Christ, but we are called to reflect him.

Second Sunday In June

Acts 2:1-11 or
　Ezekiel 37:1-14

Romans 8:22-27 or
　Acts 2:1-21

John 15:26-27; 16:4b-15

Seasonal Theme   We learn from the miracles, parables, and ministry of Jesus and grow in our faith.

Theme For The Day   The birth of the Christian Church and the coming upon the disciples of the Holy Spirit.

First Lesson   Acts 2:1-11   *The Day Of Pentecost*

From *Harper's Bible Dictionary* we find a ready-made outline for preaching. Pentecost was also known as:
A. "The Feast of Weeks," Exodus 34:22; Deuteronomy 16:10
B. "The Feast of Harvest," Exodus 23:16
C. "The Day of First Fruits," Numbers 28:26

Pentecost means the fiftieth day. It was seven weeks after Passover (our Easter). It was the beginning of the harvest of fruit as the Feast of Unleavened Bread opened the grain harvest. In later Judaism the festival took on the anniversary of the giving of the law at Sinai so it came to be a joint historical and harvest celebration. Many Jews would be in Jerusalem. The Holy Spirit came upon the disciples numbering 120. The tongues of fire (v. 3) were the same as the burning bush in Exodus 3:2. Here then is the birth of the Christian Church. Paul wrote in 1 Corinthians 16:8 of waiting until after Pentecost before his return to Corinth from Ephesus. He probably wanted to "work the crowds" of Pentecost with the new-found gospel. Psalm 29 is used liturgically for this day of celebration.

The Spirit's power was so strong that it provided those disciples a message all the people could understand.

Second Lesson   Romans 8:22-27   *Christian Hope And Prayer*

Paul the optimist tells us in verse 24 that we are saved by hope. Life, according to him, is not a dismal waiting for death in sin and decay. We could look forward to a new freedom and change brought to us by God's power in Jesus Christ. Because we Christians not only live in the sinful world, we also live in Christ, which gives us a picture of God's love and power and mercy. We anticipate life, not death; and we have a hope rather than giving up.

Verses 26 and 27 give us insight on prayer. Because we don't know what's best for us and because we don't know the future, we can't pray as we ought. The best we can do is offer a sigh and the Spirit will intercede for us. Perhaps the best prayer is simply saying to God that you submit to God your spirit and it's God's will you seek.

The Gospel   John 15:26-27; 16:4b-15   *The Work Of The Spirit*

Verses 26 and 27 tell us that the Spirit will help our hearts believe and that we are to help others believe by our witness. Then in verses 5-11 he tells his sad disciples that his leaving is best for them — because when he leaves, the "helper" or "advocate" will come to them. While Jesus was with them in person, they were confined to his whereabouts; but when he left and the Holy Spirit came, he could be with them (and us) everywhere. We then have three great words describing the Spirit's work: sin, righteousness, and judgment (see vv. 8-11). So we might say that this Holy Spirit persuades us of our sin and assures us of our Savior.

Notice verses 12-15 assure us that the Spirit will continue to reveal God, direct, and inspire us.

Preaching Possibilities

The story of the Pentecost birthday of the Christian Church is definitely in the First Lesson. Also the Second Reading or the Gospel has plenty of content for inspired, relevant preaching. These two selections are full of information about the Spirit and could be combined for a sermon on "The Work of the Spirit." Some of the content could be:

A. The Spirit of God gives us endless and boundless hope (Romans 8:24).
B. The Spirit of God teaches us to pray (Romans 8:27).
C. The Spirit of God becomes our Advocate (John 15:26).
D. The Spirit of God teaches us about sin, righteousness, and judgment (John 16:8-11).
E. The Spirit of God gives us our universal advantage (John 16:7).

If we somehow got through the Easter season without talking about witness, it is in all three readings today.

Possible Outline Of Sermon Moves

Title: A Spirit-Filled Church
Text: Acts 2:1-21

A. Introduction: Re-tell in your own words the Pentecost experience of those disciples and describe how this is the birthday of the Christian church.
B. Move to how this event shaped our contemporary church.
   1. It will be a Spirit-filled church (v. 4). Until now those disciples were afraid but now they boldly stand in the Jerusalem square.
   2. It is an inclusive church (v. 4). The message included everyone in his or her language.
   3. It was an amazing church (v. 12). God's deeds and power were evident (v. 11) and it astonished everyone.
   4. It was a visionary church (v. 17b) they prophesied and dreamed.
   5. It was a church of salvation for its people (v. 21). The gospel was proclaimed and people were baptized and saved.
C. Now talk about what this Jerusalem church has that your congregation ought work harder at.
D. Give your witness. Tell your people which elements you long for in your congregation and how you will try to work for them.
E. Invite your hearers to join you in making your congregation more like this first one in Jerusalem.
F. Frame the sermon by returning to the opening description of the Pentecost experience and end assuring the listeners this action is to be continued.

Prayer For The Day

We celebrate your Church, O God, and your spirit, which still inspires and instructs us today. Help us here at *(your congregation)* to be a spirit-filled congregation reflecting the diversity of your creation and motivated to witness to the Gospel inviting others to join us as your saved family. In Christ's name. Amen.

Possible Metaphors And Stories

I heard the Reverend Joseph Wold tell the story of a young Dwight L. Moody wanting to join a church in Boston. He had brought many poor into the worship services and the membership committee were not sure they wanted such a radical in their midst! The elders told him when he applied for membership that he should take a month and "go pray about it." He came back and said he had prayed about it to Jesus and Jesus told him not to be upset about being put off by the committee. Jesus said he had been trying to get in that church for years!

At a Memorial Day weekend speech at the Rotary Club of Des Moines, the General of the National Guard explained the use of the army rallying point. When troops go out to fight, if they get lost or scattered, the rallying point is a pre-arranged place like a fork in the road, high building, bend in river, and so forth, where they all meet again and rally before going back into battle.

Where are the rallying points of our battlefield lines? Which others meet us there to rally with us?

Did you hear about the man who bought a stationary exercise bike and hired the neighbor boy to come in and ride it for him? Or the man who joined the church but never attended? He just mailed in his offering each month.

In *The San Francisco Chronicle* (March 18, 1996): "Pepper Spray Stuns Oakland Congregation." A sixty-year-old woman was hospitalized and twenty other Oakland churchgoers were treated for eye and throat irritation after a pepper spray canister accidentally went off inside a woman's purse. It was at the Green Pasture Church. According to the newspaper, "The fumes spread, causing some church members to develop symptoms."

What might be the symptoms of the spirit being set free? Apostolic radical, infectious witness syndrome, greed appendicitis, grace co-dependency, servanthood obsessive-compulsive, and so forth?

Third Sunday In June

Isaiah 6:1-8   Romans 8:12-17   John 13:1-17

Theme For The Day   God as our parent, our Savior, and spiritual presence with us now.

Old Testament Lesson   Isaiah 6:1-8   *Isaiah's Call*

No doubt this passage was selected for Trinity Sunday because it can be considered as a precursor of the Trinity. It is the year of King Uzziah's death and the Temple was about to lose its glory — never to return to this state. The Romans would be coming to destroy it all. In verse 2 we have the fiery guardians of the Lord's holiness. Two wings covered their faces — in awe; two wings covered their feet — acknowledging the lowliness of their service; two wings were used for flying or hovering. These things were continuous. Then we have the threefold Holy in verse 3.

The fire on the altar of incense and this vision caused Isaiah to utter verse 5. And there is mercy for such a repentant person. His sins were forgiven. The way was now prepared for Isaiah to deliver his message.

This is often thought of as Isaiah's initial call to be a prophet. We ought note how strongly the prophet felt his commission from God. Being in God's presence he had no alternative but to accept this commission to preach a rather unpopular message to the people.

New Testament Lesson   Romans 8:12-17   *Children Of God*

Paul develops the metaphor of adoption as descriptive of our new relationship with God. We are adopted by God and thus become "children of God" — a part of God's family (v. 14). It is the Holy Spirit herself which is the witness to our adoption and thus our inheritance (v. 16). Paul saw our entry into God's family like a Roman adoption. We do nothing to earn or to deserve it. God takes us into God's family because of his love and mercy. All our sins forgiven, we become inheritors of God's undeserved love and glory.

The Gospel   John 3:1-17   *Nicodemus Visits Jesus*

Nicodemus was a distinguished Pharisee who served in the Jewish Sanhedrin. We only meet him in this Gospel. Perhaps he was more liberal than some and open to new ideas. In John 7:50-51 he defended Jesus from prejudicial accusations and in 19:39 he joins Joseph of Arimathea in providing a decent burial place for Jesus. Notice how each man treats the other with respect as a teacher.

According to *Harper's Bible Dictionary*, "Legends without biblical foundation tell that Nicodemus was baptized by Peter and John, and banished from Jerusalem during the Jewish uprising against Stephen. The Apocryphal Gospel of Nicodemus dates from the thirteenth century A.D."

Verses 16-17 are all this man needed to know and believe. God gave a son so he might have eternal life and that son did not come to condemn but to save.

Preaching Possibilities

Individually, there are many sermon possibilities. The Old Testament Lesson lends itself to Isaiah's call and commission and ours. The New Testament Reading will work as a rich metaphor about our new relationship to God and to each other. We are adopted into God's family and this God is our parent and we are brothers and sisters. The Gospel has three great themes: Nicodemus as a secret disciple, or at least a fair person, looking out for the treatment of some radical Jews; the "little Gospel" of John 3:16 or the assurance of John 3:17 that God doesn't want to *judge* or punish but to *save*.

After saying the above, I must remind you that this is a special Sunday in the church year. It is the only Sunday when we celebrate a doctrine rather than events in the life of Jesus and the early church and his teachings. So I think we must go with that very difficult theme of Trinity. Because the church mothers and fathers thought it important in explaining our beliefs about God, we must try our best to help our hearers come to understand this complicated belief.

Possible Outline Of Sermon Moves
A. Begin with a story about an adoption you know of or witnessed and what a difference it has made in that person's life.
B. Move to Paul's claim in the Second Reading that God has adopted us into God's family.
C. List out what you believe are the implications of being adopted into God's family:
   1. We are there by undeserved grace and mercy.
   2. We ought treat each other as brothers and sisters.
   3. There ought be an unbreakable good will amongst us no matter what happens — we are family.
D. Move to the fact that this is Trinity Sunday and these scriptures help us understand a little how our Holy Parent is.
   1. God is one who loves us so much that he gave his son for us — John 3:16.
   2. God is spirit and wants us to be born of the spirit as well as water — John 3:5.
   3. God has a mission and ministry for us as his adopted people — Isaiah 6:8.
E. Pull it all together by stating we have an adopted father who adopts us like a loving parent, gives his son Jesus for our sins, and is with us still in spirit.
F. Frame by returning to the story of an adoption you know of and how beautiful it has been over the years relating that to God and God's adoption of us.

A Teaching Sermon Alternative
A more simple approach to this doctrinal Sunday would be to use Luther's Catechism and the meanings to the three "articles" of the Apostles' Creed.
A. Introduction: Explain that this is the one Sunday in the year when we learn about a belief, the Holy Trinity.
   1. Have the congregation say the first article of the Apostles' Creed. Tell them this is God at work with us as a father and creator.
   2. Now have the congregation recite Luther's meaning to the first article.
B. Move to the second article and have them read about God as our Savior Jesus Christ.
   1. Tell them what it means to have a Savior and use the John 3:16-*17* Gospel for the day.
   2. Have them read Luther's explanation of the second article.
C. Move to the third article and have them read it together about God at work with us now as Holy Spirit and the Christian Church.
   1. Tell about being adopted by God in the Romans account and how that ought be reflected in your congregation.
   2. Now read together the meaning of the third article of the creed.
D. Sum up by presenting the Trinity: God as out Parent, our Savior, and our Spirit present with us now.

Prayer For The Day
Holy Parent who has adopted us into your saved family even though we don't deserve it, help us through your ever-present spirit to be faithful children in your special family. Show us our commission as you did Isaiah in the temple and move us beyond the academic timid discipleship of Nicodemus to loyal undeserving family members for whom Jesus was given on a cross. In the name of God our father, our savior, and our spirit presence. Amen.

Possible Metaphors And Stories

Some object lessons for today's Trinity emphasis would be the sassafras leaf's three shapes, but still all sassafras; the different forms of water: ice, liquid, and steam; the different roles a parent plays but all still our parent: father, teacher, protector, husband, etc.

It was a 32-foot wooden cabin cruiser moored next to our dock, owned by our neighbor, John Roench. At 12:30 p.m., the stern began to sink. Frantically I called John at his office. But by 2 p.m. when he arrived, the boat had completely sunk. Vessel Rescue came with two divers who went to the bottom and placed rubber bladders under the keel. Then while pumping out water from the hull they pumped air into those bladders ... and up she came! Now after being under water and the hull swelling up she floated unassisted. When we are inundated and sinking, the breath of the spirit will lift us up as well. We also have a rescue.

A recent newspaper account of a fire in San Francisco stated the fire department is looking for "suspected accelerants in the ashes." How about Pentecost accelerants? What is it the spirit of God can best use to accelerate the Pentecost fire again? Let it be us through whom a new fire is ignited in the souls of our people. Oh, that we could accelerate the fire in our soul to witness, steward, minister to, and have compassion for all God's people.

HMOs are everywhere ... health maintenance organizations. We who are God's church are SMOs ... spiritual maintenance organizations. Annual check-up, regular devotions, test the heart for capacity! What ought we do to fulfill our God-given mandate?

Fourth Sunday In June

1 Samuel 17:(1a, 4-11, 19-23) 32-49   2 Corinthians 6:1-13   Mark 4:35-41

Seasonal Theme   We learn of the Christian faith and how we are to follow Jesus as his disciples.

Theme For The Day God's presence provides us a courageous way to face the many struggles and problems that come to us.

Old Testament Lesson   1 Samuel 17:(1a, 4-11, 19-23) 32-49   *David And Goliath*

During the street fighting of 2000 and 2001 in Palestine between Israelis and Arabs, this story took on a poignant meaning. We saw daily scenes on our televisions of young Arab boys with slingshots hitting heavily armed Israeli soldiers. Notice the contrast. Goliath, 9' 9" tall with a bronze helmet and a coat of scale armor weighing 125 pounds. He had a long spear and a bronze javelin (v. 7). David, unable to wear the heavy armor of King Saul, had a sling and five smooth stones. The confrontation took place outside Jerusalem where the two armies were facing each other over the Valley of Elah. They had decided one representative from each side would determine the victor. It was a scheme that, no doubt, conserved the lives of many soldiers. It's a story that can be retold with great theatre.

New Testament Lesson   2 Corinthians 6:1-13   *Enduring Our Struggles*

Paul begins chapter 6 with a crucial plea. Don't take God's grace in vain (v. 6:1). God gives us all this love undeserved and Paul says don't make what God has done for us on the cross having been done in vain. Verse 4 continues with Paul calling himself a servant of God. Then he lists a long catalogue of troubles he has *endured* to be that faithful servant. And that word *endured* is an important one. Chrysostom calls this word, which comes from the Greek *hypomone* "the queen of virtues, the foundation of right actions, peace in war, calm in tempest, security in plots." Barclay says of *hypomone*, "It is the courageous and triumphant ability to bear things which enables a man to pass the breaking point and not to break and always greet the unseen with a cheer." So this is no passive accepting of our troubles in a fatalistic manner; but rather finding a way to turn them into strength and victory. It is a long list and there are alternatives to the bad: purity, knowledge, patience, kindness, holiness of spirit, genuine love, truthful speech, and the power of God.

This whole passage is a fine description of the struggle to be a faithful Christian and follow Christ as his disciple.

The Gospel   Mark 4:35-41   *Jesus Stills A Storm*

Here is a story told by Mark to prove the power of Jesus over nature. We could try to explain how this happened; but we would probably miss the point of Mark's relating the incident by doing so. Notice as Mark tells it the disciples scold Jesus for not being more concerned. In Matthew 8:25 and Luke 8:42, the disciples' scolding is changed to a request for help. Perhaps the peace Jesus commands is more needed by the disciples than it is by the wind and waves! In his typical fashion, Mark presents the disciples as bewildered and filled with awe. Notice, too, that the words Jesus used to address the wind and waves are exactly the words used in Mark 1:25 to the demon possessed man. Sometimes it does seem as though nature gets taken over by the power that opposes God. It's almost like demon possession.

Preaching Possibilities

This is a rare Sunday (in my opinion) when we could use any of the three readings by themselves for our sermon text, or use all three together on the topic of courage, or even use either two of the three with good results. For a possible development of the Gospel by itself, see my *The Miracles Of Jesus And Their Flip Side*, CSS Publishing, 2000, pp. 53-57. In this treatment, I have proposed the "flip side" as being: "Perhaps Jesus calming was not so much the waves and the wind on Galilee that day, but rather the fear and panic in the hearts of those sailor-disciples." The Second Reading is a rich deposit of challenges of being a Christian and the victorious ways we can get through.

Possible Outline Of Sermon Moves

A. Introduction: The two stories and a letter we read today as our Bible readings all cry out for us to have *courage*.
B. Tell in your own words of David whipping Goliath. The story of Jesus stilling the storm, then Paul's struggle in being a Christian.
C. Now invite your hearers to consider each one of these readings and what they tell us about facing adversities and coming through:
   1. The odds were against young and small David except he was on the right side. And he wasn't weighed down with armor and he had courage to do it.
   2. The disciples forgot in that storm they were in the same boat as Jesus. When they remembered it they had a new courage to get to the other side.
   3. Paul reminds us that there is a *courageous* endurance that gets us through the worst of struggles. As David took his slingshot and the disciples asked for help, so Paul says that's the victorious way we can endure our problems and difficulties.
D. Move to an illustration in your own life where at first you thought all was lost and then God gave *courage*.
E. Move to how these stories ought to affect our congregational ministries of each member here in the church and out in each individual's daily lifestyle.
   Optional: Talk about the congregation's problems and how the boat has always been a symbol of the church. We, too, as a congregation, must not give up; but have *courage* and know the peace available in our storms.
F. Frame the sermon by referring to the three lessons and their main teachings in reverse order.
   3. Paul teaches us about courageous endurance.
   2. Jesus teaches us to remain calm in the storms that come.
   1. And brave young David illustrates courage when God is on our side.

Prayer For The Day

Give us courage, O God, that we might accept our struggles with your help and do our best to overcome them. And when the forces seem overwhelmingly against us, give us the bravery of David and the peace of the storm-surrounded disciples. In Jesus' name. Amen.

Possible Metaphors And Stories

The Philistine Goliath from Gath looked so big and strong, no Israelite soldier had the courage to fight there in the valley of Elah against him. David, however, saw him so big he just couldn't miss with his trusty slingshot!

When rough seas and wild storms rage about us,
There is one who can speak the word of blessed calm,
To still the turmoils which often so threaten us.
Yet, best of all, guide us through while winds rage on. — JLS

A special program about Pope John Paul II tells about his assistant when he was a bishop and the communists demanded work stop on a church at Mora Huta. The Communists said it could not be built. His assistant said he was afraid. John Paul replied, "Nicolei, fear only poor work." Sometimes our best contribution in the circumstances is to do our work well.

John Wayne, born in Winterset, Iowa: "Courage is being scared to death and saddling up anyway." Perhaps this kind of bravado helps if one believes it deeply enough.

Fifth Sunday In June

| 2 Samuel 1:1, 17-27 | 2 Corinthians 8:7-15 | Mark 5:21-43 |

Seasonal Theme   We learn of the Christian faith and how we are to follow Jesus as his disciples.

Theme For The Day   The compassion of Jesus for those of high office and those lost in the crowd.

Old Testament Lesson   2 Samuel 1:1, 17-27   *A Poem Of Grieving*

David becomes the king over Judah and then all Israel. He becomes the true theocratic king and under his leadership the country did well defeating their enemies and prospering. We'll be reading from this book the next seven Sundays.

David's mourning publicly over the deaths of Saul and Jonathan is preserved for us in verses 19-27. This was made into a poem and titled "The Song of the Bow." Notice it opens and closes with the thought, "How the mighty have fallen." The loyalty of Jonathan to his father Saul is praised. But it was Jonathan who David especially grieved over and yet celebrated his long friendship (see v. 26).

New Testament Lesson   2 Corinthians 8:7-15   *The Genuineness Of Love*

This is one of Paul's financial stewardship letters. He is appealing to the congregation to excel in this offering as they have excelled in other ways. He sites God's self-giving as a motivation for their Christian generosity. He claims it is Jesus' coming to earth and becoming a human bringing heaven's riches to us, which should provide our motivation for sacrificial giving. Paul claims the readiness to give as proof of genuine love ... and without any reservations. The idea in verse 14 is intriguing. "Their abundance may be for your need, in order that there might be a fair balance." This fair balance is illustrated with the experience of Israel with the manna in the wilderness (Exodus 16:18).

The Gospel   Mark 5:21-43   *Jairus' Daughter And A Hemorrhaging Woman*

The following comments follow closely the material found in *The Interpreter's One Volume Commentary on the Bible*. This is two miracle stories with one contained inside the other. It is also recorded in Matthew 9:18-26 and Luke 8:40-56. The story is told to demonstrate the power of Jesus over life and death. Faith is a big part of both miracles; but in the case of the daughter, it was the faith of her father, Jairus. In the case of the woman with a hemorrhage, it was her own faith. In both cases, no doubt the role of faith was to allow God's power to work. I doubt very much it had a proportional effect on the healing. In verse 39, those of us who see this healing of misdiagnosis take the words literally. However, sleeping was a common word to designate death. "Taking by the hand" in verse 41 is the same as when Jesus healed Simon Peter's mother-in-law recorded in Mark 1:31. Verse 43 is consistent with Mark's repeated comment to the reader that Jesus did not seek publicity.

The twelve-year-old daughter of Jairus was just now old enough to be considered a woman according to Jewish custom. She was at the beginning of her womanhood, which makes it doubly tragic.

The woman with the hemorrhage had in her Talmud no less than eleven curses for this malady. Most were sheer superstitions. And this particular problem made the woman continuously unclean, which closed her out of all fellowship with friends and worship of God (Leviticus 15:25-27). In both cases, Jesus was their last resort.

Preaching Possibilities

There are a couple of ways the Old Testament Lesson could connect and provide an introduction to the Gospel healings. Like David's thoughts about Saul and how the mighty have fallen, so this leader of the Synagogue now has to give up his prestige and approach Jesus. And as David grieves the loss of Saul, so Jairus grieves his daughter's death. It's a stretch and I will not go there. The Old Testament will stand alone in a topical sermon about death and grieving. "The Song of the Bow" can be introduced with good background on David and his relationship to Saul and especially Jonathan whom he so loved. Then proceed to talk about "when we mourn," we can be sure of these things:

A. Grieving is an integral part of living and no matter how faithful we are we must go through it.
B. God knows our pain of loss and is ready to comfort.
C. We do not grieve alone — others of God's family are with us.
D. Jesus is with the one we grieve and is with us. It is the same one who would heal the daughter of Jairus and the same one who would stop in a crowd and help a wretched woman who had suffered for years.

The New Testament Reading is a good base for a sermon on financial stewardship. This is material we Americans need desperately to hear in our culture, which is rampant with wealth addiction.
Paul on financial stewardship:

A. The genuineness of a Christian's love is tested in his or her generosity in sharing money (v. 8).
B. We give our money for others because of what Jesus has given for us (his life) (v. 9).
C. If we strongly want to share and help others we need to fulfill that eagerness to do with actual sharing (v. 12).
D. We need to keep a balance between our abundance and others' needs (vv. 13-14).

In relationship to C and D above, I hope you will stress the fact that we Christians who live in this culture have a bigger need to give our money away than the church has to have it. See below section on "Possible Metaphors And Stories" for a couple of stories that can be used.

So today we have three readings which are pregnant with homiletic possibilities. Each one is full of potential for preaching God's word for our people.

Possible Outline Of Sermon Moves

Let's try a first-person monologue sermon having the woman with the hemorrhage tell the story.
A. Have the woman tell how awful it had been for her for many years because of her hemorrhaging.
B. Then she tells of all the remedies she had tried until she had no resources left and was destitute.
C. Now have her tell of hearing about a "miracle worker" coming to her town — and seeing Jairus approach him and deciding if he would go with Jairus, perhaps he would help her.
D. Have her describe her hope to just touch his robe in order to have the healing and the effort to do so ... then admitting to Jesus what she had done.
E. Now comes an emotional description of her healing and the difference in her life since.
F. Then have her describe following this Jesus to Jairus' house and what she saw there.
G. Now the "so what?" of the dialogue. Have her tell what she advised Jairus should be the response to what Jesus had done for them. That would be individually and as a congregation over which he was president.
H. Conclude by having this woman say something like: "And Pastor *(your name)*, if I could talk to your congregation, I would encourage them, because of what I have told them today, to do the following": *(Make three or four suggestions that fit your context and ministry like: we should notice the individuals lost in the crowd in our community who need Jesus' attention and help them on his behalf.)*

Prayer For The Day

Jesus, you help the proud and people of high office as well as those lost in the crowd. Help us to be the instruments through which you continue to extend your love and compassion. And open our hearts to the needs of others with a willingness to be very generous. Like Jairus and the woman with the hemorrhage, we, too, are thankful for all the ways you see us and our needs and have reached out to help. In Christ's name. Amen.

Possible Metaphors And Stories

The newspaper article simply stated, "Orphan found jewelry, becomes rich this week." A sixteen-year-old orphan found a vinyl bag by the railroad tracks near his home in Hollywood, Florida, and thought it contained costume jewelry. Now he has found out the 116 pieces are worth about $400,000 to $600,000. The boy's lawyer said Eric has dropped out of school partly because of the publicity over the find. Our lives do have underestimated treasures yet to be discovered. Also, riches can destroy our best of motivations.

Chim Pitch of Cambodia and Stella Min of Myanmar (Burma) both tell of the same practice by Christians in their countries: When they go to cook their rice, they always take the first handful of grain and put it in a special container, which is set aside to be brought to the church each Sunday. This rice is then used to feed the poor and for the victims of the annual flooding in their countries.

Death flutes wailed a morbid tune for Jairus' daughter;
At life's end our graceful God provides for us and loved ones,
By touch old woman's hemorrhage dried from compassion,
Even when ridiculed, health and wellness is our ministry. — JLS

The big fire at Thousand Oaks, California, was started by a homeless man trying to keep warm. Many million dollar homes burned to the ground. Perhaps they failed to take in the man. We pay a price whenever we ignore the poor and homeless. Eventually it comes back to our own lives and homes.

In our Hong Kong chapel service we were asked to pray for a recent graduate of this seminary, Fong, Ching Ye, who had fallen and broken a leg. After the service the seminary chaplain explained to me that her congregation would suspect she is not spiritual enough or this would not have happened to her. How easy it is to let superstition take the place of faith.

First Sunday In July

2 Samuel 5:1-5, 9-10   2 Corinthians 12:2-10   Mark 6:1-13

Seasonal Theme   We learn of the Christian faith and how we are to follow Jesus as his disciples.

Theme For The Day   God often speaks to us in the everyday familiar and we must travel light in our mission as disciples of Christ.

Old Testament Lesson   2 Samuel 5:1-5, 9-10   *David Anointed King*

David is installed king over the entire nation. He agreed to follow the requirement set down for kingship found in Deuteronomy 17:14-20. Now King David moved the capital to Jerusalem as it was on the border between Judah and the Northern tribes. Mount Zion and Mount Ophel became the city of David (vv. 5:7, 9; 6:12). The "Millo" in verse 9 is interesting. It may mean that which was filled in between the hills to level the city. 1 Kings 9:15 and 24 may indicate that it was mounds erected to protect the city from the North.

The capture of Jerusalem was a sign to all Israel that God was with him. He was no fly-by-night tribal chief but a major political power. So now we have a consolidated kingdom with a recognized powerful king.

New Testament Lesson   2 Corinthians 12:2-10   *Paul's Thorn In His Flesh*

In this passage, Paul opens himself up to us in a heartfelt honesty. Both his suffering and his glory are here. As if he is outside himself he says, "I know a man ..." Of course, this is Paul describing a spiritual experience of ecstasy and nearness to God. Paradise comes from a Persian word for a walled garden where a king would invite someone to be honored, to be his companion in the garden. So, for a time, Paul had been a companion of God. But the thorn in his flesh is even more interesting (v. 7).

William Barclay says of the word it more likely meant a stake upon which criminals were impaled (*skolops*). Many have speculated on what this thorn was:
1. Luther thought it was opposition and persecution.
2. Spiritual temptations.
3. Carnal temptations is the common Roman Catholic view.
4. Paul's physical appearance (2 Corinthians 10:10).
5. Epilepsy has been a common explanation.
6. The oldest theory is severe headaches.
7. I have always thought of it as eye trouble. Perhaps he never recovered from the Damascus Road light (Acts 9:9). Also see Galatians 4:15 and 6:11.
8. William Barclay goes for "chronically recurrent attacks of a certain malarial fever." We who have served in Africa and seen this disease can go for that theory, also.
9. I have one more theory for which there is no room to develop in this manuscript. I wonder if it might have been Paul's failed marriage that tormented him all his life?

Whatever the torment, Paul tells the Corinthians that God's grace was sufficient for him (v. 9) and that's the powerful homiletic here. Even though Paul was weakened from this problem — in his weakness God's grace made him strong. It will really preach.

The Gospel   Mark 6:1-13   *Jesus Rejected In His Hometown*

In the synagogue it was the custom to have great teachers. In this account Jesus was asked to teach in his hometown synagogue. The people were amazed and astonished. They just couldn't believe this hometown boy whose family they knew could be what he claimed to be. Verse 4 is one of the often-quoted verses of scripture.

Any pastor who has returned to the congregation where she or he grew up knows the situation well. The "amazed" in verse 6 may have been the author Mark's more than Jesus'.

In verses 7–13 we see the mission of the disciples. They were to travel light. From these verses we can see Jesus would have us disciples live simply, put our trust in him and not things, and be generous in giving of ourselves rather than demanding privileges due us. It's a message we clergy and preachers can take to heart.

Hospitality was an important virtue in the Palestinian village. Jesus told his disciples to move on if it were refused to them. It may be that the mission was so urgent that Jesus was telling them to move on if the people were not receptive. Time was short.

Preaching Possibilities

I see little connection between the three readings. And I don't think the Old Testament Lesson is very productive for preaching. One could use it to address the right and wrong idea of God being on a nation's side. Or one might talk about the divine right of the Jew to have Jerusalem. I cannot get my head around either!

Paul's writing about his religious experience and his life-long suffering is very productive for preaching to our contemporary congregations. It deals with religious experience, suffering, and somehow with God's help getting through.

A brief outline might go like this:
A. Tell about your own or another person's particular struggle.
B. Tell about Saint Paul's thorn in the flesh and what it might have been (read v. 7b).
C. Give your own idea of what the thorn was like: Malaria?
D. Now move to the fact that God doesn't remove our thorns but gives us the stuff to endure them (v. 9), which becomes your text.
E. List out how that "sufficient grace" might look now: a comforting prayer and worship life; a real presence in the sacrament; a supporting fellowship encouraging us; a knowledge that Jesus knows what it is to suffer ... etc.
F. Return to your own or another person's thorn you began with. See below a couple of illustrations for the above homiletical plot.

Possible Outline Of Sermon Moves
A. Retell the story of Jesus returning and trying to teach in his own hometown.
B. Tell what we learn from this story:
   1. God is often in the very familiar around us and we can easily overlook God's wisdom and presence.
   2. Sometimes it is the most difficult to witness to your own family.
   3. Rarely can we accomplish much on God's behalf unless it is with those who expect us to do so.
C. Move to the mission of the twelve. Tell the story in your own words. You might even put it in present language: authority to confront today's evil; don't take travelers' checks or credit cards; no large suitcases full of extra clothing, one set is enough; don't move to a more expensive motel.
D. Then move to what this teaches us:
   1. As disciples we must travel light in this world.
   2. Our mission is urgent — move on to the most promising.
   3. We are sent out just like those early disciples.
E. Consider what these teachings mean for you as the preacher and for your congregation as God's disciples now.
F. Invite your hearers to join you in one small step to carry out what you have learned today.

Prayer For The Day

Help us to see your true presence all around us in the familiar, O God, and to hear the nearby voices that speak for you. And equip us to be faithful disciples going out this week to witness to our faith and not to be discouraged by rejection. Give to us the ability to travel light as we carry out your urgent message. In Jesus' name. Amen.

Possible Metaphors And Stories

In an ad for a large insurance company, The Hartford, these words are used, "Bring it on." It is to communicate the idea that whatever life deals out to us, if we have Hartford Insurance we can say, "Bring it on!" Paul could say it, too; not because of Hartford, but because of God's "sufficient grace" (2 Corinthians 12:9).

When flying into Stapleton Airport one morning, we took a very bad jolt. The pilot explained this as being caused by "jet wash," which came from a plane which crossed our path a while back and we could not now see two miles to the left of us. We get "bumped" by the jet wash of others, their good or poor actions before us — former pastor, lover, employee, family member. When it jolts us, it is a surprise. Being able to understand this can help us adjust to the rough flying conditions.

In a D-Day special on CBS, Dan Rather was talking with Norman Schwarzkopf. He told how the paratroopers were dropped at night and given little metal crickets to use in identifying each other in the dark to find out if a troop were friend or enemy. What can we offer to identify our discipleship and allegiance?

It is told of the "Swedish Nightingale," Jenny Lind, that she always spent a few minutes alone in her dressing room before giving a concert. She would strike a clear vibrant note and then pray, "Master, let me sing true tonight." Might our prayer be similar. Let our witness sing clear and true.

Second Sunday In July

2 Samuel 6:1-5, 12b-19　　　　　　　　Ephesians 1:3-14　　　　　　　　Mark 6:14-29

An Introduction To Ephesians

For the next seven weeks our Second Reading will be from the book of Ephesians. Most believe that Paul wrote this book during his two-year imprisonment in Rome. This was sent as a circular letter to be read at worship in congregations Paul had begun including Ephesus, an important city in western Asia located at the intersection of several major trade routes. These congregations were established on Paul's third missionary journey.

No particular problems are addressed; rather, Paul tries to explain God's eternal purpose and the goals that God has for the church. A major theme is unity in the congregation as one family who ought live in love toward each other.

Seasonal Theme　　　We learn of the Christian faith and how we are to follow Jesus as his disciples.

Theme For The Day　　We are tempted in many ways and pray for the strength to resist and the wisdom to control our desires.

Old Testament Lesson　　　2 Samuel 6:1-5, 12b-19　　　　*David Brings The Ark To Jerusalem*

The ark had been separated from the places of their worship for 100 years. Now that David captured Jerusalem, he could retrieve it from Kiriath Jearim (Joshua 15:9) and bring it to the neutral place of Jerusalem, the new capital of the Kingdom. He would place it in the tabernacle he would build on Mount Zion and announce that Jerusalem is the religious center of the nation.

The ark is described in Exodus 25:10-22. Its contents were the two tablets of stone on which were the Ten Commandments, the basis of the covenant between God and the people. The ark's history reflects the history of its people, according to *Harper's Bible Dictionary* where we find the following information:

Carried by sons of Levi in the wilderness	Deuteronomy 31:9
Brought over the Jordan by the priest	Joshua 3:17
Was at the fall of Jericho	Joshua 6:4-11
Placed at Shilo	Joshua 18:1
Captured by the Philistines	1 Samuel 4
And now brought to Jerusalem by David	1 Chronicles 13:3-14

After being in a tent-like sanctuary, it is now placed in the Temple of Solomon beneath the cherubim *(Debri)*. We don't know what ever happened to it. I have seen a frieze found at Capernaum, which looked like a wagon with a small columned structure, flanked by lions, which may be a likeness of it.

Today in most synagogues, an ark is located in the east wall and prayers are directed toward it, symbolic of the Holy of Holies in the Jerusalem Temple.

The use of music in Israel's worship was common. One may find nearly the same instruments in Psalm 150.

New Testament Lesson　　　Ephesians 1:3-14　　　　*Spiritual Blessings In Christ*

These opening lines may very well be lines from some early Christian hymnody that Paul knew. It sings of God's will done through Jesus, God's wonderful forgiveness and salvation, God's desire to praise, and God's giving of the Holy Spirit as a promise of our future inheritance.

Verse 5 is significant in that Paul states we are "... destined for adoption as his children ..." The same idea occurs in a number of Paul's letters: Romans 8:15, 23; 9:4; Galatians 4:5.

This rich metaphor emphasizes both God's initiative in establishing a relationship with us and the divine character of that relationship: God's love — our responsibility. So we are created for the praise and service of our creator.

Verse 10 we read of the oneness of Christ in all things on earth and in heaven. Paul stresses the unity of God's creative and redemptive activity. We get the idea here of a plan for all of our history eventually ending in the rule of the Christ.

The passage finishes with an assurance that we are created to live for the praise of God. The "we" in verse 12 includes all the Christian community although it is tempting to consider it as Jewish Christians including Paul.

The Holy Spirit holds an important place in the theology of Ephesians. "Seal," in verse 13, refers to Christian baptism. One might also translate the term "inheritance" as future blessings.

The Gospel Mark 6:14-29 *The Death Of John The Baptist*

One can still get a glimpse of John's head as Muslims have kept it in a box and have run with it several times to keep it from being captured. The last time I saw the box was in the Muslim mosque in Damascus in elaborately decorated surroundings.

King Herod had a heck of a guilty conscience. When he heard of Jesus' activity, he imagined that the prophet, who had called attention to his seduction of his brother's wife, was alive again even though he had ordered him beheaded.

By taking Herodias as his wife, he had broken the Jewish law (Leviticus 18:16, 20, 21). To John it was an outrage and offense of morality. So, outspoken John said so publicly. At Herod's birthday party Salome danced a provocative dance which aroused him to such a state that he promised her anything. She, at her mother's prompting, asked for the head of John. Verse 26 is the saddest part of the story. Herod could not back down without losing precious prideful "face." And that's what killed John.

Consider the characters in this drama:
1. Herod, now full of guilt, easily seduced, and unwilling to reverse a promise made in the height of erotic excitement;
2. Herodias, who shows us what a vengeful person can do;
3. Salome dances like a prostitute thus arousing and manipulating men of power for her own gain;
4. And John the Baptizer who spoke the truth and took the high path morally even at the risk of his death. He was a courageous man who lived the truth.

Preaching Possibilities

The Old Testament Lesson is an opportunity to deal with "that which is holy" and talk about David's covenant based on the law compared with our "deal" with God based on the cross and God's grace. We could compare the elements of covenant worship then when singing, playing musical instruments, dancing, and the ark containing the Ten Commandments with our present liturgy, music, and the sacraments of baptism and communion. It's a thin basis on which to do it, so I won't go there — but I could using Paul's Ephesians for the basis of grace and the new covenant.

Music is an element in all three readings: the Old Testament — as they parade with the ark to Jerusalem; Paul's letter — with quotations from early Christian hymns; and in the Gospel — Salome dances a very unreligious dance!

The Second Reading easily provides a text for a traditional "three points and a poem" outline:
Title: Spiritual Blessings We Can Count On
Text: Ephesians 1:3-14
A. God chose us to be holy, blameless, and loved (v. 4).
B. God destined us for adoption into God's family (v. 5).
C. God saved us through Christ's blood (v. 7).
D. God has an inheritance for us (v. 11).
E. We are given the seal of the Holy Spirit (v. 13).
F. So What? We live in the presence of his glory (v. 12).

Possible Outline Of Sermon Moves

Title: John Loses His Head Over An Erotic Dance

A. Begin by retelling in your own words the delicious story of Herod, Herodias, and Salome.
B. Imagine what a court video camera person would have gotten on tape that day!
C. Talk about these elements in the story:
   1. Herod's guilty conscience that made him afraid of the ghost of decapitated John and how guilt can distort our lives even today. Shakespeare's Hamlet had similar distorted thinking from his guilt.
   2. Herodias' vengeful nature because she knew she was being confronted by the truth and how the truth can anger us, also.
   3. Salome's tempting dance and the use of sexual desire and her body to manipulate Herod. How often that same sexual desire is used today to tempt us mightily.
   4. Herod's pride, which would not let him back down on a promise made in the heat of sexual stimulation and desire to impress his peers. And how often pride can get in the way of our loving and doing the best for others.
D. Move to some conclusions because of the above. As a congregation we must expect to hear and support preaching that confronts the ugly truth and reveals our sins. We must, as individuals, be on guard and teach our children to be on guard against the sin of Herod, guilt and pride; of Herodias, of being revengeful; and of Salome, using sex to tempt others to sin.
E. Frame the sermon by returning, in your own words, to the story of the dance and beheading. Then tell that John's head is now in a box entombed in a Muslim mosque in Damascus. We could only imagine what it would say to us today if it could speak!

Prayer For The Day

Help us in the times of temptation, God. Give us the strength and character to resist adultery and sexual abuse. Help us to recognize our motivation of pride or vengeance or the desire to use our bodies to manipulate others for our gain. And above all, teach us to confront sin and wrong with the truth you teach us. In Christ's name. Amen.

Possible Metaphors And Stories

There is a little steak house named Toppers in Des Moines, Iowa, between Mercy and Lutheran Hospitals. When I have my collar on, they always slip an extra piece of steak under the regular order (special). It's a real bonus just for being there.

What are the bonuses of our regular lives?

According to the *Minnesota Star* newspaper, they train the Metro Transit Authority bus drivers by using a video of the route the driver will be driving. Oh, that the older Christians might serve as that videotape of the route the younger will transit.

I saw a rerun of the film *Gandhi*. A Hindu man came to him and confessed he had killed a Moslem boy. Gandhi said he knew a way out of his hell. Find a parentless boy and raise him as a Moslem. "When we follow 'an eye for an eye' we end up with a world which cannot see" (Gandhi).

Two Jews went to synagogue on Yom Kippur. They hated each other. Now all is forgiven. They came out the door and one said to the other: "I wish for you all you wish for me." The other replied, "You're starting it again!" (told by George Forell at a field seminary in Tucson, Arizona). How easy it is to harbor a grudge and nurse a hurt rather than do the hard work of radical forgiveness.

Third Sunday In July

| 2 Samuel 7:1-14a | Ephesians 2:11-22 | Mark 6:30-34, 53-56 |

Seasonal Theme   We learn of the Christian faith and how we are to follow Jesus as his disciples.

Theme For The Day   The radical nature of Jesus' compassion for us and our need to have compassion for others on God's behalf.

Old Testament Lesson   2 Samuel 7:1-14a   *God's Covenant With David*

David is now established in Jerusalem and his thoughts turn to building a permanent structure in which to install the ark. Compared with his own dwelling, the tent in which the ark was kept was no longer appropriate. David talked it over with the prophet Nathan who at first approved and then later reversed himself and said the Lord would build David a house instead. He promises David offspring, a kingdom forever, and that David would be God's son. So David is promised a dynasty of kings. It would begin with him and go on forever (v. 16).

New Testament Lesson   Ephesians 2:11-22   *One In Christ*

The key word here as Paul talks about unity in the church is peace. It describes a two-fold harmonizing in Christ.

A. Verses 11-12: Paul always claimed circumcision was inward. See Romans 2:25-29. This book of Ephesians tells the Gentile Christians that this Jewish heritage is also theirs within the church.
B. Verses 13-18: Because of Christ's death the Gentiles are also God's people. Perhaps Paul was remembering Isaiah 57:19 here. Jew and Gentile are now one in the church.
C. Verse 2:14b: This metaphor may have been the wall erected in the Temple in Jerusalem. What is said is that reconciliation with our God means necessary reconciliation with our fellow believers. There can be no separation wall in church. We are partners in receiving God's saving grace in Christ.
D. Verses 15-18: The unity in the church is like a new person, a new humanity. When we remember the image of the church's being the "Body of Christ" present in the world, we have rich preaching possibilities. Unity is further emphasized in verse 18 with "one Spirit."
E. Verses 19-22: "Saints" here probably refers to all Christians. "Household" pictures the church as God's family who are bound together under God's parental care.
F. Verse 20: Another metaphor here describes the church as a building with Jesus Christ as the corner stone. The Greek could mean either cornerstone or foundation stone.
G. Verses 21-22: Here one could use the metaphor of Christ as the mortar of the building. It's also an interesting concept that we Christians are built together to form the church.

The Gospel   Mark 6:30-34, 53-56   *Sheep Without A Shepherd*

The disciples have returned from their mission and at this time Jesus is very popular. Rest for Jesus and his disciples was impossible. They went across the northern tip of Galilee for some peace and quiet; but there was a crowd waiting for them. I think any other person would have been aggravated and resented this intrusion on his/her privacy. The key for me in the whole passage is verse 34, "... he had compassion for them." So back to work trying to make a difference for these who were like a bunch of sheep without a shepherd.

Verses 53-56 describe this compassion in action at Gennesaret. Picture that crowd bringing sick of all kinds and laying them out on mats so that Jesus might see them and do something. The whole pericope reeks of compassion. One could impute all sorts of wrong motivation to this crowd. Most came to use Jesus for some purpose. Get healed, get fed, get entertained. Still Jesus had compassion. It's a big element in the radical apostolic of discipleship.

Preaching Possibilities

If you have not used any of the Samuel passages yet, this could be a good Sunday to teach some history.
A. Proper 4: Samuel is called (1 Samuel 3:1-20).
B. Proper 5: Samuel anoints Saul as king (1 Samuel 8:4-20).
C. Proper 6: The choice and anointing of David (1 Samuel 15:34—16:13).
D. Proper 7: David takes on Goliath (1 Samuel 17:(1a, 4-11, 19-23) 32-49).
E. Proper 8: David grieves over Nathan and Saul (2 Samuel 1:1, 17-27).
F. Proper 9: David is anointed king (2 Samuel 5:1-5, 9-10).
G. Proper 10: David brings the ark to Jerusalem (2 Samuel 6:1-5, 12b-19).
H. Today (11): God's covenant with David (2 Samuel 7:1-14a).

The New Testament Reading is also pregnant with possibilities. It is an opportunity to teach about the Christian church in the time of Paul and in our contemporary time right here and now. A number of Paul's metaphors for the church will work as your outline:
A. Circumcision and non-circumcision
B. Far off have been brought near
C. Christ is our peace
D. He has torn down the dividing wall
E. One new humanity
F. Access in one Spirit to the Father
G. No longer aliens but citizens
H. Members of the household of God
I. Jesus Christ as the foundation stone
J. We are building blocks of the church

There is a wonderful opportunity to plead for peace in your congregation and to confront racism there and in your community as well. Anti-Semitism should also be held up as wrong spirited for all Christians.

Possible Outline Of Sermon Moves

Let's use my sermon outline based on audience reaction and apply the Gospel for today.[1]
A. Build a fire. There are times when crowds disgust us. They are there for the wrong reason and we are simply being used.
B. Build a bridge. All of us here today get tired of the constant badgering we receive from homeless or helpless or organizations who send mail pleading for help.
C. Make your point. The point is that a disciple of Christ has a model of compassion that is way beyond considering the legitimacy of the request for help.
D. An example. Now retell the story of Jesus at Gennesaret from the Gospel for today. He called the crowd sheep without a shepherd. Explain its meaning.
   1. Sheep without a shepherd are helpless to their many enemies. They are very vulnerable animals as we are.
   2. Sheep without a shepherd get lost easily. Life can be very bewildering without our shepherd to lead us.
   3. Sheep without a shepherd will have a tough time finding pasture and thus sustenance for life. We need a shepherd to point us to life's sustenance also.
E. Witness. Admit your own feelings sometimes as people continually beg for help. And admit you need to take seriously this compelling story of compassion for others.
F. Action. List out some ways the congregation together and members individually might be more compassionate in your community. Don't forget money and how it can act in compassion for others.

G. Frame. Return to the opening "fire" listed above or a metaphor listed below used as the fire and make your summary of what you have said in reverse order.

Prayer For The Day

Help us, O God, to feel and act with compassion as Jesus modeled for us along the Sea of Galilee's shore. When we are tempted to give in to weariness and feel our privacy invaded, show us the way to be your instrument of kindness in a cruel world. And as Jesus taught us, move us to help even those who will never appreciate our efforts. In Jesus-the-shepherd-of-the-lost-sheep's name. Amen.

Possible Metaphors And Stories

To go with the New Testament Reading: A *New York Times* article by Natalie Angier, August 26, 2000, was headlined, "Race Is Only Skin Deep." She wrote that scientists say it may be easy to tell at a glance whether a person is African or Caucasian or Asian but the differences dissolve at the DNA level. (May they dissolve at our church's level as well!)

Dr. Craig Venter is quoted as saying, "We all evolved in the last 100,000 years from the same small number of tribes that migrated out of Africa and colonized the world." Venter and scientists at the National Institutes of Health have unanimously declared *there is only one race.*

So equatorial populations developed dark skin, presumably to protect against ultraviolet radiation, while people in northern latitudes evolved pale skin, the better to produce vitamin D from pale sunlight.

Dr. Harold Freeman said that only about .01 percent of your genes is reflected in your external appearance like skin color, nose width, shape of eyes, etc. We ought think about *ethnicity* rather than *race*. Ethnicity encompasses both genetics and culture.

One Saturday in Hong Kong, my computer crashed and I could not get it started again. The Norwegian professor worked on it and finally got it going. Then all the directions were in Norwegian! Words like *arkiv, rediger, innhold, elikett,* and *spesilt* appear. My hearing aid stopped working on the same day but I was afraid to ask him to fix it! What a marvelous worldwide universal church we have with many languages but all one people!

An ad for Pioneer in *Newsweek* shows a man and a woman in pajamas reclining on a couch reading the newspaper. The caption is: "We bring the revolution home." Under the picture are the words: "Sunday morning. Time to kick back, get comfortable and perfect the art of doing nothing. Ideal compassion. Pioneer's new six-disc CD player." We know a different peace and compassion.

In the medical lab where I had to give some blood I noticed a tongue depressor and a capsule of smelling salts taped to the wall near the chair where I was seated. It was there obviously "just in case" of an emergency. We often practice our Christian faith in such a fashion. It is there "just in case." But we rarely think of ourselves as the "just in case" — it's for someone else. God wants to use us to help because the need in someone else's life is now.

---

1. For more on this type of sermon structure, see my *The Preacher's Edge*, CSS Publishing Company, 1996.

Fourth Sunday In July

| 2 Samuel 11:1-15 | Ephesians 3:14-21 | John 6:1-21 |

Seasonal Theme   We learn of the Christian faith and how we are to follow Jesus as his disciples.

Theme For The Day   Our inner-self can be renewed with the presence of Christ, which will produce a life based on God's love.

Old Testament Lesson   2 Samuel 11:1-15   *David And Bathsheba*

In the spring after the rains when the armies often resumed their battles, David sent his military out to attack Rabbah, the capital of Ammon. For some reason David did not go with them. One night he spotted Bathsheba taking a bath and he decided he must have her. It could be that Bathsheba was bathing at the conclusion of her period of "purifying" herself. Some commentaries written by men place some blame on this woman who in the proximity of the palace would put on such a display. I will not go that chauvinistic route.

After intercourse with David, Bathsheba discovered she was pregnant. David tried two different schemes to make her husband believe he was the father: he brought Uriah back from the front to report to David, hoping he would then go home and sleep with his wife. That not working, he tried to get him drunk so he would sleep with her and that didn't happen. So he arranged to have him killed by placing him in the front of the battle and then abandoning him.

So we have this turning point in David's reign which began with his temptation when he saw a beautiful woman taking a bath one hot night and yielded to his desire and power. Then the worst part of all, he tried to cover up his adultery. It's a downhill slide starting with getting a peek at a naked woman and progressing to the murder of her husband. Sounds like one of our television "soaps."

New Testament Reading   Ephesians 3:14-21   *Prayer For Readers*

Verses 2-13 have interrupted the prayer of Paul begun in verse 1. Verse 16's "inner being" is the same word as Romans 7:22. We could think of it as our inner real self, which can become an entirely new personhood when yielded to God's Spirit (2 Corinthians 4:16). Then this idea is expanded by saying that the "made new" happens as Christ is accepted and the new life is "rooted and grounded in love" (v. 17). This is the fullness of God and is the widest, longest, etc. knowledge of God.

In verses 20-21 we have a magnificent doxology, which brings to a close this doctrinal portion of Paul's letter. "In the church and in Christ Jesus ..." continues Paul's emphasis that the church is the body of Christ. It's quite a prayer for all us who read and hear it.

The Gospel   John 6:1-21   *The Feeding Of The 5,000*

This very familiar story is also told in Matthew 14, Mark 6, and Luke 9. Here are a few background facts that may enrich your preaching on this event. William Barclay helps us here.
A. Because of the Feast of Passover, there would be many people on the roads on their way to Jerusalem.
B. Philip was from Bethsaida (John 1:44) and he would know about the area.
C. A denarius was about a day's wages.
D. The boy had his picnic lunch along.
E. The fishes were no larger than sardines.
F. At a Jewish feast the participants always left something for the servants. It was called the *Peah*.
G. Each of the disciples would have along their basket (*koplunos*).

There are several ways to interpret this miracle:
A. Jesus literally multiplied loaves and fishes.
B. It was a sacramental meal.

C. It was a miracle of convincing by example everyone to share what they had along with them. (I like this one.)

Now a different miracle (vv. 16-21) when Jesus walked on water. The Greek here is crucial: *epi tes thalasses*, which is precisely the same as John 21:1, where it is translated "at the sea." He was walking on the seashore. So here is a story John the fisherman would love to tell: the appearance of Jesus and his strong voice of reassurance as they reach the Galilean side. The wonder of the event is that when we are in trouble Jesus sees and comes to help and brings us to safe haven. It's a grand fisherman's story told by an old fisherman and faithful disciple.

Preaching Possibilities

Each of the three readings is so compelling and rich in content it is very difficult to decide what to do for today's sermon.

The Old Testament has all the elements of temptations and sex to hold our hearers' attention.

The New Testament Reading is rich in theological content and has so much to teach us.

The two Gospel stories are so compelling and are ones our hearers delight in hearing retold.

One might try using all three but I believe it would lack focus and would be trying to cover far too much. It could look like this:

A. The sin of David's adultery is still tempting and as disastrous as it was then (2 Samuel).
B. The need for a new inner-self is still very much present in our lives (Ephesians).
C. Miracles of sharing can still take place in our day.
D. God still comes to us when we are in need of his help (Gospel of John).

Another approach in using all three readings would be to use the personalities in the stories. It could be titled: *Their Story Is Ours Also*.

A. David and Bathsheba's temptation is ours also.
B. Paul's prayer is our prayer also.
C. Andrew's and Philip's response may be our response also.
D. The disciples' boat is our boat also.

For a treatment of the two Gospel miracles, see my *The Miracles Of Jesus And Their Flip Side*, CSS Publishing, Lima, Ohio, 2000.

Possible Outline Of Sermon Moves

Title: Our Inner-Self
Text: Ephesians 3:14-21

A. Introduction: Tell of the background of the words, "inner being," which Paul uses in this prayer for us.
B. Tell a story to illustrate your own "inner being" in contrast to your outer being. You looked brave but were scared to death or you smiled a happy face but were crying inside.
C. Now move to what Paul prays for our inner being and how we can be changed:
   1. We might be strengthened so as to resist the sexual temptations all around us. Use King David and Bathsheba as an example.
   2. We can have Christ in our inner being. That means compassion for others like the hungry in the Gospel today.
   3. This will result in our being grounded in God's love. Use Paul's portion of the prayer following in verse 19 and/or Jesus' love for his disciples in trouble in the boat so his coming to them.
D. Move to what this prayer for us ought to issue into in our congregation and our ministry in the community.
   1. We ought to pray for and love each other.
   2. We ought to share our resources and feed the hungry.

3. We ought to take specific program steps for renewal of our "inner selves" in our congregation.
4. We ought to locate those in danger or any need and come to them with help.
E. Conclude with Paul's benediction in verses 20-21.

Prayer For The Day

O God of the inner-self, as well as the outer more observable self, renew and change us with the power of your Spirit that we might also be grounded in your love right down to the core of our being. Teach us how best to resist temptation all around us, give us the spirit of sharing, and come to our aid in the scary times of our lives just as you expect us to do on your behalf for others. In Christ's name. Amen.

Possible Metaphors And Stories

According to Ken Burns' special, *Jazz*, on public television, it was a Jewish family in New Orleans who took an eleven-year-old black youngster, the son of a prostitute, out of the notorious Storyville portion of the city and had him ride their coal wagon and blow a tin horn to announce coal for sale to the thieves and prostitutes who populated the neighborhood. And so their compassion for the young lad developed into the greatest jazz musician the world has ever known — Louis Armstrong.

A bridegroom was arrested after allegedly shooting his new wife in the stomach soon after their front porch wedding, authorities said. Luarette Kenny, 38, and Raymond Brunson, 50, apparently got into a fight as the reception wound down. She pitched a plate of macaroni salad at him and then got shot with a .22-caliber handgun, police said. Friends said things seemed to be going fine and they weren't sure what happened (*Oakland Tribune*, April 18, 1992). Life goes sour even with the highest motives.

We came upon the scene of an accident at Big O Tire Store in Pittsburg, California. We could see the corner of the building marked from the vehicle's missing the curve, skid marks on the street, antifreeze stain from a ruptured radiator, pieces of chrome and glass on the street. Sunglasses and a blood-stained cap, shrubs broken down, and the inside of a headlight were there. An accident had happened. How often we see the signs of the accidents of people's lives. Can we who are Christ's find a way to prevent them and give comfort to those to whom they happen?

What a story on *NBC Nightly News*! It was about Russian and American troops in prisoner of war camps. Americans would receive Red Cross packages and share them with Russians at risk of death. The Russians would not tell the guard when a prisoner died but would hold up the body in line so as to get their food allowance.
We are without risk and the saints' bodies are held up that we might feast on their food.

First Sunday In August

2 Samuel 11:26—12:13a　　　　　　　Ephesians 4:1-16　　　　　　　John 6:24-35

Seasonal Theme　　　We learn of the Christian faith and how we are to follow Jesus as his disciples.

Theme For The Day　　The unity in the congregation that is possible by following Paul's advice to his congregations.

Old Testament Lesson　　　2 Samuel 11:26—12:13a　　　　*King David Is Confronted And Confesses*

The story of King David continues from last week. After Uriah's wife Bathsheba was finished making public mourning for him, she went to David and became his wife. The child born to them was a son. God promised David that this would cause him problems until his death. The effect of David and Bathsheba's sin not only would bring them sorrow for the rest of their lives, but also would bring trouble upon their people.

Nathan the prophet confronts David with a hypothetical story, which he admitted is really David. The punishment promised to David for his crime of adultery and of murdering Uriah was that David would suffer from the sword and his wives would be taken from him (vv. 10-11). This was fulfilled by David's own son Absalom when he slept with David's concubines (16:22).

David may not have been punished because of his contriteness and confession (Psalm 51). God's grace was at work. But the effect of this sin continued and brought sorrow to David and his nation.

New Testament Lesson　　　Ephesians 4:1-16　　　　　*Unity In The Body Of Christ*

The Interpreter's One Volume Commentary on the Bible introduces this reading as the basis for Christian ethics. Victor Paul Furnish writes: "These are introduced by an appeal to the true basis for Christian ethics: God's call to unity, peace, and love (vv. 1-6) and his bestowal of spiritual gifts for the common good" (vv. 7-16). In 1 Corinthians 12:4-11, Paul writes of gifts of the Spirit. This writer talks of gifts of Christ (v. 7) and tries to prove it by quoting Psalm 68:18. He takes this Old Testament reference to Moses and changes it to Christ.

The lower parts of the earth are a reference to Jesus' incarnation and his descent into Hades as recorded in 1 Peter 3:18-22.

The gifts listed in verses 11-16 are not only for the individual but also the community of faith. It is the body of Christ we call the church that may reach a certain maturity (v. 13).

We are to refrain from immaturity like children and grow up maturing in the faith so that we speak the truth in love. Over and over Paul states that our unity and building up must be in love (v. 16b).

The Gospel　　　　　　John 6:24-35　　　　　　　*Jesus Is The Bread Of Life*

These people searching for Jesus couldn't get their eyes above seeing him as a wonder worker. They were entirely focused on bread to eat — right now. One could call them entirely earthbound. Jesus confronts them on that (v. 27). Perhaps these folks represent ourselves who are very rich in material things, yet very poor in spiritual things. One could say that after being fed on the Galilean hillside, they were back for "seconds." We also have a hunger for love, and life, and truth. Only the Christ can satisfy this kind of hunger we all have.

Verses 28-29 are interesting. No doubt the Jews expected a list of good works they could render to gain favor with God. Instead Jesus told them "... that you believe." God wants us to have faith and that means a relationship with God — the kind of relationship that ensues in obedience, love, and trust, for we now view God not as our feared judge but, rather, our friend and parent.

In verses 30-34, we remember that this manna was always thought of as God's bread (see Psalm 78:24 and Exodus 16:15). Jesus reminds them that it was not Moses but God who gave the manna. Here Jesus' bold claim was that the only real satisfying element in this life is God.

In verse 35 we have one of the highlights of John's Gospel. We shall continue its implication next week.

Preaching Possibilities

If we have not yet dealt with David and his sins at all, today's confrontation by Nathan is ready for an expository or narrative sermon.

Briefly it could go like this:
A. Tell David's story from anointing to Bathsheba to Nathan's confrontation and David's remorse. Then ask what this teaches us about humans.
   1. Power corrupts us, too.
   2. We have sexual desires that can bring misery upon us and others.
   3. Temptation to sin is everywhere and we must resist.
B. Then move to what this teaches us about our God.
   1. God sees all our secret acts and schemes.
   2. God has messengers like Nathan who speak for God.
   3. God is full of grace and forgiveness if we "'fess up" and are truly sorry for our actions.
C. Now apply these truths to our life together as a congregation.
   1. There will be temptations as we live together.
   2. Our life together is lived out not expecting perfection but, rather, forgiveness.
   3. Like Nathan we must confront sin in our community and call for repentance.
D. Today's Gospel begins a too-long series of readings from John's Gospel about bread. You will need to decide which Sunday you will use this theme and then concentrate on other themes the other Sundays. I will not go with living bread this week yet. The Second Reading is just too inviting.

Possible Outline Of Sermon Moves

Title: Paul's advice for our congregation (name your church)
Text: Ephesians 4:1-16
A. Introduction: Ask the question why is it that Christians gathered together as congregations fight, quarrel, suffer with dissension?
B. Remind your hearers that when we became a Christian and member of the body of Christ, we still remain sinners. (Look at David, called and anointed by God, deeply religious and he still committed adultery and murder.)
C. Now move to Paul's advice of how a congregation of sinners might get along better and be unified as Christ's body.
   1. Lead a life worthy of our calling.
   2. Practice humility and gentleness.
   3. Be patient in love with each other.
   4. Work hard at maintaining unity and peace in the congregation.
   5. Remember we all have one baptism.
   6. Remember we all have an undeserved gift: God's grace.
   7. Acknowledge that each one has their (his/her) gift from God to share with the rest.
   8. Grow up and abandon childish ways.
   9. Speak the truth but always in love.
   10. See yourself as a part of Christ's body on earth and work to promote the growth of that body.
D. Give your own witness as to how you feel the congregation misbehaves or carries out the above advice well.

E. List some of the steps you prayerfully have discerned the congregation ought take because of the above advice from Paul. Examples might be: Start a prayer group for congregational unity; begin a pastoral relations committee; ask some visitors to explain how they view this congregation, etc.

F. Conclude by returning to your opening asking again the questions about dissension in Christian congregations. Then assure your listeners we have a remedy and read verses 15-16.

Prayer For The Day

Bring peace, love, and unity to our congregation, O God, and show us the way to grow up in our relationship to you and mature together as your body and presence in this community. We celebrate your grace, which binds us together and your Son who forgives us. Keep us mindful of our unity in one baptism and one Almighty God. In Christ's name. Amen.

Possible Metaphors And Stories

According to Mei, Yee Pang, another Hong Kong student, the word for "leader" in Chinese means collar and arm. It means to link together all the parts of a shirt, the parts that protect the main parts of the body. Sounds like Paul's definition of the church as "the body of Christ."

Ads for cars are interesting.

Toyota claims: "Every day belongs to you, make it count." A good stewardship of life itself. Every day we have been given to minister on God's behalf. Let's make it count.

Saturn says: "A different kind of company, a different kind of car." Let our congregations be able, with God's help, to say the same thing. Not a service club or country club — as nice as they are — but a different kind of company, one which follows the Christ and ministers on his behalf and celebrates his presence with us now.

Cadillac touts: "Live without limits," as if that is a happy way to enjoy our lives. Not really. A disciplined life lived carefully and consistently with Christ's example is where real joy will be found.

Today I saw a crew of men with air hammers tearing out the front steps and the approach to Debra Heights Methodist Church in Des Moines, Iowa. There are those who work on behalf of the power which works against God to wreck the approach to the church. They hammer away with the power of the world. Sometimes it is on purpose. Other times it is without knowing what they are doing.

There is a little white frame church on Martin Luther King, Jr., Boulevard in Oakland, California. There is a Better Homes and Gardens Realty sign in front. It led me to muse how one would describe a church for sale:

Abundance of forgiveness
Precious fellowship
Security in eternal life
Assurance of companionship
Help for difficult decisions
Real presence of Jesus at meals
Life-changing worship
Will throw the building in free!
Need not have good credit record or references
No shirt, no shoes, still service

Second Sunday In August

2 Samuel 18:5-9, 15, 31-33   Ephesians 4:25—5:2   John 6:35, 41-45

Seasonal Theme   We learn of the Christian faith and how we are to follow Jesus as his disciples.

Theme For The Day   Jesus is our source of real life as bread is our source of real food.

Old Testament Lesson   2 Samuel 18:5-9, 15, 31-33   *Absalom's Defeat And Death*

David's men convinced him to stay behind rather than lead the army as he wanted to do. He commanded his officers not to harm his rebel son Absalom in battle. The elements of the terrible region (v. 8) were even worse for Absalom than the swords of David's army. He was trying to get away on a mule and got entangled in the lower branches of an oak tree, which suspended him in midair. Joab killed him. Absalom had already erected a memorial to himself in the Kidron Valley east of Jerusalem. One can still see it below and from the pinnacle of the Temple mount. David was crushed by the news of Absalom's death as announced to him by the Cushite. He poured out his grief to God. So two of David's sons, Amon and Absalom, died violent deaths ... because of their father's transgressions?

New Testament Lesson   Ephesians 4:25—5:2   *Rules For Life In Christ*

First, let's look at what Paul forbids as we take up a new life in Christ:
1. Do not lie.
2. Do not be angry overnight.
3. Do not steal.
4. No evil talk from your mouth.
5. Don't grieve the Holy Spirit.
6. Get rid of any bitterness, wrath, anger, wrangling, slander, and malice.

Those things that Paul writes we should do:
1. Speak the truth.
2. Work honestly.
3. Build up in your speech.
4. Be kind to one another, forgiving one another.
5. Be imitators of God.
6. Live in love, as Christ loved us.

Verse 25 seems to be key here. We are all part of the body of Christ, the church. This new life is one of love. This, says Paul, should shape how we are as a congregation.

The Gospel   John 6:35, 41-45   *The Bread Of Life Again*

Last week it was one of John's bread passages; this week is one, and the next week after that will also center on bread. It goes on and on even using the same passages over again! Today's passage is one of the great passages of John's Gospel. The metaphor of Jesus as the bread of life says to us that as bread gives us physical life, so Jesus gives us real life, which is a different relationship to our Holy Parent, God. This new relationship with God is only possible through Jesus, the Christ.

There are different ways of living for us. We can just merely exist and we can really live the full abundant life in Christ. So Jesus' claim that he is the bread of life. He can satisfy our hunger for real life here and on into eternity.

The Jews' reaction to Jesus' message (v. 42) warns us to be very careful lest we reject a message from God because we don't like the human messenger!

William Barclay tells us of the background of the verb "drawn" in verse 44. It usually implies some resistance to God's attraction. Drawing a net to shore (John 12:6, 11) Paul and Silas being drawn before the magistrates in Philippi (Acts 16:19), drawing a sword from its sheath (John 18:10). In each case there is resistance to the draw (*heikuein*). Our resistance can defeat God's draw. It will preach! To resist the offer of Jesus is like refusing bread when we are starving. It is the very essential of life we are resisting. Life here and life in eternity are turned down.

Preaching Possibilities

If you have not yet dealt with the story of David, it could be done this week as we move on from him next week when we go from 2 Samuel to 1 Kings. It's a sad story of one called by God who was corrupted by power and whose sins caused much suffering for his family and friends.

The Second Reading is rich with content as it describes the new life in Christ lived in love of God and each other. It lends itself to a heart-to-heart sermon that talks to the congregation about how they live together as the body of Christ. It could begin by describing Paul's advice on how we ought treat each other, talking about how far from this ideal we sometimes get as a congregation, and then holding up the doctrine that God still loves the sinner, and because of that grace we ought do better in loving God and in loving each other. A very simple outline could be:

A. Tell the background of this book of Ephesians: that it was written for Paul's congregations to read at worship.
B. Tell what Paul said we should refrain from being and doing as individuals and as corporately as the body of Christ.
C. Tell what Paul said we should be and do.
D. Now share your own feelings as to where we could do better.
E. Now read it re-written in your own words and addressed to your congregation as if you were Paul and you were writing Ephesians to your own congregation.

Possible Outline Of Sermon Moves

Title: The Living Bread *or* Pass The Bread, Please
Text: John 6:51

A. Introduction: Tell a story about bread and then move to the claim of Jesus that he was "... the living bread that came down from heaven."
B. Move to explain what Jesus meant. He must have had in mind the manna provided the Jews in the wilderness. And because in that time bread was even more so the very foundation of what was eaten, so Jesus was the foundation, too.
C. Explain the metaphor further.
   1. Bread nourishes our lives. It is essential.
   2. Jesus sustains our spiritual lives, which is a radically new relationship between us and our God. Use Paul's writing in the second reading to illustrate this new relationship.
   3. Without Jesus, real life, which is more than just existence, is not possible.
   4. You have to have Jesus for life as you have to have bread for nourishment. Only he can end the insatiable hunger for real existence.
D. Give your own witness of how it was before you knew and accepted Jesus when your life was mere existence. Then share the wonderful new life now with the bread of life. If you cannot do this, perhaps you can tell of someone else's witness (or have him/her tell it).
E. Now move to action the hearers ought take because of the above Gospel:
   1. Be certain you have a steady diet of this bread by removing your resistance to God "drawing" you. (See comments on the Gospel.)
   2. As a congregation be sure that the real bread of life is served up every week for all to feast on. (There are many substitute foods.) Paul well describes a congregation without real bread.
   3. "Pass the bread." Be sure this bread is not hoarded but shared with all who will take it. And in the sharing of it, we value it even more.

F. Frame the sermon by giving a summary of what you have said about Living bread and sing (or have sung) a verse of the hymn "Living Bread From Heaven." (See below.)

Prayer For The Day

Help us, O God, as a congregation and as individual Christians always to dine on you, the living bread. Show us the way to a new relationship with you and also with each other. We rejoice in how much you love us even to give your son on a cross that we might be forgiven and know that love. Help us to "pass the bread" as well as feast on it. In Jesus-the-living-bread's name. Amen.

Possible Metaphors And Stories

Eddie Chan, one of my Chinese students in Hong Kong, was translating from my English into Cantonese and called it, "I am the life of bread." I'll take that mistake in translation and think about it.

O Living bread from heaven, how well you feed your guest!
The gifts that you have given have filled my heart with rest.
Oh, wondrous food of blessing, Oh, cup that heals our woes!
My heart, this gift possessing, with praises overflows!
(Text by Johann Rist; Tune: AURELIA)

A town put on the passion play and recruited a non-Christian to play the part of Jesus Christ. While carrying the cross, the crowd taunted him and he attacked them the very first night. After further coaching he just gritted his teeth and said: "Okay for now, but just wait until the resurrection!"

Think how Jesus could have reacted to his arrest, trial, and crucifixion. He could have come down off the cross, pulled it up, and thrown it down the hill at them.

I tried to use my power skillsaw recently. The round blade was just a fraction of an inch off center, so when the saw started, it vibrated and shook me and the lumber. I centered it and it ran like a top! It was smooth, and it cut great as well. Now what must I do to get back on center in my spiritual life? What is so off the center it vibrates others' lives as well?

While the basic elements are the same, one has only to look at the bread section on the grocery store to see that there are many varieties: whole wheat, rye, white sandwich, German black bread, pumpernickel, sourdough, oatmeal, cornbread, (potato bread is pretty good, too) etc. So Jesus is our nourishment in many varieties and forms.

Third Sunday In August

1 Kings 2:10-12; 3:3-14　　　　　　　Ephesians 5:15-20　　　　　　　John 6:51-58

Seasonal Theme　　　We learn of the Christian faith and how we are to follow Jesus as his disciples.

Theme For The Day　　The real life-giving presence of the Christ in the bread and wine of communion.

Old Testament Lesson　　　　1 Kings 2:10-12; 3:3-14　　　　　*David Dies, Solomon Reigns*

David, at the age of seventy (2 Samuel 5:4), died. The scripture describes it in a lovely way in verse 10, "... David slept with his ancestors." The remarkable king for forty years was a poet, warrior, musician, military genius, administrator, and man of God. His son Solomon succeeded him. Beginning with 3:3 we have Solomon's prayer for wisdom, which was granted. It sounds like because Solomon was generous in his sacrifice at Gibeon (five miles north of Jerusalem), which was the most popular and largest "high place" in the kingdom, God was generous to Solomon and told him to ask whatever. He must have surprised God because instead of asking for power and wealth, he asked for wisdom so he could rule the people well (v. 9). So God promised him wisdom with which to rule the people and added the bonus of honor and riches ... and long life if he remained faithful. Solomon was twenty when he began his reign and called himself a child, admitting his inexperience (1 Chronicles 22:5; 29:1). The Hebrew word for wisdom here literally means "a hearing heart."

New Testament Lesson　　　Ephesians 5:15-20　　　　　　　*A Spirit-Led Life*

We continue the advice on Christian living given by Paul, their former pastor and teacher, to the congregations he began. This short reading lists things to do and not to do.

Don't:　　　　　　　　*Do:*
Be unwise people　　　　Watch how you live
Be foolish　　　　　　　Make the most of your time
Get drunk　　　　　　　Understand the will of God
　　　　　　　　　　　　Be filled with the Holy Spirit
　　　　　　　　　　　　Make melody to the Lord
　　　　　　　　　　　　Give thanks to God
　　　　　　　　　　　　Be careful

In verse 16, "making the most of the time" comes from Colossians 4:5 where it means to pass up no opportunity to make your witness to those outside the church. We are admonished to live a Spirit-led life of praise, which, in Colossians 3:16a, meant in Christian worship, but here is expanded to mean all of Christian life.

The Gospel　　　　　John 6:51-58　　　　　　　　　*More On Bread*

We have yet another passage about bread. John is doing here what he often does: not giving Jesus' actual words as he spoke them, but rather, the meaning and inner significance of his words. In that day of mystery religions, which offered communion and even identification with some God, these words would be so hard to understand.

William Barclay tells how ancient sacrifice usually included the offering of an animal in the temple. A portion was burned on the altar; but a portion was given to the priest and the rest given back to the one who offered it. That person then would have a feast for himself and his friends in the temple precincts. They would depart actually feeling they were filled with God. To these people this passage made sense. They would not read these words with a crude and shocked literalism. One could say Jesus meant by these words we should take his life into ours until it becomes ours. We then think of Jesus as not something we should debate about but rather something we should take on as ours and be changed by it.

Also said here is that the bread Jesus is talking about is far more than the manna furnished the Jews in the wilderness. This is bread, which eaten gives eternal life (v. 58).

Preaching Possibilities

The Old Testament Lesson can be the basis for a sermon on prayer as Solomon sets the example of not presenting a "laundry list" of things he wanted for himself. Paul's comments in the Second Reading about being wise will connect with Solomon's request to be given wisdom. If you do go with the Old Testament, I think the literal translation of the Hebrew word for wisdom, "a hearing heart," is a beautiful description of what Solomon, God, and Paul all had in mind. A hearing heart:

A. Listens in a centered way to others' feelings.
B. Listens in a spirit of love and not judgment.
C. Listens wanting the best for the other person.
D. Listens discerning the best in God's sight.

The Second Reading will lend itself to an expository sermon on Christian living; but we must guard against legalism as we compose it. It will be repetitious if we have used Paul's words any of the last few weeks as they are on the similar theme of "do's and don'ts" for living the Christian life as an individual or as a congregation of believers. The outline in Comments on the Scripture above might be helpful.

I'll go with the reading from the Gospel of John and a teaching sermon on Holy Communion. If you have not done this for a while and your congregation will celebrate it at these services, I recommend it to you.

Possible Outline Of Sermon Moves

A. Begin by describing one of the most delicious meals you have ever eaten and why it was so good.
B. Move to the meal of Holy Communion and why Jesus said in the Gospel this is such a wonderful meal.
   1. Those who eat it have eternal life (v. 54).
   2. Those who eat it abide in Jesus (v. 56).
   3. We will live because we eat it (v. 57).
   4. This is much more than a gift of needed food like the manna; this is Christ's actual presence here with us.
C. Move to your own witness by returning to the best meal you ever had and how much better this meal is for you.
D. Move to how people have emphasized various interpretations of communion:
   1. A time of remembering what Jesus did for us.
   2. A time when we actually handle his body and blood.
   3. A time when he is actually there with us.
   Each theory tells a little more of the mystery of this meal with our God.
E. Frame your message by returning again to the best meal your ever had and why. Then tell how this one is even better because ... *(Give a summary of your points in reverse order: 4, 3, 2, and 1.)*

Prayer For The Day

Thank you for your delicious supper laid out before us today in order that we might be together and be with you again. We celebrate your actual presence and all that you have done for us that we sinners might have forgiveness and eternal life. Let today's meal be as you would have it — full of love and kind-hearted to all. In your name. Amen.

Possible Metaphors And Stories

While worshiping at Saint John's Lutheran Church in Antioch, California, I watched a little boy go forward for communion. He took the wafer and individual cup, and instead of eating and drinking there, he returned to his seat and held a little picnic back there. How might we take the true presence from our church's altar out into the world where we live, work, and play?

The movie *Places in the Heart* is the story of a southern woman trying to survive with her family after her husband is shot. It opens with the gospel hymn "This Is My Story" and closes with "In The Garden" as they all gather for communion in church. You see the murderer, the Ku Klux Klan, an adulterer, a black and a white couple all there for the bread and wine.

One of my Hong Kong students from Cambodia and one of the first Christians there after the Pol Pot regime writes: "Almost my entire childhood facing only killings and hatred since 1975 to 1989. The communist ideology — atheism is still influenced and widely practiced ... and Christians understood as human flesh eaters ... I went with my elder sister who spoke to me about Jesus Christ. She was one of the first Christians in Cambodia" (Yi, Narith, Cambodia).

From Robert Fulghum's book, *Uh-Oh*: "A Hudson Bay start meant the frontiersmen always camped the first night a few short miles from the company headquarters. This allowed the gear and supplies to be tried out, so if anything had been left behind it was still easy to return. A thoughtful beginning spared the travelers later difficulty."
A prayerful beginning to each day's journey will also make the trip go better equipped all day.

Fourth Sunday In August

1 Kings 8:(1, 6, 10-11) 22-30, 41-3   Ephesians 6:10-20   John 6:56-69

Seasonal Theme   We learn of the Christian faith and how we are to follow Jesus as his disciples.

Theme For The Day   Our own battle, and equipment for the battle, against evil in our individual lives, life of the congregation, and life of the community.

Old Testament Lesson   Joshua 24:1-2, 15-18   *Joshua's People Pledge Loyalty*

Joshua gathered the tribes of Israel in Shechem and spoke on God's behalf reminding them of all God had done for them bringing them out of Egypt and into Canaan. It was a recapitulation of Israel's history. The conditions of the covenant are stated in verses 14-15. They now must choose whether to worship the god's of Ur whom their ancestors worshiped, the gods of the Amorites in Canaan, or Yahweh. Whatever their choice would be, for Joshua it would be Yahweh. So he adds an example to his oratory. It's a good example of leadership for us who preach many words.

The people were moved by Joshua's argument and his example (v. 16). Because of all Yahweh had done for them they will follow Yahweh. Yahweh shall be their God. For preaching there is here the proper loyalty to a God who has done much for them. Not bad for an emphasis yet today.

Alternate Old Testament Lesson   1 Kings 8:22-30, 41-43   *Solomon's Prayer*

In this passage, Solomon offers an inclusive prayer of dedication of the temple. He would have offered this prayer kneeling on a special bronze platform that was constructed in the courtyard just for this occasion (2 Chronicles 6:13). In verse 23 the word for love is *hesed* meaning loyal love (1 Kings 10:9). *The Bible Knowledge Commentary* lists nine requests Solomon made for his people:

1. God's presence and protection.
2. Forgiveness of trespasses.
3. Forgiveness of sins that had caused defeat in battle.
4. Forgiveness of sins that had brought on drought.
5. Forgiveness of sins that had resulted in calamities.
6. Mercy for God fearing foreigners (amazing!).
7. Victory in battle.
8. Restoration after captivity.
9. Attention to every prayer.

Solomon called on God who had been faithful in the past. Confession and petition would result in God hearing the petition. Hearing occurs thirteen times in the prayer and forgiveness occurs six times. Got the focus?

New Testament Lesson   Ephesians 6:10-20   *The Whole Armor Of God*

In the Old Testament, God is portrayed in armor (Isaiah 59:17) but here Paul is portraying the early Christians as through God's strength they might arm themselves for battle against the powers that oppose God. Our confidence to even try to battle against such an enemy is the fact that these forces are all subject to Christ (Ephesians 1:21). We put on God's mighty strength as we put on a whole new nature (4:24). I like the feet. They are to be shod with the gospel of peace.

Worth noting is verse 16, which the footnote indicates might be translated, "In all circumstances"; but Goodspeed translates it "... besides all these." I like the translation, "Above all ..." which gives the shield of faith and the helmet of salvation and the sword of the Spirit higher rank than the rest. In order to do battle and remain strong, we must most of all have faith, salvation, and the Holy Spirit.

In verses 18-20 we have the importance of prayer where we get the strength to do battle against the power of evil. The saints are all other Christians, for whom we ought also pray. In verse 20 we have a great sermon title in "An Ambassador In Chains."

The Gospel   John 6:56-69   *The Words Of Eternal Life*

We have yet another reading with the bread of heaven! See last week's "Comments on the Scripture" for some introductory information. John doesn't give us an account of communion. He refused to limit Christ's presence to one liturgically correct service. Our practice of the faith would be a lousy one if we just thought of Jesus with us when we took the bread and wine in church.

As Jesus was teaching in the Capernaum synagogue, the disciples found his teaching difficult not so much to understand but as to accept. It's the thought of surrender to Christ and accepting him as our authority for life that is tough to accept. And the demand of moral living is not so easy either!

Jesus claims it is the spirit in which something is done that's important. The life-giving power of *the* spirit is of supreme importance.

In the remainder of the passage are sad words. One gets the feeling of the approaching end. Judas will betray. Already disciples are defecting (v. 66). When Jesus asked for some assurance of continued loyalty from the twelve, Peter (as usual) utters that statement we often use in our liturgies of worship (v. 68). It must have been discouraging to Jesus as many who had crowded to him were slipping away. It is John's version of Peter's great confession found in Mark 8:27, Matthew 16:13, and Luke 9:18. Barclay's summary comment on this passage is moving: "In the last analysis Christianity is not a philosophy which we accept; it is not a theory to which we give allegiance; it is not something which is thought out; it is not something which is intellectually arrived at. It is a personal response to Jesus Christ. It is an allegiance and a love which a man (person) gives because his heart will not allow him to do anything else."

Preaching Possibilities
A. If you have not yet dealt with the "living bread" of the last many weeks, better do it today. See the two preceding Sundays for suggestions for a sermon on communion and a sermon on living bread.
B. There can be the foundation today for a sermon on prayer. In the Old Testament, 1 Kings passage we have Solomon's model prayer, which includes important elements of confession and forgiveness. In Paul's letter we have praying in the spirit (v. 18), pray for others (v. 19), and pray for boldness (v. 20).
C. The Gospel might be approached from the angle of how tough it is to be a faithful disciple even like those early ones. A sermon on discipleship would be well supported here.
 1. Real disciples will have real life with Jesus abiding in them.
 2. Real disciples will have a difficult code of ethics to follow in this world.
 3. Real disciples will have the Spirit's help to live out their discipleship.
 4. Real disciples will have eternal life. They know Jesus is the Holy One of God.

Possible Outline Of Sermon Moves
Title: The Battle We Fight
Text: Ephesians 6:10-20
A. Begin by describing your own maturing about the idea of evil and the devil. Mine would go: As a little boy I thought of the devil as a man with pitchfork and red underwear; in college I discarded the idea all together and believed humans had to take on full responsibility for any evil; after years in ministry I am convinced there is an organized power that works against God in the world.
B. Now move to Paul's ideas for fighting this power of evil.
 1. We must arm ourselves for it is a life-long battle. Our best armor is: truth, righteousness, gospel of peace, faith, acceptance of salvation, God's spirit, and God's word.

2. We must be constantly in prayer in the Spirit. That means we pray for others and we pray for boldness.
   3. We are also to proclaim the gospel boldly as a defense of the evil that would overcome us (v. 20).
C. Now return to your own witness and some of the ways you observe evil's presence in the world, your community, your congregation, your own self.
D. Describe how you believe we might keep alert and persevere in our culture and congregation and how we might as disciples and ambassadors continue to be in prayer.
E. Tell a story from below "Possible Metaphors And Stories."
F. Close with a specific prayer.

Prayer For The Day

In our battle against the evil that tempts us, O God, give us your powerful presence. Help us to know evil when it sneaks up on us and teach us the most effective way to expose it and battle it in our own lives and in our congregation and community. Give to us alertness and your power to do the battle. In Christ's name. Amen.

Possible Metaphors And Stories

On *60 Minutes*, March 14, 1982, Theodore Hesburgh, President of Notre Dame University, quoting Dante said, "The worst place in Hell is reserved for those who remain neutral during a moral crisis."
Saint John talks about neither hot nor cold which he spit out.

Dr. Hellman, a psychiatrist on a television show titled *Relentless Mind of a Murderer*, said this: "Life is the process of finding out too late what should have been obvious at the time." But the life of faith can help it come out differently.

On Speedway Avenue in Tuscon, Arizona, there is a store with a large sign hanging out front: "Gospel Equipment." I wonder what they sell in there. Could it be helmets, breastplates, sandals, belts, shields, and swords which Paul recommends in Ephesians 6:11-17?

Home Depot's Behr paint now comes with a lifetime guarantee. They claim, "When you are done painting, you are done painting." What are the lifetime guarantees for baptized Christians? Never alone, belonging to a worldwide family which will not desert us, eternal life, inner peace, and a wonderful joy.

In Shakespeare's *Othello*, the king states, "On horror's head horrors accumulate; Do deeds to make heaven weep, all earth amazed."

Fifth Sunday In August

Song of Solomon 2:8-13   James 1:17-27   Mark 7:1-8, 14-15, 21-23

Seasonal Theme   We learn about Christian growth and the way of discipleship.

Theme For The Day Sins of the heart we must guard against and being a "bleeding heart and do-gooder" is true religion.

Old Testament Lesson   Song of Solomon 2:8-13   *The Joy Of Being In Love*

In this book, which may have originally been a collection of wedding songs to be used at various stages in the ceremony, we have a famous passage of the joy of love in the springtime. There is an appreciation of nature here and throughout which is unparalleled anywhere else in the Old Testament. The woman's lover invites her to come away into the beautiful nature outside. The passage holds before us the delightfulness of being in love and the beauty of God's natural world.

New Testament Lesson   James 1:17-27   *True Religion*

As is usually the case in James, we have a string of admonitions for living the Christian life:
Verse 17: Gifts given and received are from God.
Verse 18: We are the best of God's creation (first fruits).
Verse 19: We should listen, being careful about what we say, and refraining from anger.
Verse 21: We are to welcome God's word, which is powerful.
Verse 22: Don't just talk about it; but act on God's word.
Verse 25: Acting on God's word gives us freedom.
Verse 26: Our religion is worthless unless we control our words.
Verse 27: Real religion in God's sight is caring for others who are in distress and guarding against the temptations of the world.

Two words in verse 21 bear further comment. "Sordidness" is an attempt to translate the Greek *ruparion*. When this was used in medical terms it meant "wax in the ear." So James may be saying to get the wax out (anything impeding hearing) so we might hear the true word of God. The second word, which is called meekness in this translation, is the Greek *prautes*, sometimes interpreted as being able to keep all emotions under control. "Blessed are the meek ..." So we have James telling us to keep ourselves under control so that we might have Christian serenity and make our decisions not by wild emotion but by right reason.

The Gospel   Mark 7:1-8, 14-15, 21-23   *Jesus And The Law*

For the Pharisees and, especially, the scribes, religion was reduced to many, many rules and regulations. For instance, not to wash one's hands before eating was to be unclean in the sight of God. When the Pharisees questioned Jesus about why his disciples failed to wash properly, he used the occasion to distinguish between those who honor God with their words but do not by their hearts (see v. 6).

Then in verses 14-15, Jesus makes the same point by telling them that it was not what *went in* the person but what *came out* of them that counts. Verses 21 and 23 continue the teaching by making a list of heart stuff that brings evil and defiles us (v. 21). Jesus is saying that *things* cannot be clean or unclean in religious thinking. But *people* can by their own actions. This was a new idea for that day.

William Barclay, in his *Daily Study Bible*, gives an explanation of the Greek words used for that which defile us:
1. Evil intentions — *dialogismoi* = Evil thought from which the evil action comes
2. Fornication — *porneiai* = Every kind of sexual wrong
3. Theft — *klopai* = A mean, deceitful pilferer

4. Murder and adultery — Their meaning is quite clear.
5. Avarice — *pleonexiai* = The accursed love of having. That lust for having that is in the heart of the person who sees happiness in *things* instead of in *God*.
6. Wickedness — *poneriai* = In whose heart is the desire to harm
7. Deceit — *dolos* = The word for bait in a trap. It is crafty and treacherous.
8. Licentiousness — *aselgeia* = One sins without a qualm
9. Envy is literally *the evil eye*, which looks on another and would cast an evil spell on another if it could.
10. Slander — *blasphemia* = Insulting persons or God
11. Pride — *huperephania* = Contempt for all except oneself, which developed into meaning invading God's prerogatives
12. Folly — *aphrosune* = It means moral folly.

Preaching Possibilities

I do not see much possibility of linking the Old Testament Lesson with either the New Testament Reading or the Gospel. It could stand by itself and one could try to awaken in our hearers a love for our natural world and recapture a love for spouses, etc. It would be a stretch, but one might develop a sermon on love of various kinds: sexual, of brother, God's, etc. I won't go there this week!

The New Testament Reading and the Gospel do fit nicely together. We could develop the theme: "Advice for Christian Living." James lists advice both negative and positive and Mark has Jesus correcting the Pharisees about clean and unclean (we could make a list of these in our day and community) and he also tells them about religion of the heart.

We will have to be careful this Sunday lest our preaching be too heavy with warnings and legalistic admonitions.

Important moves putting the two together could be:
A. James tells us that our deeds are more important that our words (v. 22).
B. He lays out for us what makes for a teachable heart (v. 21).
C. Who are the orphans and widows in their distress in our communities?
D. Jesus, in Mark's Gospel, gives us some warnings against those things which can corrupt us still.

Possible Outline Of Sermon Moves
Title: Warnings For Christians
A. Introduction: Speak of the many rules and regulations of the orthodox Jews in Jesus' day and how astounded they were when Jesus disciples did not go through the elaborate procedure of washing before they ate. Jesus quoted to them their Bible by using Isaiah: "This people honors me with their lips, but their hearts are far from me ..." (Mark 7:6b).
B. The warnings: This experience gave Jesus an opportunity to teach the people about the many ways we can be trapped by our own evil intentions. Let's see what warnings are here for us Christians today.
   1. Evil intentions come from within us — our own heart. There is a point where we *decide* and then *do*. So we must guard against the evil within us motivating us to bad behavior that hurts others and us as well. This is so because we are both saints and sinners. We never reach the state in our lives where we don't any longer have to guard against that evil which tries to possess us. This argues for lifelong:
      a. self-examination and confession
      b. Christian education and Bible study
      c. regular worship and prayer

Use the first from "Possible Metaphors And Stories" below.
   2. Jesus warns us about what the Bible calls *avarice*. The Greek word means "the love of having." It's when we see happiness in things rather than in God. Let's examine ourselves in our consumer culture and see if that is us.

3. We are also warned about *envy*. Tell your listeners how envy can destroy one's self and take all the joy out of our lives. Use number 2 below under "Possible Metaphors and Stories."
4. We are warned about *fornication*. The original word meant every kind of sexual wrong. Tell how, in the Song of Solomon, we read a beautiful description of erotic love. But here we are warned against that strong sexual desire, which can pervert and distort our sexuality to the place of reducing us to animals, taking our instant gratification whenever we can. Let's present sex as a wholesome part of being a human Christian, yet warning against undisciplined handling of our sexual lives.

C. Now move to the James account and point out that James might have the best answer as to how one guards against these things that can corrupt us: do good things on God's behalf for others. Make the point that being a "do-gooder and bleeding heart" is exactly what Jesus asks us to do!

The reason might not be as obvious as we first think when we read James 1:25. Not only do those who have need get helped, but we who do the helping are changed. To give to those in need on God's behalf is to fill our own hearts with God's love and, thus, often drown out those sins Jesus warns us about.

D. Now frame your message by returning to how you began with Scribes and Pharisees being amazed at the disciples who failed to wash their hands ceremoniously before eating. The heart is the key here; it is from the heart that the hands are motivated to do and not do that which is true discipleship and religion.

Prayer For The Day

Give to us the insight, O God, to keep our hearts from avarice, that love of having which makes us love things more that people. Fill us with a right, wholesome attitude about our sexuality and remove from us envy so we can enjoy all our blessings from you. As a congregation, motivate us to be people of loving and compassionate hearts who help others on your behalf. In Christ's name. Amen.

Possible Metaphors And Stories

Former Bishop George Anderson of the Evangelical Lutheran Church in America told a summer conference of returned missionaries that on his way to his office in Chicago he read a sign a homeowner had erected: "Forget the dog, beware the owner!" and that recently had been added "No trespassing."

In *Newsweek*: "Executive Robert McDonald, after cleaning up after his dog, took literally a mugger's demand to 'give me what you got.' He must be New York's dumbest mugger!" (November 9, 1987, p. 21).

We almost always overvalue what the other person has.

Lexus has a television ad for cars which ends with "... ever miss a great opportunity? Buy a new Lexus now." They show someone being ignored when suggesting bottling water to sell, or setting up coffee shops like Starbucks, or manufacturing a silicon chip to store information. It ends by saying we ought to redeem ourselves by buying a Lexus. James says we miss a chance to practice true religion by not ministering to widows and orphans.

On the outside of the Anthropological Museum in Mexico City are the words: "God is as invincible as the night and as untouchable as the wind ... They were able/knew how to dialogue with their own heart" (Aztec).

First Sunday In September

Proverbs 22:1-2, 8-9, 22-23   James 2:1-10 (11-13) 14-17   Mark 7:24-37

Seasonal Theme   We learn of the Christian faith and how we are to follow Jesus as his disciples.

Theme For The Day   The compassion of Jesus and the inclusiveness of the gospel. Our faithful petitions of prayer can heal others.

Old Testament Lesson   Proverbs 22:1-2, 8-9, 22-23   *Treatment Of The Poor*

This collection of wise sayings is straightforward and understandable as written.

Verses 1-2: Riches are useless if in getting them we ruin our good name. Even if we acquire wealth it does not separate us from the poor as we both come from the same creator. God is concerned about us all whether rich or poor.

Verses 8-9: The difficulties that wicked people bring on others will come back on those who caused it. Trouble comes from sin (Hosea 10:13; Galatians 6:7). This verse probably was encouraging to people suffering and oppressed. In verse 9, "those who are generous" is literally "a good eye" and elsewhere of those who are stingy is literally "an evil eye" (see 23:6 and 28:22). So we have the promise that the person who looks at the poor with an eye to help and not to take advantage are blessed. See more on generosity to the poor: Deuteronomy 15:10, Proverbs 14:21, 31 and 28:27.

Verses 22-23: Here is a strong warning against taking advantage of the poor. The Lord defends them. And God takes from those who take unjustly from the poor. I immediately think of those who legally take from the poor because they can afford to do so in court when the poor cannot!

New Testament Lesson   James 2:1-10 (11-13) 14-17   *Warning Against Partiality*

This follows the Old Testament Lesson well. James warns against showing favor to the wealthy and reminds us that the poor have a special place in God's heart. It all sounds as if James is having a dialogue with us and scolding us for our unseemly behavior being more partial to those of wealth. Regard for outward appearance is inconsistent with our Christian faith. Jesus modeled a life of concern for the poor and refused to cater to the wealthy (Philippians 2:6-11). The well-dressed should not be favored in the church.

In verse 8 we have the "royal law," which refers to the whole law in the Old Testament and as interpreted by Jesus. It is summed up in the commandment to love your neighbor (Leviticus 19:18b and Romans 13:8). James then takes it one step further which we cannot mistake. To show this partiality is to sin. I wonder if it is true of showing partiality to the poor as well? I think so. I think this is radical stuff that says no partiality toward *anyone*. All are God's people.

The Gospel   Mark 7:24-37   *The Syrophoenician Woman And A Deaf Man*

First the woman (vv. 24-30): Jesus is in the Gentile country of Tyre, a city that had one of the great natural harbors out of which some of the world's great sailors who steered by the stars came. The word "dog" is an insult. It was often used of women as we hear "bitch" used in our culture. Jesus' use of the word might be explained a couple ways. He used the diminutive, which meant "puppy." Or perhaps he said it in a way that was reflecting what others nearby were thinking. Tone of voice does make a difference.

This woman was a Greek. She had the gift of repartee. People often wiped their soiled hands at the meal with chunks of bread and then gave them to the dogs. So she said that even after the children eat, there is that which the dogs get. This was a faith Jesus admired — she would not give in or give up.

Symbolically, this woman represents the Gentile world, which accepted the "Bread of Heaven," which the Jews had rejected.

Now the deaf man (vv. 31-37): The journey here described would have taken at least eight months. It's a lovely story demonstrating Jesus' compassion again. No matter how tired of how many competing situations, if an ill body was presented to Jesus, he wanted to help. And not to prove anything either — just because the person needed it. Notice he was considerate of the man and took him aside. Then he acted out what he was doing since the man could not hear his words. Back then it was thought saliva had a curative quality. He treated him not as one of the many hounding him for healing but as an individual with specific needs.

The judgment of the crowd reminds us of Genesis 1:31 when God said a similar thing of God's creation. So we have a miracle of Jesus that best illustrates Jesus' sensitivity in treating people.

Preaching Possibilities

The proverbs in the Old Testament Lesson and the James passage lend themselves to a sermon on the Christian's responsibility toward the poor and the danger of worship of money. It's a good opportunity to preach again on financial stewardship. Some of the great teachings are these:
A. Proverbs assures us that God is the creator of all, rich and poor. And that the generous are blessed (v. 9).
B. Proverbs tells us God is on the side of the poor. We ought not take advantage of our power of wealth over the weakness of the poor.
C. James states that the poor of the world are often rich in faith (v. 5). And that we ought follow the royal law of loving neighbor as we love self (v. 8). Here we have guidelines for sharing our wealth.

If we preach on the Gospel for today, we'll have to decide if it will be a topical sermon using both miracles of healing on something like Jesus' compassion and ours; or if it will be a narrative sermon based on one of the two miracles. I will provide an outline of sermon moves on each of the two miracles using my formula for preaching a narrative sermon on miracles.[1]

Possible Outline Of Sermon Moves

Title: An Under The Table Grace
A. Tell the story in your own words of Jesus' confrontation of this "foreigner" woman the only time he was out of the country.
B. Tell what it teaches about God. God is gracious and sympathetic to all kinds and sorts of people. There are no foreigners in God's sight. God has compassion for us when we are in need.
C. Explain what it reveals about us. Like the disciples we also can have racial prejudices and must confront them.
D. Prayerfully discover why the author wanted this story preserved. Mark probably told this to illustrate that Jesus came to the Gentiles as well as the Jews.
E. Look for a flip side focus. Jesus still can work miracles on others when we prayerfully request it. Or what demons can possess our daughters and sons in our culture and time? Drugs, sex, greed, self-centeredness, wealth addiction?
F. Answer the "so what?" (What do we do about it?) So we must continually pray for others and Jesus' intervention in their lives. We must find a way to overcome our racial prejudices. We must find ways as a congregation to reach out with the gospel to others not at all like us.
G. Frame by returning to the first few sentences. Now refer back to your opening sentences and what you will do because you have preached this story this day.

Option 2: Jesus cures a deaf man
A. Tell the story in your own words. Be careful not to use the old terminology "deaf and dumb" as that is demeaning to these challenged folks.
B. Tell what it teaches about God. God has compassion and sees us in our needs even in a crowd of humanity. God is considerate and loving in dealing with us in our pain.
C. Explain what it reveals about us. We are tempted to overlook the one hurting person in the crowd. When we witness genuine miracles in our lives (or others') we just can't keep quiet about it.

D. Prayerfully consider why the author wanted this story preserved. Mark probably heard Peter preach it as an example of Jesus' tender compassion and his power to heal.
E. Look for a flip side focus. Jesus can open our closed mouths in order for us to speak the gospel to others. And he can open our ears to hear the cries of those who need our help.
F. Answer the "so what?" (What do we do about it?) We might see if there is a need for a ministry to the deaf in our community. We can discover what compassionate ministry we can do on God's behalf in our community and set up a task force to explore how we might organize to do it.
G. Frame by returning to the first few sentences. Recap the story again in your own words sharing your own feeling as you tell it.

Prayer For The Day

Help us to be instruments of your compassion, O God, and when people hurt in our midst, help us to hear their cries for help. Remove from us all racial prejudice and forgive us from the many ways we have been racist in the past. Open our mouths to speak the good news to others. Above all, show us the ways to minister to all in need. In Christ's name. Amen.

Possible Metaphors And Stories

After preaching on the miracle of healing the deaf man, we were moved to hire an expert on sign language and begin a ministry to deaf adults in Des Moines, Iowa. I will never forget Giselle Berninghaus one day telling of a newly-found deaf man who had been hearing disabled for many years prior to coming into our school. She discovered his ears were completely full of ear wax! After it was removed, his hearing was partially restored! So Jesus "... put his fingers into his ears ..." After that Giselle went to seminary and now conducts an ecumenical deaf ministry in Appleton, Wisconsin. And the people are "astounded beyond measure."

A pastor told of having old church records of a Norwegian congregation which listed membership as: "52 souls and 2 Swedes."
Something in our very genes keeps us narrower than we ought to be.

On the *CBS Evening News*, concerning the helping of Vietnam refugees some years ago, the newscaster said, "Americans are suffering from 'compassion fatigue.' " Probably the disciples were suffering from it also up there in that house in Tyre when the woman with the demon-possessed daughter was brought in.

On the January 28, 1988, television show *Night Court:* Bull is hit with lightning and thinks God tells him to give everything to the poor. Actually Art, the maintenance man, over a walkie-talkie was saying to Bull who was helping mount a television antenna: "Give it everything and pull."
In the last scene, after Bull has given everything away and finally finds out it was Art speaking, God comes to him and Bull says, "But I have the joy of giving to others and that's the way we get close to you — by giving away. Thanks, God." God replies, "You are welcome. Sorry about the polyester underwear."

On the CBS news with Dan Rather, Bill Moyers said regarding the twenty-fifth anniversary of the Peace Corps, "We carry two passports. One is American and the other is human being." Let's never let the former block out the latter.

---

1. See *The Miracles Of Jesus And Their Flip Side*, CSS Publishing Company, 2000, by the author.

Second Sunday In September

Proverbs 1:20-33   **James 3:1-12**   **Mark 8:27-38**

Seasonal Theme   We learn of the Christian faith and how we are to follow Jesus as his disciples.

Theme For The Day   The giving away of our lives for others is where real life here is to be found. We must expect to carry Jesus' cross as part of our discipleship.

Old Testament Lesson   Proverbs 1:20-33   *Wisdom Rejected*

Here we learn of disaster which accompanies the neglect of wisdom. Wisdom is personified as a woman who appeals to everyone (vv. 20-23). Verses 24-28 tell us only a fool ignores wisdom and it's at his own risk (vv. 29-33). We can, however, respond to wisdom's scolding and thus become wise.

When troubles come, as they always do, wisdom won't help if we have ignored her up till then. It's a tough saying and seems to claim that if we reject lady wisdom we can't reclaim her after she has withdrawn her invitation. Fools must suffer the consequences of their actions (v. 31). Galatians might support this idea (Galatians 6:7). In 3:23 we learn the flip side of this idea. Heeding wisdom gives safety and peace. These introductory words set the tone for the rest of the book.

New Testament Lesson   James 3:1-12   *Taming The Tongue*

This is a passage full of metaphors. James' point is that even though the tongue is small, its behavior can (and does) shape our entire lives. He uses these metaphors:
1. The bridle with bit guides the horse's direction.
2. The rudder of a ship guides the entire ship.
3. A whole forest is set ablaze by one flame.
4. Wild animals can be tamed but not the wild tongue.
5. A spring cannot give out fresh and brackish water.
6. A fig tree cannot give off olives.
7. A grape vine cannot yield figs.
8. Salt water cannot give us fresh water. (Before the process of desalinization!)

So the tongue controls the person. We are unable to control it. The author is close to giving us the doctrine of original sin (v. 6). See also Paul in Romans 7. This tongue is our worst enemy. We sense something is wrong because out of the same mouth comes blessings and curses. Watch your mouth. I might add not only does what we say hurt or help others; it also shapes our own behavior. James, you really are on to something here!

The Gospel   Mark 8:27-38   *Peter's Confession And Jesus' Cross*

Jesus and his little band of disciples are now in Caesarea Philippi where we find today the source of the Jordan River. There was also at that place a temple to Caesar, the Roman Emperor. It was in this setting that Peter finally got it right. This carpenter from Nazareth is the promised Messiah. Here in the middle of Mark's Gospel we now learn that this Jesus had ahead of him the inescapable cross. So Jesus had to determine if anyone realized, understood, who he was. Peter told him what others were saying (v. 28) and then he said what became clear to him.

Jesus saw he had a lot of teaching to be done for these disciples before he departed so he told them to keep this discovery a secret for a while longer. No doubt Peter spoke the very temptations attacking Jesus at that moment (v. 32). Not wanting to die, Jesus was re-fighting those temptations in the wilderness following his baptism. It's often true that a friend concerned about us gives voice to our temptations.

Beginning with verse 34 we have the sheer honesty of Jesus about discipleship and following him. They "deny themselves," literally meaning to "say no to self." We must say no to our natural inclination to take the easy, safe way. We say "yes" to Christ's way, which may involve suffering; but in doing so we find freedom.

Verse 36 tells us that it is most often so in the Christian faith that we find real abundant life by giving ours away for others. Mother Teresa often quoted: "Unless life is lived for others, it is not worthwhile." It's so easy to sacrifice eternity for the pleasure of the moment (v. 37).

Preaching Possibilities

All three readings will go together by using the following emphasis:
A. Old Testament Lesson: God has given us brains and we are encouraged to use them on God's behalf.
B. New Testament Reading: We must be careful lest our natural inclination to sin is enhanced by what we allow ourselves to give voice to.
C. Our words to others, like Peter's, can be the instrument through which the power that works against God may try to work (Mark 8:33).
D. To be a Christian and disciple means some sacrifice (Mark 8:35).

The Second Reading lends itself to standing alone and talking about our words and how they can destroy or build up others. And also how our words can shape who and how we are. Some moves could be:
A. Such a little instrument that has such a big effect on our and others' lives — the tongue. Examples — rudder of a ship, flame starting a fire.
B. What we say can be a ministry of encouragement and/or a tool of character assassination of others.
C. What we allow our tongue to say can also shape us and our attitudes in this life.
D. Our tongue's instinctive inclination is to cause trouble and tear down rather than to build up.
E. We have the potential to bring others to Christ with this instrument called the tongue.
F. We can curse God or love God with our tongue.

We also could base our sermon for today on the scripture verse Mark 8:28, asking how would we answer this question if Jesus asked it of us today?
A. A "just in case I need you for help" Jesus?
B. A "save my soul for eternity" Jesus?
C. A "make me loved by others" Jesus?
D. An "escape from my many problems" Jesus?
E. A "teacher of wise things" Jesus?
F. A "Savior my parents worshiped" Jesus?
G. A "person admired by my significant other" Jesus?
H. A "make me well" Jesus?

You add to the list from your experiences in your ministry.

Possible Outline Of Sermon Moves

Title: Discipleship For These Days
Text: Mark 8:34b-36
A. Introduction: Give the setting of this story. Jesus is teaching his disciples after Peter confessed Jesus was the Messiah.
B. Now move to what he taught. These things he wanted his disciples back then and us disciples to know about discipleship:
   1. Mark 8:34b To follow Jesus will mean some hard times of sacrifice and pain (story below).
   2. Mark 8:35 To gain real, full, abundant life one must take risks and give (his/her) life away (story below).
   3. Mark 8:36 We must guard against striving to get rather than to give away. A life of doing for others is where real life is to be found.

See below for three metaphors that can be used to illustrate the above three moves.
C. Move to your own witness and how you have gradually matured in age and faith to realize the truth of the three above teachings of Jesus.
D. Frame you sermon by returning to your opening and how these words must have stunned the disciples and then how they teach us as well.

Prayer For The Day

O God, help us to do better at sharing our lives with others and bearing your cross in our discipleship. Move us far beyond the striving for things for ourselves to a life of concern for other people. And when the call for sacrifice comes, let us accept it with graceful hearts. In Jesus' name. Amen.

Possible Metaphors And Stories

In the movie *The Thorn Birds*, after telling the story of the thorn bird, the priest says to Maggie: "... for the best is only bought at the cost of great pain." Jesus bought our at-one-ment with God at great pain on the cross.

I noticed on a cold winter day that the Life Flight helicopter has a heating blanket around its engine to keep it warm and ready to fly at any moment the call comes to do so. We need to keep warm our motivation to serve others no matter how cold our own lives may be.

William Sloane Coffin said that there are two ways to be rich: "One is to have a lot of money; another is to have few needs."
Our culture foists on us so many false needs for which we sacrifice too much.

In a little general store on Kings Ranch Road in Gold Canyon, Arizona, there hangs a plaque. Burned into the wood are these words: "Cowboy etiquette: Better to taste your words before you spit them out."

The pastor was visiting in the parlor. A young farm boy had just killed a big rat and came running into the room to tell his mother, "... and I stamped and stamped on it," then, noticing the pastor for the first time, added, "... and God called it home."
We often have one language for the church and another for the world, and fail to connect the two.

Third Sunday In September

Proverbs 31:10-31 James 3:13—4:3, 7-8a Mark 9:30-37

Seasonal Theme We learn of the Christian faith and how we are to follow Jesus as his disciples.

Theme For The Day Humble service wanting to serve others and rejecting the natural ambition for rank and prestige.

Old Testament Lesson Proverbs 31:10-31 *The Noble Wife*

This last section of Proverbs is sometimes called an acrostic poem. Each of the verses begins with a letter of the Hebrew alphabet in order. Solomon seems to be the author of this passage which honors a good wife. 31:10 indicates that they were rare. Some of her attributes listed which make her so desirable were these: the husband has confidence in her, she supports and encourages him, she delights in her work, she is good at shopping, she manages the household well, she works hard and invests well, she plans ahead, she gives to the poor, keeps her family warm, dresses well, respects and builds up her husband, appears dignified, is wise and faithful, her children love her, she "fears the Lord," which seems to be the key to her capabilities. I wonder if the husband matched her in all the above attributes? This might be a good passage to use on Mothers' Day. No matter how much I try to approach it without prejudice, it seems to be chauvinistic.

New Testament Lesson James 3:13—4:3, 7-8a *Two Lifestyles*

This passage also speaks of wisdom. Virtues commended are understanding, gentleness, not envious, selfish, boastful, or untruthful. Verse 17 continues the list of virtues: pure, peaceable, gentle, full of mercy with no partiality or hypocrisy. Verse 18 commends God's peace. Then we are admonished against coveting — that upon which our system of merchandising is based. The reading ends with a partial remedy for all the ills listed above. If we draw near to our God, God will draw near to us. Of course, it is God's Holy Spirit that enables us to draw near to God.

So we have here a preachable contrast: true wisdom, which is a divine gift (3:13) and selfish ambition, which is evil's instrument (3:14-16). Paul makes a similar contrast in Galatians 5:19-23.

The Gospel Mark 9:30-37 *The Greatest Disciple?*

The reading begins with Jesus informing his disciples that he was now heading for the cross but that he would rise again. Of course, they didn't understand!

Then comes this heart-breaking incident of the disciples arguing about who would be greatest at the very time Jesus was trying to tell them of his crucifixion. They were still thinking of Jesus establishing a worldly kingdom. How could they live with him and hear him teach all this time and be so far off the truth? Notice in verse 35 that he sat down. This was a posture of serious teaching by a rabbi.

Some have thought this little child in verse 36 might have been Simon Peter's son. Wouldn't that be a nice picture? Jesus here takes the ambition to rule and changes it to the ambition to serve. Instead of wanting people to do for us we ought want to do for others. Think how this principle would enhance our economics, politics, ministry, and peace within our congregations!

The point about the child must further emphasize the fact we don't befriend the powerful because of what they can do for us; but rather, we befriend the helpless in order to be some help to them (because of what we can do for them). Jesus said a similar truth in Matthew 10:42.

The whole passage is very unflattering to the disciples as Mark often reported. Matthew usually rewrote the account to protect the disciples' reputation.

Preaching Possibilities

The only way I would approach the Proverbs lesson is to transpose a noble wife to a noble spouse and present it as the virtues needed in both wife and husband. It could go: A capable spouse who can find? They are far more precious than jewels. "The heart of their spouse trusts them and will have no lack of gain ..." etc.

One could use the Old Testament Lesson as an example for preaching on the James reading on two kinds of wisdom: one of gentleness and one of envy.

Verse 16 in James does also hook into the Gospel and those disciples arguing over rank. If we used all three readings, an outline might look like this:

A. Selfish ambition does not enrich a good marriage (Old Testament Lesson).
B. Selfish ambition does not bring peace to us or our congregation (New Testament Reading).
C. Selfish ambition destroys our discipleship (the Gospel).
D. Jesus teaches us a different ambition: that of serving others (the Gospel).

Now go over the above four points relating each one to your congregational, individual, and family life. It will preach.

Possible Outline Of Sermon Moves

A. Begin by relating a story of selfish ambition or by confessing to your own selfish ambition in being a pastor and preacher.
B. Move to the Gospel account of the disciples arguing over who would be greatest. Read from a Bible (that people can see in your hands) after telling it in your own words, Mark 9:33-35.
C. List out the ways selfish ambition can destroy peace in:
   1. A marriage
   2. A community
   3. A congregation
   4. An individual relationship
D. Move back to the scripture account of Jesus' answer to the problem. Tell in your own words then read Mark 9:36-37.
E. Relate what this means to you. That we ought substitute the ambition for power and rank with the ambition to serve the helpless and ones who may never appreciate our help. Tell a story or two that illustrate this theological idea.
F. Pray for the strength to overcome the ambition for power and prestige with the ambition to serve the helpless on God's behalf listing some examples of such helpless in your community.

Prayer For The Day

Move us to seek out those who need our help in our community, O God, and to resist seeking prestige in doing it. Help us to do humble service bridling that devilish desire for rank and power that sneaks into our lives so easily. Bless our discipleship with peace and harmony as we seek to do your will as your followers. In Jesus Christ's name. Amen.

Possible Metaphors And Stories

The women of the Lorla clan of the Kpella tribe of Liberia wanted a health center so much that they carried two building blocks at a time on their heads across the Saint Paul River in "dry time" to build the walls. It so shamed the men that they finally got busy and helped build the building. The nurse, Korlawu Togba, R.N., who trained at Lutheran Phebe Hospital in midwifery and emergency room techniques, is the medical help for the clan. During the war of 1990 the building was burned and the men of the village were killed. The women and children ran to escape into the bush. How brutal we humans can be to each other!

Lee Kalmer, Dean of ISU College of Agriculture, told of a farmer buying a new tractor. He had it delivered at night so he could put on it old decals so it would not look new. He didn't want to "lord it over his neighbors." What an example of humble stewardship.

The author of *Ironweed* states: "It's a short distance from the 'Hallelujah' to the 'hoot.' " So it is we can come down fast and hard and painfully.

A Rolaids ad on television has Henry VIII saying the words, "Who is king around here? It's enough to give a man heartburn."

We can ask of our lifestyle and priorities: Who is the king around here? We have a savior-king waiting for our allegiance and service.

A special on *60 Minutes*, October 18, 1987, was about Sister Emmanuel who lives in the garbage dump of the city of Cairo. She claims she has "married the slums." Sixty-two years old, her theory is that you must live with the people you serve. They raised one million dollars and built a hospital. She has to fight the parents to get the children in school. One of her concerns is the women beaten by husbands she calls "beaten slaves of the garbage." This woman began life as a pampered daughter of a rich businessman.

What is it that moves some to help?

Fourth Sunday In September

Esther 7:1-6, 9-10; 9:20-22   James 5:13-20   Mark 9:38-50

Seasonal Theme   We learn about Christian growth and the way of discipleship.

Theme For The Day   The seriousness of temptation and warnings of danger.

Old Testament Lesson   Esther 7:1-6, 9-10; 9:20-22   *A Reason For Purim*

I don't believe this is a familiar book to most Christians and it will need an introduction to the congregation. Page 538 of the *New Revised Standard Version* of the Bible does it well.

While God is not mentioned in the entire book, it does seem to indicate that God cares for his chosen people, the Jews. The passage we have today related the background and justification for the Jewish festival of Purim. This has been written to help future generations remember the great deliverance of the people under the reign of Ahasuerus.

The gifts to the poor in verse 9:22 is rather natural for such an observance of joy. It is still a part of the Jewish festival today.

New Testament Lesson   James 5:13-20   *Priesthood Of All Believers*

A ministry of prayer is called for by James. Ways are described that give opportunity for ministry to each other: Pray for each other, pray for the rich, and pray for forgiveness. Then in verse 17, James gives an example of Elijah, who prayed it would not rain and it didn't for three and one half years! I'll bet Elijah was not popular for that prayer! On the other hand, when he then did pray *for* rain, it really did (1 Kings 17:1 and 18:42). We are also to rescue each other when we stray into sin (v. 19). So, according to James, we are a singing, praying, confessing, and forgiving church. We care about each other.

The Gospel   Mark 9:38-50   *Advice On Temptation*

Verses 38-41 don't seem to be related to the rest of the passage. Evidently there were wonder-workers using Jesus' name as their formula of power and John was concerned what the twelve should do about them. Jesus' answer is that anyone who uses his name and power will be unable to say anything bad against him. He adds in verses 40-41 that whoever isn't against them is for them and anyone who does the good thing on Jesus' behalf will be rewarded. It is not an answer John expected.

Now follows a passage about temptations and how to deal with them. It says:

We must not cause new Christians to be tempted (v. 42). "Little ones" could mean children or young in the faith or (I prefer) Jesus' followers of any age. See Matthew 18:6 and Luke 17:1-2.

Then drastic measures are called for when facing temptations, even if it is hand, foot, or eye. Hell is the Hebrew *gehenna*. This was the valley near Jerusalem where infant sacrifice to the Ammonite god Molech was practiced and was called Hinnon valley. The name became a symbol for hell. Verse 48 comes from Isaiah 66:24 and it symbolizes the finality of God's judgment.

The three sayings on salt are unrelated in verse 49. They teach us: suffering is a normal experience, we can lose our usefulness, and we should be at peace with each other. See Romans 12:18.

Preaching Possibilities

The New Testament and the Gospel will combine together nicely for our preaching this weekend. We would use the theme of "this is our ministry" from James and tell about:
A. A ministry of prayer for each other, the sick, and for others' and our forgiveness.
B. James tells us our ministry ought produce a singing, confessing, and forgiving church.
C. Jesus tells us disciples that we ought partner with anyone who ministers in his name. (Identify who that may be in your community.)

D. Then add Jesus' words about temptation. We must not be the one who brings temptation upon someone else.
E. And this is so serious we must take drastic measures to halt whatever the temptation, like cutting off a limb of our bodies.
F. Christian disciples are to be at peace with each other.

This could be a marvelous sermon about our practice of the faith. We ought use some humor and stories to keep it from being too dour.

Possible Outline Of Sermon Moves
Title: These little ones
Text: Mark 9:42
A. Introduction: Down through the years, there have been a number of theories about who Jesus meant when he talked of "little ones." Some have thought children, some have thought new Christians, and some have thought all Christian disciples.
B. Sermon moves:
   1. "Little ones" has most often been thought of as children. It is true that one of the worst sins is to teach or seduce a child into such behavior.
      Recent research has revealed that drug addicts are often made by "using" with their own parents.
      Other ways we might cause children to stumble are by our own example in language, in cheating, in ugliness toward our spouse or children, by our unfaithfulness toward church, etc. Children are watching us! Are we fulfilling the vows we made at our children's baptisms to raise them in the faith?
   2. More and more scholars have called attention to the fact that Paul and John called new converts to the faith "little ones." We can cause new members to stumble by not doing out part in welcoming them into the congregation. Or advising them not to be "radical" in their discipleship, or by considering them second-rate members in the congregation.
   3. Some would claim "little ones," according to Jesus, were all his disciples. In John's Gospel, Jesus calls the disciples "little ones." So in this case, we are not to do anything that would discredit the church or each other. Frying the pastor for Sunday lunch is not recommended. Explain the Greek word for "stumble," which meant a bait stick. It was the enticement in a trap. Our behavior inside the church and outside all week long must not set traps for other Christians, but, rather, help them to grow in the faith.
   4. Now give examples of "little ones" in your congregation — a child, a new member, and one of the long-time faithful. All are "little ones" in Jesus' view. He loves them and we must also.

Prayer For The Day
There are so many temptations all around us, dear Holy Parent. Help us to resist them in whatever form they come. And, most of all, give us the motivation and insight not to ever, ever bring a temptation to others, whether they are children, new Christians, or old faithful disciples. Thank you for considering us your "little ones." In Jesus, the Christ. Amen.

Possible Metaphors And Stories
Dan Rather announced on *CBS Nightly News* on March 31, 1987, that the AIDS virus "resurrects itself." Kill it and it somehow starts again. So the bad can resurrect as well as the good! Addictions, prejudices, bad habits, greed, and so forth.

The palm tree outside my office window on the seminary campus must have the dead fronds removed every so often so new ones will grow. The Christian life does call for the removal of the dead that new might grow. Let's see, what ought we remove?

prejudices old enemies
wealth addiction saved-up hurts
selfishness jealousy

On a Northwest Airlines plane they place a plastic cover over the engine intake while loading the food from a truck to the plane's galley.

I wonder what we ought to cover and with what to keep from contaminating our intake which propels us through life?

Andrew Hsiao, former President of Lutheran Theological Seminary, Hong Kong, told me of his mother in Hunan Province, People's Republic of China, during the Cultural Revolution. As an old woman, she was called into their Lutheran church building, put on trial for being a Christian, and forced to renounce her faith in the sanctuary of her own church. She never recovered from it. I am not sure he has either. An important thing for us to ask is if we have even been faithful enough that they would try us as they did her.

A Suggestion:

With the first Sunday in October, we begin readings from the New Testament book of Hebrews for seven weeks. Thus, a couple suggestions you might consider: place in the worship bulletin a brief introduction to the book of Hebrews or announce it verbally before reading the New Testament reading. Consider using material provided at the beginning of the book found in the *New Revised Standard Version* (p. 265). The second suggestion is to conduct a Bible study[1] over the next seven weeks using the readings for the day. I, personally, think this is very rich doctrinal theology better learned in Bible study than in preaching. An outline might go like this:

Hebrews 1:1-4; 2:5-12
    Jesus, pioneer of salvation
Hebrews 4:12-16
    Jesus, our high priest
Hebrews 5:1-10
    Jesus compared with the temple high priest
Hebrews 7:23-28
    Jesus as guarantee of our better new covenant
Hebrews 9:11-14
    The contrast of perfection, performance, and completeness. We have an eternal redemption.
Hebrews 10:11-14
    Once for all sacrifice and resurrection and coming again. And a summary of the seven weeks study of Hebrews.

Possible Worship Bulletin Announcement:

Beginning with the first Sunday in October, we will read from the book of Hebrews as the New Testament Reading for seven Sundays. Written to Jewish Christians who were considering returning to Judaism, the writer tries to persuade them to hold fast in their faith in Jesus Christ. The book was written prior to the fall of Jerusalem. The author may have been Apollos or Barnabas.

The central theme is the sovereignty of the Christ. The practical applications of this we'll find in the Second Lesson readings. As I read from this book, however, it sounds to me like a missal to teachers of the Christian faith as to what content to teach. It would be like a theologian writing to Sunday school teachers.

---

1. William Barclay's *Daily Study Bible*'s volume on Hebrews will be a very helpful reference on conducting this study.

First Sunday In October

Job 1:1; 2:1-10   Hebrews 1:1-4; 2:5-12   Mark 10:2-16

Seasonal Theme   We learn about Christian growth and the way of discipleship.

Theme For The Day   God's Kingdom is childlike and Jesus loves the children.

Old Testament Lesson   Job 1:1; 2:1-10   *Job, Satan, And The Lord*

In this narrative-prose section of Job, we have a blameless and upright man, who fears God, having to endure undeserved suffering. Job's distresses seem so unfair. Even Job's wife struggles to the misery by suggesting he should denounce his God (v. 2:9). Job's answer to her is that if we receive good at the hand of God we should also expect to receive bad (v. 2:10). I'm sure our hearers can identify with this good person who is a supreme example of affliction that defies human explanation. "Skin for skin" (v. 4) is a proverbial saying which had to do with trading animal skins and implied that Job had traded the lives of his children for his own. Scholars have guessed the disease in verse 7 may have been smallpox or elephantiasis. When Job needed comfort and support from his wife, he got, instead, evidence of her acridity toward God. In 27:5 we learn that Job told his friends that "... until I die I will not put away my integrity from me."

New Testament Lesson   Hebrews 1:1-4; 2:5-12   *Jesus: Pioneer Of Salvation*

The first four verses introduce the theme of the book and connect it with the traditions as well as presenting Jesus the Christ as working out the purpose of God. Verses 1:2-4 present Jesus as God's ultimate revelation. The word "imprint" is even more interesting. It is the impress of a seal on the wax or clay. This metaphor comes from the practice of one imprinting one's personal seal in hot wax to seal a letter. So, when we see the Son, we have the imprint of God the Father. Verse 1:3b gives us for the first time the central theme of the entire book — he made "purification for our sins."

In verses 2:5-12, we have Jesus' work in salvation. In verse 6, we have the claim that Jesus' life and mission was the fulfillment of Psalm 8's prophecy. Jesus becomes the true man who causes the wonder of the prophet. Jesus is God's initiative in our salvation (v. 10). Notice while the author stresses defilement by sin, he/she also tells us of human's origin in God and how Jesus relates to us sinners.

The Gospel   Mark 10:2-16   *Divorce And Little Children*

While the motive of the Pharisees for asking this difficult question about divorce is suspect, nevertheless it is a subject in which our hearers will also be interested. In Jewish law, a woman was considered a thing who was at the complete mercy of the male. So, a man could divorce his wife on almost any grounds. But a wife could not. The Jewish law is based on Deuteronomy 24:1. So Jesus is striking a blow for women by restoring marriage to where it ought to be.

Matthew's account of Jesus' advice on this subject is quite different. In Mark, Jesus says absolutely that there is to be *no* divorce and re-marriage. In Matthew 19:3-9 he is quoted as forbidding remarriage but allowing divorce on the basis of adultery, which certainly dissolves the bonds of marriage anyway. Perhaps the heart of this passage is that Jesus emphasizes that the loose sexual morality of the day be repaired. We are reminded that marriage is a life-long promise of fidelity and carries with it a heavy responsibility. Jesus is strengthening the Christian home and family.

Verses 10:13-16: As Jesus makes his way toward the cross, his followers are trying to protect him. They mistakenly think he would not want to be bothered right now with mothers wanting their children blessed. For us who have raised many, the passage is not altogether clear. Children have all kinds of traits and some of them are certainly not what I think of as the Kingdom of God. Verse 15 may be the key. The kingdom is a gift, not something we earn like the Protestant "justified by grace through faith." Some traits of children that we could affirm as kingdom worthy would be obedience, trust, and the ability to forget and forgive.

Perhaps we learn something about Jesus here. He must have been liked by children as well as he liked them. A kind, warm, joy-filled person with compassion and love for others, the kids were attracted to him.

Preaching Possibilities

I'm not sure I can find any significant connection between any of the readings for today. I think any of the three readings will provide a marvelous topical sermon:
- A. *Old Testament:* Why Good People Suffer
- B. *New Testament:* God's Imprint And Ours
- C. *The Gospel:* Let's Hear It For The Family or Children As Kingdom Samples

In our culture the question of suffering is as real now as it was back then in Job's day. We can draw the difference for our hearers between what God *allows* to happen to us in order to not break God's natural law, and what God *wants* to happen to us because of demonstrated love for us on the cross.

The metaphor in the Second Reading of the hot wax and the imprint of the seal lends itself to an extended metaphor sermon.[1] We can build our sermon moves on what we think a seal of Jesus would look like — Jesus feeding the hungry, blessing the children, dying on the cross, coming out of the grave, ascending, healing, etc. — and what each one of those means to us personally and corporately.

One other approach is to wonder out loud what those who selected these three readings wanted to communicate to us today on God's behalf. It's a stretch, but we could answer:
A. The Old Testament tells us even good people will suffer.
B. The New Testament tells us we have a God who really cares about us through what Jesus has done.
C. The Gospel relates God's great interest in families, marriages, and children.

Then you could suppose why these were of interest to these people who selected them. Perhaps on the committee was a woman who had a fine husband dying of cancer (Old Testament). Maybe there was a man who was worried about the Christian example he has set for those who know him (New Testament). And one of the committee might have gone through divorce and felt guilty about it and the way his children now saw him and God's kingdom. It will preach.

Possible Outline Of Sermon Moves

A. Introduction: Tell a story of children you have or know acting terribly. Better yet, relate an event in your own childhood like this.
B. Now question if that is what Jesus meant when he claimed the kingdom as a little child (Mark 10:14). Transition by relating how Jesus was on his was to the cross, the disciples tried to protect him, and he scolded them, asking that the children be brought to him.
C. Then move to Jesus' words about the kingdom in verse 14 and question if selfish, sometimes mean, noisy, and messy children can ever be how God's kingdom is.
D. Relate a story of a beautiful child, like the first one listed in "Possible Metaphors And Stories" below. Then give what child-like traits Jesus was commending: humility, obedience, very trusting, forgiving. There are stories below for illustration of these kingdom traits.
E. Frame your sermon by returning to your opening story and contrast it with the kingdom traits summed up in reverse order. Finish by quoting again verses 15-16 by reading them from a Bible all can see.

Prayer For The Day

Help us, O God, to refrain from being childish and show us the ways to be childlike, just like in your kingdom. And bless our congregation in all its attempts to bring the little children to you. In the name of the one who took them up in his arms and blessed them. Amen.

Possible Metaphors And Stories

Danny only had one arm. He came to the second grade Sunday school class for the first time. When the teacher thoughtlessly asked the students to fold their hands and sing, "This is the church, this is the steeple," Hannah, next to him, saw his dilemma. Putting her fingers and hand in his, she remarked, "Come on, Danny, you and I will be the church together."

Oh, if we could only live it out as adults! Let's put our hands together and be the church.

On flight number 981 (United Airlines), there were storm clouds all around the horizon. The captain announced, "Fasten your seat belts, because we do have some turbulence even in the friendly skies."

It's true even as God's people and in God's care there are storms and rough roads to travel.

Missionary Barry Lang at Bong Mine, Liberia, told that when a Liberian Christian lives the wrong way or when two people have a difference of opinion and have strong words, or one proves the other wrong, then the offender kneels on the floor and takes the foot of the other and begs for forgiveness. When the offended puts a hand on his shoulder, it is finished, "cut" — no more can either bring it up again. It is completely over! On the cross Jesus put his hand on our shoulder and proclaimed "it is finished" ... we are forgiven.

Martin Luther said in the sixteenth century at one of his famous table talks after looking at his son Martin: "In all simplicity ... children believe that God is gracious and that there is eternal life. These natural affections do not cease in the pious, as those who are without feeling and are hardened imagine, for such affections are the work of divine creation. Children live with all sincerity in faith, without interference of reason, as Ambrose says: 'there is a lack of reason but now of faith' " (*What Luther Says*, p. 142).

---

1. See Schmalenberger's *The Preacher's Edge*, CSS Publishing Company, 1996, chapter 7.

Second Sunday In October

Job 23:1-9, 16-17   Hebrews 4:12-16   Mark 10:17-31

Seasonal Theme   We learn about Christian growth and the way of discipleship.

Theme For The Day   How the Christian manages wealth. It's all about being a good steward.

Old Testament Lesson   Job 23:1-9, 16-17   *Job Complains*

Job was trying to find God and plead his case before him like a lawyer would argue before a judge. The Hebrew word used is *yakah*, which means to argue, debate in court. He was sure the judge would acquit him and his troubles would be over.

Job was terrified (dismayed) not because of his sins, but because of the Lord's awesome nature. Sounds like Job is a good candidate for regular Prozac. He needs something to remove the "thick darkness."

New Testament Lesson   Hebrews 4:12-16   *Our High Priest*

First the word of God is presented as something living and vital. It is sharp and will cut through our pretense and lay us bare to see ourselves as we really are (vv. 12-13). Then we have Jesus portrayed as a high priest who was an ordinary human being with an extraordinary call from God (v. 14). This high priest has empathy for us (v. 15) so that we can approach him confidently that we might have mercy and grace when we need it (vv. 15-16).

The Gospel   Mark 10:17-31   *The Rich Man*

Some things to notice about this graphic story. It sounds as if the rich man had kept all the "you shalt nots," but had not done any "thou shalts" like giving to the poor. Being respected was not enough. Jesus was saying spend yourself and your possessions on others, then you will find the fulfilling life (v. 21).

Now comes a severe warning in verse 23. It is very difficult for a person to enter the kingdom of God and have wealth. The word for money is *chremata*, which Aristotle defined as, "all those things of which the value is measured by coinage." Jesus must have had in mind the following dangers for us who have wealth:

A. When we have so much invested in this world it is difficult for us to think beyond this world or of leaving it.
B. We begin to think of everything in terms of price.
C. Wealth is a test of us. For many who can stand adversity only a few can handle wealth. It is an enormous responsibility. The person who trusts in himself and his possessions can never be saved and the one who trusts in God's redeeming grace can enter into salvation.

Good old Peter saw his chance and reminded Jesus that the disciples had given up everything to follow him (v. 28). For that, Jesus promised them a person will receive back a hundred fold (v. 30). We will deal with that needle and camel in the "Possible Outline Of Sermon Moves."

Preaching Possibilities

I think we would be straining the original meaning to put these readings together in any configuration. Perhaps those who selected them did so with the idea of a series on Job or a series on Hebrews, which could have easily been done these weeks.

The Old Testament account of Job's discouragement and inability to find God can sound very contemporary with our people today. Perhaps we could describe the depths of despair Job was in and then point to Hebrews 4:15 to give an assurance to our people that God is available and is sympathetic to us.

If we do use Job, it will take an introduction as to how Job got to this discouragement before we can use today's portion of scripture.

Easily, the Hebrews passage will lend itself to an old fashioned doctrinal sermon. The outline might include the following points:

A. *Verse 12:* The word is much more than printing on paper.
B. *Verse 13:* The word can reveal to us how we really are.
C. *Verses 14-15:* We can hold fast to our beliefs for we have a high Priest who is able to sympathize.
D. *Verse 16:* God has mercy and grace for us in our time of need.

To finish in a very traditional way, we can use as a poem William W. How's hymn "O Word Of God Incarnate" (*Lutheran Book of Worship*, #231).

Possible Outline Of Sermon Moves
A. Begin by retelling the story as told in the Gospel. "It happened right after that sweet picture of Jesus blessing the little children ..." etc.
B. Now explain the metaphor of the camel through the eye of a needle:
   1. Eye of the needle could be the attempt to put a ship's hawser cable through a real sewing needle.
   2. The eye of the needle could have been the name for the little door in the city gate, which was closed at night.
   3. The eye of the needle could be just an exaggeration — a hyperbole with a bit of humor mixed in. In Burma, my students tell me, camel is translated "elephant"! Jesus made his point: It is almost impossible for a rich person to get into the kingdom (read v. 25).
C. Give some examples of the same point using contemporary hyperbole — it is tougher than kicking a 75-yard field goal. It is tougher than freezing over the Mississippi in August, etc.
D. What's so dangerous in being rich?
   1. It's addictive and we always want more.
   2. Our hearts are fixed on the world.
   3. We look at everything in terms of price.
   4. Wealth brings with it tremendous responsibilities.
E. Talk about mistakes we could think as we hear this sermon:
   1. We think of ourselves as the disciples rather than the rich man in the story.
   2. That we think of the kingdom as far off in heaven, rather than here on earth where we pray for it to come.
F. Now emphasize that the one *who gives is always the one even more blessed* than the one who receives. So if we don't share our wealth we are robbed of the great blessings of giving it away.

   Then punch hard on the idea that there are two ways of being rich: One is to have lots of money and the other is to have few needs.
G. Now frame your sermon by returning to the words of Jesus about the camel through the needle and then review your moves in reverse order. It will preach.
H. A bonus for this Sunday. Challenge your hearers to use their imagination and guess what happened to that rich man. Here are some ideas:
   1. He left, never to return, and died a bitter, selfish, unhappy, greedy old man with no friends but lots of wealth he could not take with him.
   2. Or, perhaps, he returned a few weeks later having sold off most of his possessions and giving the money to the poor of Jericho. He and James became leaders in the church in Jerusalem.
   3. Or, perhaps, he became one of the money changers in the temple courtyard whom Jesus drove out and so angered them that they engineered his crucifixion.
   4. Or (I like this one), perhaps, when he left Jesus, he went back to his vineyard and paid everyone the same wage even though some had worked just a little.
   5. Maybe he was so insulted that a few weeks later he joined others in shouting, "Crucify him!"

6. Or, one more possibility: he took Jesus' advice seriously and, one day, met a widow at the temple in Jerusalem who had just given her last mite in the offering. They married and became the characters mentioned in Acts 5: Ananias and Sapphira, who tried to reserve too much for themselves — the old temptation had returned and once again it was "much harder" (Mark 10:25).

Prayer For The Day

Dear God, teach us how to share the wealth that we have. Make our hearts generous that you might bless others through our giving. And do bless us with acceptance into your kingdom here on earth and at last with you in heaven. Amen.

Possible Metaphors And Stories

In my class on stewardship in Hong Kong, the students were to define stewardship in their own language and culture. Stella Min from Myanmar (Burma) said, "In my language, to be a steward means a treasurer; (Branda Soe) ... the one who keeps valuable things for others." In Cambodia, Chim Pitch wrote, "For Cambodia, steward meant chief of royal palace and also it meant servant." This is the kind of servant who brings a blessing to others.

A sign in the Sizzler Steak House in Albany, California, said, "No sharing. Please, do not put us in an awkward position." What is awkward for that restaurant is surely basic for discipleship.

I saw on *CNN News* that a man had won six million dollars in the state lottery. He told all he would do with the money, including spoiling his grandchildren. His wife said he forgot to buy her a valentine this year. The first time in forty years of marriage! He had bought a recreation vehicle that weekend and was out driving it around. How easily wealth can help us change our priorities.

Third Sunday In October

Job 38:1-7 (34-41) Hebrews 5:1-10 Mark 10:35-45

Seasonal Theme We learn about Christian growth and the way of discipleship.

Theme For The Day The call, responsibilities, and blessings of discipleship.

Old Testament Lesson Job 38:1-7 (34-41) *God's Rebuke*

Last week we read Job 23 and the week before that chapter two. So we have the essence of the book.
A. Two weeks ago Job 1:1; 2:1-10: A blameless man is suffering; why?
B. Last week Job 23:1-9, 16-17: Job is going through tough, severe suffering and pleads his case to God.
C. Today God gives as much of an answer as God is ever going to give for Job's suffering: 38:4. Where was Job when the world was created? Who is Job to question the wisdom of our creator God? When some irony is used to point up Job's foolishness: verses 4, 5, 18, 34-41, Job can't do all this which God does, so he shouldn't question God.

New Testament Lesson Hebrews 5:1-10 *Jesus The High Priest*

This is a beautiful simile. In verses 1-4 the author points out that priests are called by God to offer sacrifice for the people's sin and their own sins as well. The author makes the point that because of the priests being also human and sinners, they are sympathetic to their people whom they serve (v. 2).

In verse 5, the point is made that because Jesus became a human, there is a similar situation. He understands what it is like to be human, is sympathetic to us, and he offers himself as the final sacrifice for our sins. Thus, Jesus becomes our source of eternal salvation (v. 9). But we should obey him! It will preach.

In verse 2 we have the beautiful word "gently" describing how the priest will deal with his people. The Greek is *metriopatheia*. It is the mean between two extremes: anger and laziness. It means the ability to help folks when they are foolish and do it without becoming annoyed with them. It means an attitude of never giving up on someone but being patient with him or her. A nice word for ministry and a nice description of how Jesus is with us.

The Gospel Mark 10:35-45 *James And John's Ambition*

When we look at the other synoptic Gospels, we see that when Matthew tells this story, he puts the blame on James and John's mother. It was just too embarrassing to tell about two of the disciples and so Luke omits it altogether. "Drink the cup" (v. 38) meant martyrdom. Baptism is symbolic for death (see Luke 12:50 and Romans 6:3-4). Verse 39 probably indicates their martyrdom. Acts 12:1-2 reports James' death. There are conflicting reports in John's narrative.

Now we have the meaning of discipleship (vv. 42-45). It is *serving* rather than receiving *privilege*. Jesus is our best example of that service. And his best service was giving himself as a ransom. References that help develop this idea are found in Isaiah 53, 1 Corinthians 6:19-20; 7:23, and Galatians 1:4 and 2:20.

Preaching Possibilities

If you have not done so yet, Job and his suffering will preach this Sunday by looking back to the Old Testament Lesson for the two previous Sundays and then presenting this Sunday's reading as the best answer we are going to get on why good people must suffer. See Old Testament Lesson comments.

I believe we could use all three readings today in this fashion:

Old Testament Lesson: Job's question is ours: "Why must we suffer?"

New Testament Reading: We can count on Jesus being sympathetic to our struggles. God will not give up on us.

The Gospel: Serving and suffering is a part of being a disciple of Jesus just as it was for James and John.

The Second Reading and the Gospel are so rich that I believe we may want to just center on one, avoiding a "lack of focus," which flaws much of our preaching.

The Hebrews passage gives us advice on being a disciple and on doing our ministry in the world where we work, live, and play. Jesus is our best example.

A. We must deal gently with each other (v. 2).
B. We refrain from seeking honor for our service (vv. 4-5). The Gospel may be a good example here.
C. We must be constantly in prayer (v. 7).
D. We must learn to be obedient (vv. 8 and 9b).
E. The one we follow gives us eternal salvation. (v. 9).

However, I will go with the Gospel for today and focus on ambition and discipleship.

Possible Outline Of Sermon Moves

A. Introduction: Because the Gospel is about brothers James and John, let's try a biographical narrative sermon seeing what the lives of these two Galilean fishermen and sons of Salome and Zebedee have to teach us. They were well connected. Salome was probably the sister of the Virgin Mary, so James and John were cousins of Jesus. Zebedee was prosperous and had a home in Jerusalem and was a friend of the High Priest, Caiaphas. The two disciples are always coupled together in the Gospels. Jesus called them "sons of thunder."

John was the youngest of the disciples and was called the "beloved disciple." Some have called him "the apostle of love." He was one of the inner circle of disciples along with Peter and James. He may have been the only disciple who died a natural death, his brother having been martyred by Herod Agrippa (Acts 12:2). Before that, some believe he had written for us the Gospel of John, the three letters of John, and the book of Revelation.

B. These two brother-disciples teach us a lot about discipleship.
   1. Discipleship is not about position and glory (Mark 10:38).
   2. Discipleship may involve sacrifice (Mark 10:39).
   3. Discipleship is service to others (Mark 10:43).
   4. Discipleship means loyalty to the Christ was gave his life on the cross as a ransom for us (Mark 10:45).

      You might want to add above that a disciple is eager to learn using John's reputation as recorded in John 13:23 and 1 John 2:9.

C. Now frame your sermon by returning to information about the brothers. James' name is the English for Jacob and means the supplanted or follower-after. John means Jehovah has been gracious.

In their own way, they both did drink of the same cup as Jesus. James died when Herod Agrippa had him run through with a sword. John lived to the age of 100 and served with a long, hard life the Christ. So one gave his life by martyrdom and the other by long, long service. (See Mark 10:39.)

Prayer For The Day

Like brothers James and John, help us also to hear your call to discipleship, O God. Show us the way of sacrifice and service. Accept, too, our thanks and praise for what the Christ has done for us on the cross that we might know eternal salvation here and now, and after the grave. We pray in Jesus the Christ's name. Amen.

Possible Metaphors And Stories

I taught a course in Hong Kong called Discipling in the Parish. At semester's end, each student wrote a paper on "What discipleship means to me." The following are some quotations from students from various countries:

"And my grandmother was real inspirer who spend her whole life in ministry through going to places in a boat to the villages on the bank of the great south Indian river Godavari" (Geddada, Sarah Joy, India).

"... the most effective way to win a person to Christ and to make disciples is to live a life of word and deed consistency" (Milanie S. Catolico, Philippines).

"Almost my entire adulthood facing only killings and hatred since 1975 to 1989. The Communists ideology — atheism is still influenced and widely practiced ... and Christians understood as human flesh eaters ... I went with my elder sisters who spoke to me about Jesus Christ. She was one of the first Christians in Cambodia" (Yi, Narith, Cambodia).

"Last Monday was traditional Chung Yan Festival. In that day we used to go to the grave of our ancestors to memorize (sic!) them ... worship dead spirit will bring good luck to the living ... After my husband and I became Christian, we are more and lass fall in trouble. If we participate such festival which caring ceremony of idol worship. I still trying to find a way which Jesus will agree with" (Man, Suk Yee, NT, People's Republic of China).

Fourth Sunday In October

Job 42:1-6, 10-17   Hebrews 7:23-28   Mark 10:46-52

Seasonal Theme   We learn about Christian growth and the way of discipleship.

Theme For The Day   Jesus as our high priest and/or Jesus and our compassion for those less fortunate than we are.

Old Testament Lesson   Job 42:1-6, 10-17   *Job Repents And Is Content*

This is the second reply to God by Job. The first (40:3-5) he admitted he was finite and God does display many wonders of nature. In this reply, he now confesses his pride and God's sovereignty. Verse 42:2a emphasizes Job's foolishness in questioning God's ability. In verses 4-5, Job admits he cannot answer God's questions of him in 38:4, 34-41. However, the dialogue has deepened his idea of God. So his awe was deepened and his arguing was intensified. Now that he has gained insight (v. 5) into God's character and ways, he confesses and repents. Finally Job was ready to trust the Sovereign even though he could not understand. The dust and ashes in verse 6 are a way of showing self-deprecation. See Genesis 18:27.

New Testament Lesson   Hebrews 7:23-28   *Jesus The Priest, Continued*

The writer continues to illustrate that Jesus is the best High Priest, superior to the old Levitical priesthood. In verse 22, just before this reading, he claims Jesus is a "... guarantee of a better covenant." The old covenant between the nation and God is explained in Exodus 24:1-8. It was based on keeping the law. Jesus guarantees a new and much better covenant. It is a new kind of relationship between people and God. This one is based on love and in the sacrifice Jesus made.

William Barclay tells us about the word for guarantee. The Greek is *egguos*. It meant one who promised on behalf of someone else the loan, bill, bail would be paid. Jesus, in our lesson today, is presented as the one who guarantees the love of God. Wow, wonderful theology that begs to be proclaimed from our pulpits today!

In the passage for today, the writer also claims Jesus' priesthood is forever. Other priesthoods are ended by death. The Greek word is *aparabatos*. It is something which is permanent or non-transferable to anyone else. So Jesus has the power to enable us access to God ... and it is not for a while, but forever (v. 28). Jesus forever serves as on earth he gave his life for us and in heaven he remains to plead our case before God.

The Gospel   Mark 10:46-52   *The Healing Of Bartimaeus*

Bartimaeus means, in Aramaic, "the son of Timaeus." Luke doesn't tell the man's name and Matthew tells it as two blind men. Here, Mark introduces Jesus as "Son of David." This emphasizes the Messiah as coming out of the lineage of David. Paul affirms this in Romans 1:3. This is a confusing claim we might as well not dwell on here. The final verse may be the climax of the story: he "followed him on the way" (v. 52b). This implies discipleship, but we never hear of him again. In presenting this story we must be sure to tell our people that Jesus was on the way to the cross now. He was heading for the Passover in Jerusalem about fifteen miles away.

Preaching Possibilities

If we dealt with Job last week, then we can move on to the wonderful theology of Hebrews or to the beautiful story of healing in Mark. I probably would have each stand alone, although one could stress the compassion and love of the perfect priest, Jesus, in Hebrews as illustrated in the way he treated this blind beggar in Mark.

Please permit me to present two alternative outlines of preaching moves for this set of readings.

Alternative #1: Possible Outline Of Sermon Moves
Title: Jesus as our high Priest
A. Introduction: Tell how the writer of Hebrews was writing to teach the Jews about who Jesus was and what he had done for them and continues to do for them. A good comparison for them was to point to their high priest and say that Jesus was far, far greater that this! This is a different kind of Priest (see v. 26).
B. Sermon moves:
   1. His priesthood is permanent, not dependent on humans coming and going.
   2. This priest is our guarantee of a better covenant (v. 22). Now explain the old and new covenants.
   3. His sacrifice on the cross for our sins was forever. It need not be done again.
   4. Jesus continues to serve us by making intercessions for us in heaven. We have an advocate.
      Between each of the above moves, have someone else offer a prayer thanking God for this kind of a priest. Or sing a hymn that is illustrative of the emphasis just made. Or tell a story that illustrates the truth.
C. Now frame your sermon by giving your main points in reverse order.

Alternative #2[1]: Possible Outline Of Sermon Moves
A. Begin with a description of the life of a beggar in Jesus' day. Tell how the crowds would be there lining the streets, watching the pilgrims on their way to Passover in the Holy City Jerusalem. Unlike the Levite in Jesus' parable of the Good Samaritan, Jesus did not pass him by on the other side. I'll bet the disciples would have preferred that!
B. Now move to what this story teaches us:
   1. It demonstrates how we are to treat those in our day who are challenged by some handicap. They are special in God's sight.
   2. Tell how Jesus was on his way to the cross and still took time to have compassion. We must be careful lest we think we are too busy to help someone else.
   3. There is a precious love of the unlovely here by Jesus that makes it a powerful moment on that Jericho road.
   4. Bartimaeus' persistence paid off. He did not give up. Thus he won the prize of sight.
   5. His healing was deeply appreciated — so much so that the scripture says he followed Jesus on the way (v. 52).
   6. Discipleship is like this. It begins with our need, continues with gratitude, and is completed with unswerving loyalty.
   There is even more to consider in this healing miracle:
   7. Think what it meant to Timaeus that Jesus had compassion on his blind beggar son. We often forget the suffering of the caregiver like Timaeus.
   8. Timaeus and his son must have often asked, "Why me, Lord?" just as Job did. Will the same answer suffice for both?
C. Frame your sermon by guessing what Bartimaeus did after he got his sight — traveled with Jesus to Bethany for the raising of Lazarus? Went with him into Jerusalem on Palm Sunday? Watched the crucifixion? Joined the disciples in the upper room after Easter?
   And what have we done in response to our Savior's compassion?

Prayer For The Day
Help us to be persistent in our praying to you, O God, and come to us and heal in our time of need. We pray today you would bless those who struggle with sight, and those who care for them, with patience and strength. And might we follow you on the way just as Bartimaeus did. In Jesus, the Christ's, name. Amen.

Possible Metaphors And Stories

Home Depot's Behr paint now comes with a lifetime guarantee. They claim, "When you're done painting, you are done painting." What are the lifetime guarantees for baptized Christians? Never being alone, belonging to a world-wide family that will not desert us, eternal life, inner peace, and a wonderful joy.

One of my Burmese students in Hong Kong told how an older Buddhist man in their tribe had glaucoma and needed eye surgery. All the Christians contributed all the money they had and took him to Rangoon. The surgery was successful. He asked to be baptized and now is one of their best evangelists. "Rice Christian," you say? I'm not so sure.

A child named Amy was asked in Sunday school what she was doing. She replied she was "drawing a picture of God." Her teacher told her she couldn't do that; no one knew what God looked like. She replied: "They will when I get done." Perhaps the way we live out our discipleship helps paint a picture of God for those who see us.

The radio and television ads in Des Moines for Reichardt's clothing store have owner Bill say: "No sale is ever final here. We'll see you are completely satisfied here. I will see to it myself, because I'm here — I'm Bill Reichardt and I own the store." In the incarnation the creator of all promises us that our lives are secure. God never throws us out or away. The owner of the store is here with us and we have God's promise.

---

1. For a dialogue sermon by this author on this miracle, see *The Miracles Of Jesus And Their Flip Side*, CSS Publishing Company, 2000, p. 65.

First Sunday In November

Ruth 1:1-18 **Hebrews 9:11-14** **Mark 12:28-34**

Seasonal Theme   We learn about Christian growth and the way of discipleship.

Theme For The Day   Loving our God and our neighbor.

Old Testament Lesson   Ruth 1:1-18   *Ruth's Love And Commitment*

This week and next week we will read from the book of Ruth. Ruth was the great-grandmother of David and was included in the genealogy of Jesus. The book gives us some intimate glimpses into the lives of people in an Israelite family. Here is an account of a remnant of faith and piety at this time. This book is a beautiful example of love and devotion. The story begins with this reading today.

Naomi's husband died. Her two sons married Moabite women, Orpha and Ruth. The sons died. Naomi was now a stranger in a foreign land. She decided to return home to Judah. She was astounded when Ruth said she would go with her. It was a loving choice. In verse 8, we have the word "kindly," which is a translation of the Hebrew *hesed*. It is a significant word in the book of Ruth. See 2:20 and 3:10. It has to do with grace which is given when not deserved. In this passage both God and humans were doers of *hesed*.

Verses 9-10 indicate a need for security, which meant, for a woman, to have a husband. Ruth's eventual decision to stay with her mother-in-law meant a very slim chance of getting a husband. Verse 16 is the lovely words of Ruth pledging loyalty to Naomi. They are read often at weddings. Ruth chose to return home with Naomi over her family, national identity, and her religious idolatry. It is a beautiful expression of commitment. What follows shows that this commitment was lived out by her as well.

New Testament Lesson   Hebrews 9:11-14   *Christ As High Priest*

We continue our reading in Hebrews and continue the analogy of Christ as the High Priest contrasted with the Old Testament priests. It is a contrast of perfection, permanence, and completeness. The analogy continues in verses 13-14, claiming Jesus' blood sacrificed for us is much more effective in purifying us than the Old Testament blood of bulls and heifers. The result is an eternal redemption. As partakers in this self-offering of Christ, we share true worship and God's service.

The Gospel   Mark 12:28-34   *The First Commandment*

In an answer to a question put to Jesus about what was the most important of all, Jesus quoted the creed of Judaism. It's called the *shema* and is still used by Jews to open their worship (v. 29). It is written on a scroll, placed in a Mezuzah, and fixed to the door post of all Jewish homes. (See Deuteronomy 6:4.)

It is interesting here that in its original language it meant to love other Jews (see Deuteronomy 6:8) but Jesus quotes it without limitation. Religion for Jesus was loving God and humans. Perhaps by putting these two together, Jesus is saying that the *only way* to love God is by loving neighbor!

Preaching Possibilities

Each one of the three readings can stand alone. We might preach on "love" and use all three, also:
A. Our love for each other: Ruth and Naomi. The Ruth account might also be an opportunity to talk about love across racial barriers that we humans have artificially constructed.
B. Jesus' love for us; he sacrificed himself for us: Hebrews.
C. Our love of God carried out by loving neighbors: Mark.

Then there is the possibility of a sermon where we talk about marriage and commitment in a more topical way. Many will recognize the Ruth passage as being sung or read at their wedding (or someone else's).

A. Tell the story of Ruth and Naomi and the commitment they held for each other.
B. Talk about the commitment of life long fidelity in marriage.
C. Explain that the same qualities Jesus teaches us in church we ought extend toward spouse at home! Go the extra mile, turn the other cheek, pray for those who abuse you, love the unlovely, and be kind to one another.
D. Drive home the fact that we remain sinners and must assume while we are not perfect, we are forgiven.
E. Now frame it with how Ruth's life came out as we will read next week.
F. Arrange for someone to sing "The Song Of Ruth."

Possible Outline Of Sermon Moves

A. Begin by telling how scribes and Pharisees had been questioning Jesus, trying to corner and embarrass him. But now there seems to be a real sincere question. What's the greatest commandment? Jesus gave them their own scripture answer: Deuteronomy 6:4-5 and then added Leviticus 19:18b. It is to love God and love each other.
B. Now let's talk about what it means to love God. Tell the story of Stella Min (see "Possible Metaphors And Stories" below). To love God is to put God before everything else in our lives and to refrain from having other gods like money, position, power, sex, creature comforts, etc.
C. Now talk about what it means to really love our neighbor.
   1. In the parable of the "Good Samaritan," Jesus said our neighbor was anyone in need of our help.
   2. List out for your hearers who some of the neighbors would be for us today. In addition to those who live nearby, they would be:
      a. Those who are not at all lovable or who will ever appreciate our love for them.
      b. Those who are our national or personal enemies.
      c. Those whose culture and race is quite different from ours.
      d. Those who have hurt us severely and continue to make our lives miserable.
      e. Those whose religion is different from ours.
      f. Those whose sexual preference is contrary to accepted norms in our culture.
   3. Now explain that often the only love we can have for those listed above is God's *agape* love.
D. Make the point that in loving neighbor, we who do the loving are even more affected than those who receive God's love through us!
E. Frame your sermon with a story in your own life when it was hard to refrain from hating and instead of loving someone you didn't even like and who certainly didn't deserve your, or God's, love.

Prayer For The Day

You love us in so many ways, God. Please help us to return that love to you and teach us ways to love each other. Remove from us the desire to hate and get even and put in its place the motivation to love and forgive. We pray in the name of Jesus who loved us even from a cross. Amen.

Possible Metaphors And Stories

During my class on "Teaching the Catechism," Stella Min, from Myanmar (formerly Burma), became very quiet and almost panicky. She kept watching the window and door. After class I asked what was wrong and she explained that as we were considering the first commandment and its meaning, she could never teach them at home. Stella said the military had asked the Buddhist monks to go through the Bible and announce why it was all wrong. Since that time it had been very dangerous to make the claim that our God was the true God and that we should "have no other gods." If she did so, it might mean her arrest and the closing of the school there, where she will soon teach. She had forgotten for a while that she was not under the home military government and looked as if they would come to get her any moment. The words whispered at home but openly spoken by these students were so scary for her to hear.

The editor of *The Lutheran* magazine, in addressing a summer missionary conference, said, "We are not just loved, we are delighted in" by God according to our Bible. I delight in the very thought.

In Columbia, guerrillas massacred an entire busload of people according to one of our missionaries. One of the survivor's relatives served in prison ministry where he had to minister to the one who led the killing. Now that's undeserved love!

In my Discipling class, I learned of the Korean ways of sustaining their families by two ethical principles: the first is *heo*, which means respect for old age. The second is *jaae*, which is love and care of the young.

Second Sunday In November

Ruth 3:1-5; 4:13-17   Hebrews 9:24-28   Mark 12:38-44

Seasonal Theme   We learn about Christian growth and the way of discipleship.

Theme For The Day   Financial stewardship including sacrificial giving.

Old Testament Lesson   Ruth 3:1-5; 4:13-17   *Ruth And Boaz*

It's a lively tale. Last week we read how Ruth and Naomi returned to her home and now Naomi arranges for Ruth to offer herself to a relative of Naomi (Boaz) to become his wife. This would give both of these widows security. So Ruth approached Boaz as he slept on the communal threshing floor. In verse 7, Ruth uncovers Boaz's feet and lies down there. This was a ceremonial act and proper for that day. There might have been a bit of seduction here, but many will try to find ways to disclaim it. And what if it were? It's a nice love story. The second part of the reading finishes up the book and the story with the main purpose of telling the narrative. It proves Jesus' lineage (v. 4:17). Obed — then Jesse — then David, in whose lineage Jesus must be born.

New Testament Lesson   Hebrews 9:24-28   *Once For All Sacrifice*

We continue the analogy of Jesus the Christ as our high priest. In that day, once a year, the high priest entered the holy place (v. 25) and made a sacrifice of blood from a bull for the people. But he claims Jesus entered once and made a sacrifice for all people and all times and with his own blood. Then in verse 28 he gives the assurance that Jesus will appear again. This time it will be for those who are waiting for him to save them.

It's an interesting idea that the author has, that Jesus entered not into a church sanctuary, but into the presence of God. So we ought to think of our Christianity less in terms of church membership and much more in terms of intimate fellowship with God.

There are marvelous assumptions here: a human will rise again and the hope of the second coming of Jesus the Christ.

The Gospel   Mark 12:38-44   *The Widow's Mite*

The first portion of this reading is a denunciation of hypocrisy and formalism. When Matthew recorded this event, he expanded on the criticism by Jesus a great deal (Matthew 23:1-36). This passage warns us against using our religion for our own prestige, our own self-gain, and our desire to gain the power of respect. Instead we are to think of ourselves as servants.

But the gem is the story of a poor widow who gave all she had in the temple offering. Perhaps it was put here to make a contrast between the Scribes' offering, which was done with lots of show but took advantage of widows, and this woman who was a widow who had it right, according to Jesus, when it came to humility, sincerity, and financial stewardship.

The offering boxes were thirteen in number and outside the building proper, in what was called the court of the women. The coins are *leptons* (thin ones); the lepton was the least coin in the Greek-Syrian system. Mark adds in verse 42 that these two coins were worth about one penny in Roman coinage called a *quadran*.

This poor woman has a lot to teach us about Christian financial stewardship:
A. There is a certain daring or venture that ought to be present in our giving. This woman was uncautious when she threw in her last two coins.
B. The offering didn't have to be coaxed out of her and yet it was a sacrificial offering. So often we will only give grudgingly and if we get something back for it.
C. Even though what she had seemed so inconsequential, she gave it, trusting God could do great things with it. God can and does do great things with gifts given like that.

Preaching Possibilities

If you have not preached on the Ruth narrative, this would be the Sunday to do it.
A. Last week we read Ruth 1:1-18, which told of the tragedy in the lives of Naomi and Ruth and of Ruth's devotion to Naomi — it sets the stage for his week.
B. The lesson today tells of Ruth going to Boaz and becoming his wife and bearer of his son in the lineage of David.

So we have at least two kinds of love: Familial love between Naomi and Ruth and erotic love between Boaz and Ruth. And (God's) *agape* love in both situations. You might also hook the Old Testament story of Ruth and the Gospel story of the widow who gave her all together in a topical sermon on "Women in the Church." Two examples here are of faithful women: Ruth, who gave her loyalty to family and to marriage, and the widow (wouldn't that be nice if Mark had told us her name) who gave in the right way her offering.

I don't believe we can hook together all three readings, but certainly the New Testament Reading can stand alone.

It is an opportunity to teach about "Sacrifice: Ours and Jesus'."
A. Begin by telling about the once a year sacrifice done by the High Priest in the temple in Jerusalem and then move to the much better sacrifice of Jesus on the cross, which never need be repeated.
B. Now tell of what that sacrifice means for us today 2,000 years and half a globe away from us:
   1. It means God loves and forgives us still.
   2. It means we have Jesus in heaven pleading our cause before God.
   3. It demonstrates the amazing concern the creator has for us, God's children.
   4. It means we need not live our lives doing acts in order to be forgiven; but, rather, we live our lives doing acts because the sacrifice was done for us. (You might use the widow's offering as an example.)
   5. It means Jesus will return one day (v. 28). I think this happens at our individual deaths (John 14), but there are many theories about when and how this will happen (or perhaps he already returned on Pentecost in spirit).

After saying all of the above, I'll go with the lovely story of "The Widow's Mite." It comes at the time of year when financial stewardship is called for in our parishes.

Possible Outline Of Sermon Moves
A. Run the story. Tell of the offerings required in the temple and how the wealthy made such a show of it. Now contrast that with this widow's act of offering.
B. Now move to what is the proper way to give our offering:
   1. Humbly, without calling attention to it.
   2. In large amounts, in order that we might realize the joy in giving it.
   3. Off the top of our income, rather than from the left-overs.
   4. Consistently, regardless or whether we like the preacher or the hymns or other Christians in the congregation.
C. Then we move to the "flip-side" of the parable. The widow's need to give those two coins was much greater than the Temple's need to have them. And that's always the case for us. No matter how desperate our church's need is to have our financial offering, our need in our wealthy, blessed culture is much more to give our money away. Make the point that the *giver* is always more blessed than the *receiver* of the gift. That's just the way it is in being a steward and a disciple of Jesus.
D. Now return to the widow's story and frame your sermon by telling what the disciples learned that day near the women's court at the temple as Jesus pointed out this little poor woman who was a giant in the faith: rich in other ways than money.

Prayer For The Day

As we bring our offerings to this church today, O God, teach is how to give like your disciples. Let the gift be sacrificial, help us to present it with joy, and help us know the blessings of being a generous steward in our discipleship. We pray in the name of the one who pointed to the widow in the temple court, Jesus the Christ. Amen.

Possible Metaphors And Stories

The IRS here in the U.S. now requires that churches and non-profits must prove that "no goods or services were provided for this gift" in order for it to be a legitimate deduction on our income tax returns. That's the way the steward gives, as Jesus did. Nothing asked in return. We give as a response to what God has done for us on the cross and out of the grave.

Director of the Division for Global Mission of the ELCA, Rev. Bonnie Jensen, told of seeing in an interview room an old Japanese sign from before 1850 which announces the price paid for information on Christians:

    500 pieces of silver for a Jesuit,
    300 pieces for a Protestant minister,
    200 for a believing Christian.

A good reminder of sacrifice for new missionaries going overseas. Bonnie added that thirteen Lutheran missionaries have given their lives in the last ten years.

An employee of the church who had been stealing from the offering was caught by using a powder which showed red on the hands of the culprit when placed under a special light. There are many ways we steal from the church and park the getaway cars in the church parking lot. Giving much less than a tithe of our income to Christ and the church would certainly be one of the ways.

A small town was trying to raise money to bring the big city symphony to their high school gymnasium for a concert. One ticket seller went into Joe's barbershop. Joe said he would be out of town and was sorry he could not be there "... but I'll be there in spirit." The ticket seller responded, "And would you like your spirit to be in the $12 or $15 seats?" It's a matter of stewardship to put our money where our spirit wants to be.

Patek Philippe Geneve watches have an advertisement right now which pictures a father embracing his young son. Below the picture are these words: "You never actually own a Patek Philippe, you merely look after it for the next generation." How about that for stewardship?

Third Sunday In November

| 1 Samuel 1:4-20 | Hebrews 10:11-14 (15-18) 19-25 | Mark 13:1-8 |

Seasonal Theme   We learn about Christian growth and the way of discipleship.

Theme For The Day   The struggles and blessings of being a disciple.

Old Testament Lesson   1 Samuel 1:4-20   *Hannah Prays For A Son*

Hannah had a problem. She could not conceive a son for her husband Elkanah and that was a disaster in the Hebrew culture of that day. A man's posterity was dependent on having a son. The Israelites considered it a curse from God if a wife could not bear a child. (See Deuteronomy 7:13-14.) So Hannah went to Shiloh and prayed, pouring out her soul to God. She promised to give her son to God if God would bless her with a conception. The Nazirite vow she promised for her son is described in Numbers 6:1-8. Eli, the high priest, thought Hannah might be drunk because of the fervor of her prayers! Then he assured her that God would answer her prayer to conceive. And she did, and she named her son Samuel = *samua'el* which meant "heard of God." She had asked the Lord for him and God heard her prayer.

For more on the Nazirites' vow, see *Harper's Bible Dictionary*, page 480. There we are told that the word meant "to dedicate" or "one consecrated." Some took these as life long; others carried them out for success in some endeavor. They are also mentioned in New Testament times: John the Baptist in Luke 1:15; Anna in Luke 2:36; and Paul in Acts 21:23-26.

New Testament Lesson   Hebrews 10:11-14 (15-18) 19-25   *Our High Priest*

We are still contrasting between the High Priest in the temple and Jesus as our High Priest. We finish reading from Hebrews today (whew!) after seven Sundays in a row. In this passage we have the first part finishing up the long comparison between Jesus and the high priest and the sacrifice they offer. Then we have, beginning with verse 19, the right response to Christ's sacrifice: have confidence, approach with a true heart, with clean hearts and conscience, hold fast to our confession of hope, not wavering, loving each other, doing good deeds, meeting together and encouraging each other. The reference to "sprinkling" (v. 22) has to do with the Old Testament sacrifice when blood was sprinkled on the altar as an atonement for sin. In verse 22, the reference to washing our bodies may be a reference to Old Testament ceremonial cleansing, symbolizing inner purity. It most certainly refers, here, to the washing of Christian Baptism.

So, stated simply, we have in the first past of the reading what Jesus, our high priest, did for us, and in the second part, the behavior that ought to cause in us as a result. It will preach!

The Gospel   Mark 13:1-8   *The Destruction Of The Temple*

This is the longest speech of Jesus in Mark. The temple was destroyed in A.D. 70 by the Romans, but without the end of the age. According to Mark, only the four senior disciples (v. 3b) received these secrets of the end of the age, so this wasn't an original feature of public preaching and teaching. The expectation of disasters at the end was a common one in apocalyptic thinking. This is more developed in Revelation. The word "birthpangs," sometimes translated as "sufferings," means the beginning of the new age.

Perhaps a very important element to note here, if we look at verses 9-13, is that Jesus never presented Christian discipleship as easy or comfortable: they will be tried, beaten, called before councils, and even their own families will turn against them (v. 12). They will be hated. My students have described all this in their home countries of Myanmar (Burma), Cambodia, Indonesia, Mainland China, and Nepal. (See "Possible Metaphors And Stories" below.) Notice verse 13b, the one who endures will have salvation. What a closer! And what strengthening hope!

Preaching Possibilities

None of the readings is easily proclaimed today. The end of the church year is drawing near and the more prevalent theme is eschatological. In Mark we even hear apocalyptic words!

The story of Hannah praying for a son is an opportunity to preach about the power of prayer from several angles:
A. Prayers of faith change our insight on our situation.
B. Prayers of faith deepen out relationship with God — and with other of God's people.
C. Prayers of faith may bring great miraculous results.
D. Prayers of faith help us discern what is God's will and be part of it.

A whole different approach to this Old Testament story would be to talk about the blessings and stewardship of conception and giving birth to children. Subjects such as abortion, family planning, parenting, artificial insemination, responsibility for infertility (it's not always the Hannahs of the world!), the blessings of adoption, etc. It will take the preacher's prayers as fervently as Hannah's!

If you have gone with the seven week Bible study on the book of Hebrews as suggested earlier, this would be the Sunday to conclude and to summarize the seven weeks by preaching on the theme of Jesus as our High Priest and his sacrifice for us all, once and for all.

Possible Outline Of Sermon Moves

Title: Persecution and Endurance
Theme: Being a follower of Jesus isn't easy.
A. Tell a story of someone suffering now because if being a Christian (see "Possible Metaphors And Stories" below). Tell how it wasn't easy in Jesus' day either.
B. Now share where you, as the preacher, find the most difficulty in being a disciple.
C. Look at the struggles of congregational members in being a disciple, like:
   1. Worshiping when everyone else in the family or neighborhood or dorm stays home.
   2. Tithing when we could use the money in so many other ways.
   3. Not cheating at work when everyone else around you is cheating.
   4. Continuing to believe when there is so much violence and war, hunger, and disease all around.
D. Now talk about how Jesus warned against putting one's faith in what we humans can build and do — earthquakes where I live disprove the belief in human structures!
E. Now move to our hope — jump ahead to verse 13b — we can endure — we will be saved. Let's frame all our life circumstances with that.
F. Close by returning to your opening story of suffering and give assurance to that person that they are not alone, God will help them endure and, best of all, we will be saved.

Prayer For The Day

Help us, O God, not to put our trust in earthly things and places, but to rely on you for strength to endure whatever comes, confident that you have saved us for all eternity. In Christ's name. Amen.

Possible Metaphors And Stories

I was presiding at the worship service at St. John's Lutheran Church, Antioch, California, just after returning from a year as a volunteer missionary in China. Arriving at the last minute, the assistant minister grabbed a written prayer from several weeks ago. She prayed for me in China and I was standing right next to her in Antioch! Liz Hall's granddaughter noticed it and whispered to her grandma that she liked it. She could see the results of a prayer while they prayed it.

Missionary Tim McKenzie from Japan told, at a missionary conference I attended, of a Takieo (very old) man in the hospital, unresponsive and in a coma. McKenzie whispered into his ear, "This is your pastor, your family is here and we want to pray for you." Slowly his hands came out from underneath the sheet and gently folded. He died later that day.

In my homiletics class, Tshering Kabo brought me to tears when she told in her practice sermon of how almost all the people of her homeland, Nepal, are Hindu. It's against the law to evangelize. One neighbor boy converted to Christianity and his Hindu father tried to kill him because of his disgrace in the community. The father would have succeeded but for her intervention.

One of my students, Man Suk Yee, met me at the door of Ming Chien chapel in Hong Kong. She was to preach her senior sermon that day and said she was so nervous that she was afraid her shaking legs would collapse under her. I told her I would sit with her in the chancel and when she got up to preach I would pray for her to have strong legs. And I did pray for that woman's legs for the first time in church. They shook terribly, but as she preached and I prayed they got stronger and stronger. Within five minutes she could have played linebacker for the Oakland Raiders!

After the sermon, I offered a prayer for preachers everywhere that they might be *strengthened* in their proclamation.

The Dean came up to Suk Yee and complimented her on a fine sermon. She smiled with a twinkle in her eye, looked at me and said, "It's all in the legs!" After that, my Chinese students called me *Keng chong ga ka*. It means "Old strong legs."

Thanksgiving Day, USA

Joel 2:21-27   1 Timothy 2:1-7   Matthew 6:25-33

Seasonal Theme   We learn about Christian growth and the way of discipleship.

Theme For The Day   Giving God proper thanks for all our many blessings, including our Savior Jesus the Christ.

Old Testament Lesson   Joel 2:21-27   *God Gives Rain*

This is a passage about God's blessings and how we should celebrate them. The pastures will be green, the trees bear fruit, the vine yields well, and it's all because of both early and late rain. It's abundant rain ... a real blessing in that part of the world. And because God gives the abundant rain there will be a great harvest and the people will eat well. The author says all this prosperity proves to the people that God is with them (v. 27) and is their God. Verse 25 seems to indicate that this abundance makes up for the years of insects that had marched on them like an army. So *maybe* this blessing of rain will move the people of Israel to a right relationship with their God. In my opinion this will be a "tough sell" to the poor of our day: to indicate that prosperity is a sign that God is in their midst! And then what do we say about the times and people of draught? However, the "be glad and rejoice" will work for a day of Thanksgiving. Some have regarded verse 23 as the seat of the Qumran Essenes' title of their leader: "Teacher of righteousness" (*moreh*). I doubt this is the place, as did the *New Revised Standard Version* translators.

New Testament Lesson   1 Timothy 2:1-7   *Pray With Thanksgiving*

It's an easy interpretation. Paul says to Timothy:
Verses 1-2: We should pray for everyone and with Thanksgiving.
Verses 3-4: We have a Savior who wants all to be saved.
Verse 5: That Savior is our mediator between us and God.
Verse 6: He gave himself as a ransom for *all*.
Verse 8: Paul was called to be a herald and apostle of this truth to us Gentiles.
The theme of thanksgiving is found in verse 1, "... and thanksgiving."

The Gospel   Matthew 6:25-33   *The Birds Of The Air*

No doubt this passage would be more palatable to those who have plenty, than to those who live on the edge of starvation! Perhaps the theme is not to worry (v. 25) and the rest are illustrations of how God provides for us, and that worrying doesn't improve the situation anyway. Verses 26-30 must have been a Hebrew poem in which the lines rhyme in their sense even though not in their sounds. The message is obvious: If God has given us our lives, God will surely provide what we need to sustain them. Our emphasis according to verse 33 is to work for God's Kingdom and for God's righteousness — the bonus is that all these other things will be added, too! By the way, when I read this Gospel to the congregation and put it in the worship bulletin, to be a little more inclusive, I'll use the footnote translation for verse 35 and instead of "*his* righteousness," I'll say "*its* righteousness."

Preaching Possibilities

Because this is a national holiday in the U.S., we will have to go with a topical theme of Thanksgiving. All three readings can easily stand alone. But probably the easiest homiletic is to use all three readings, making the following emphasis:

A. *Old Testament:* God's blessing us through abundance is cause of our rejoicing. Just to have enough to eat is a great cause for thanking God.

B. *New Testament:* Because God came as the Savior Jesus who made all things right between us and God, we also celebrate with thanksgiving. And, like Paul, we need to tell others about it.
C. *The Gospel:* Because God cares for even the birds of the air, we can be sure God will care for us. So we ought not worry so much and, rather, concentrate on the things of God's kingdom. And share this Good News with others, too.

While it's not so much in the spirit of Thanksgiving, the Gospel's words of Jesus about worry surely will hit home with our people. It could be a very meaningful sermon for people of American lifestyles. You could begin relating some of the things that really worry you, the preacher, like your own and the church's finances, your children, crime in the community, your old age, your present health, etc. Then move to Jesus' words in Matthew 6:25, 27, 31. Be open about the fact that telling someone not to worry doesn't necessarily help him to stop. The answer is in verse 33. We strive to be faithful disciples in the kingdom and, thus, just don't have the time to worry about little things like what to wear, etc. It might work.

Possible Outline Of Sermon Moves

I'll try a letter sermon for this day.
A. It will begin by being addressed to a relative to whom I am turning down an invitation to celebrate Thanksgiving with his family because I have to preach at our service.
B. Then I'll tell him what I will do in my sermon:
    1. I'll begin with a review of the story of the first Thanksgiving in America, which I'll find at our town library.
    2. Then I'll tell them about three personalities in the Bible and their reasons for thanksgiving. They are *Joel* in the Old Testament Lesson, *Paul* in the New Testament Reading, and *Jesus* in the Gospel. Their reasons are listed above in the "Preaching Possibilities" section.
    3. Then I'll tell them my reasons for being thankful this year and remind them of the many reasons that the congregation ought be thankful as well.
    4. Next, I'll explain that, while my relative and I can't be together this Thanksgiving, we will join together over the miles when we take the bread and wine of the Eucharist (the "thanksgiving"). This will prepare our hearers to receive communion today if it is going to be offered.
C. Then I'll frame the letter sermon by mentioning again the first Thanksgiving in America and sign the letter from me.

Note: A letter sermon ought to be in an envelope with stamp, etc., and pulled out in the pulpit and read in letter form: "November 23, 2002, St. Mark's, Lima, Ohio, Dear Uncle George, Sorry I cannot be there today," etc. It will preach!

Prayer For The Day

Our hearts are overflowing with thanksgiving for all the ways you bless us with food, clothing, a place to live, and this precious community called a congregation. Now help us to respond by being the instruments through which you bless others much less fortunate than we are. And give us lots of bravery to tell others about your blessings. In the name of Jesus the Christ. Amen.

Possible Metaphors And Stories

According to Kenneth W. Morgan in his book *Reaching for the Moon on Asian Religious Paths*, Buddhists believe "... what we think and desire as well as what we do shapes what we become."

Yi, Narith from Cambodia wrote in a paper for me, "... we produces one to two hundred local congregations between 1989 to 1993. (He got a video of Jesus' life and went around Phnom Phen with a few fellow Christians.) I used to pray, fasting once a week, and lived a most simple life. Not many people want me to marry their daughters. I had nothing, not even proper dress and shoe, but relation with congregational members and joy in God." Jesus says, "Strive first for the kingdom ..." (Matthew 6:33a).

Chim Pich of Cambodia and Stella Min of Myanmar (Burma) both tell of the same practice by Christians in their countries. Before they cook rice, they always take the first handful of dry grain and put it in a special container, which is set aside to be brought to church each Sunday. This rice is then used to feed the poor and for the victims of the annual flooding in their countries.

If you own just one Bible, you are abundantly blessed. One third of the world does not have access to even one.

If you woke up this morning with more health than illness, you are more blessed that the million who will not survive the week.

If you have never experienced the danger of battle, the loneliness of imprisonment, the agony of torture, the pangs of starvation, you are ahead of 500 million people around the world.

If you attend a church meeting without fear of harassment, arrest, torture, or death, you are more blessed than almost three billion people in the world.

If you have food in your refrigerator, clothes on your back, a roof over your head, and a place to sleep, you are richer than 75% of this world.

If you have money in the bank, in your wallet, and spare change in a dish someplace, you are among the top 8% of the world's wealthy.

If your parents are still married and/or alive, you are very rare, even in the United States.

If you hold up your head with a smile on your face and are truly thankful, you are blessed because the majority can but most do not.

If you can hold someone's hand, hug them, or even touch their shoulder, you are blessed because you can offer God's healing touch.

If you prayed yesterday and today, you are in the minority because you believe in God's willingness to hear and answer prayer.

If you believe in Jesus as the Son of God, you are part of a very small minority in the world.

If you can read this message, you are more blessed than over two billion people in the world who cannot read anything at all.

Fourth Sunday In November

| 2 Samuel 23:1-7 | Revelation 1:4b-8 | John 18:33-37 |

Seasonal Theme   We learn about Christian growth and the way of discipleship.

Theme For The Day   Jesus is our ultimate king and wants to rule in our hearts.

Old Testament Lesson   2 Samuel 23:1-7   *The Sweet Psalmist Of Israel*

Just before the list of David's mighty men, we have these seven verses, which are written in poetic form and are called "the last words of David." He is anointed and thus God speaks through him (v. 2). Verses 5-7 are centered on the covenant of David.

Verse 4 rings a bell for us who live in the Bay Area of San Francisco where the rain clears away the fog and smog and pollution and for a while the day is clear and we can see the "gleaming from the rain on the grassy land." The evil people are like many thorns that will be destroyed by God's judgment (see Matthew 13:30, 41).

New Testament Lesson   Revelation 1:4b-8   *King Of The Earth*

On the island of Patmos where the author John is in exile, he has a vision recorded here, of the Risen Christ speaking to him. He writes it to the seven churches in Asia. In this passage, he first greets John with a blessing of grace and peace. He calls himself a "faithful witness, the firstborn of the dead, and the ruler of the kings of the earth" (v. 5). The claim is then made that Jesus loves us, freed us from our sins, and made us a kingdom (a rich idea) and priests serving God. Then the passage comes to a crescendo with the Greek metaphor for "A-Z": Jesus is Alpha and Omega. It means a certain completeness. The second part of this verse 8 probably refers to God's name in Exodus 3:14: "I am who I am." The word "witness" in verse 5 is translated, also, as "martyr." This Jesus was for us. Verse 7 reminds us of Daniel 7:13. For preaching we must note the three titles for Jesus: witness or martyr, firstborn of the dead, and ruler of the kings of the earth (see Psalm 89:27). This is a claim that Jesus is the Messiah. In verse 7, John writes the theme of the rest of the book. He is confident of the triumphant return of the Christ, which will rescue Christians from their enemies. See Daniel 7:1-14 and Zechariah 12:10.

The Gospel   John 18:33-37   *The King On Trial*

The theme of King is continued in the Gospel Reading by turning to the story of Jesus before Pilate when he asks Jesus, "Are you the king of the Jews?" etc. Let's look at what is added to the King concept from this passage.

1. Pilate asks Jesus if he is the king of the Jews (v. 33).
2. Jesus responds that his kingdom is not of this world (v. 36).
3. Pilate asks again if Jesus is a king (v. 37).
4. Jesus answers that it was Pilate who said he was a king (v. 37).

An issue has become more clear as the trial proceeds: Jesus' kingship is threatening the kingship of Caesar. We see Jesus here as having the dignity and decorum of a king.

Preaching Possibilities

The readings for today can be all used together:
A. *Old Testament Lesson:* The greatest of Israel's Kings, David, was anointed by God. He rules justly (2 Samuel 23:3b).
B. *New Testament Lesson:* The writer of John's revelation claims that Jesus made us a kingdom of serving priests (Revelation 1:6) and he is our Alpha and Omega (v. 8).

C. *Gospel:* At the trial of Jesus before Pilate, the idea of Jesus as a king is further strengthened with his own claim that his kingdom "is not from this world" (John 18:36).

Possible Outline Of Sermon Moves

While I sometimes think that the book of Revelation is a dangerous one to hold up before our hearers, I do think on this Sunday that a sermon based on the Revelation passage will be one full of imagery and encouragement for our people. It will inspire and change us preachers as we preach it, also!

A. Begin by asking how many can name a king presently ruling in the world.[1] And then ask if we even know the names of any famous kings down through history. And, perhaps, ask who were some of the kings mentioned in the Bible. (David is mentioned in the Old Testament Lesson.)
B. Now turn to the Revelation reading and talk about what it teaches us about Jesus the Christ.
   1. From him comes grace and peace (v. 4b).
   2. He was a true witness for God and a martyr (v. 5).
   3. Jesus was the first example of how it is when we die (v. 5).
   4. Jesus rules over the earth as well as heaven (v. 5).
   5. He loves us and frees us from sin by his crucifixion (v. 5).
   6. (Best of all) He made us a kingdom of serving priests (v. 6).
   7. He will come again (v. 7).
   8. He is all we need. Our completeness. Alpha and Omega (v. 8).
C. Move to your "So what?" Tell your people what they and you, the preacher, should do about all this. *Do it in reverse order*, which is always a good speech communication technique.
   8. We surrender our entire life to Jesus, who is all we really need.
   7. We are prepared and ready for his return anytime.
   6. All God's people are priests and ought be serving God and each other as a kingdom.
   5. We celebrate our freedom from sin by living our full created potential and come to the Eucharist to celebrate it with others.
   4. Our lives are not on our own but we kneel often before our King, Jesus.
   3. We have a renewed confidence that we are safe beyond the grave. Our funerals will be a witness to that.
   2. Because we have all this promise and hope, we become witnesses to others about this good news.
   1. From him we are conduits of the grace and peace out in the world where we live, work, and play.
D. Now frame the sermon by returning to your opening questions and name some kings, closing with the assertion that above all those we have one who is Alpha and Omega — Jesus, the King of All.

Prayer For The Day

King Jesus, we thank you that you are our ultimate object of loyalty and that you want to come into our hearts and rule there all week long. Help us this week to be instruments of God's peace and grace, and to be faithful witnesses and subjects in your kingdom. In the name of the Christ. Amen.

Possible Metaphors And Stories

There is a computer company who used to advertise on television, "In Gateway country, *people* rule." In Christ country, *Jesus* rules.

The Chinese term *difang guannian* means a sense of place. They will say they are from Shanghai even though they have never been there. Not their father, either. But their grandfather was born there and left at the age of 25 never to return! The Bataks of Sumatra have a similar idea with their village of origin, *Bona ne Pinisa*. We, too, have our place ... our church, the place of our baptism, God's kingdom.

At a worship service all in Chinese and without an interpreter, I really felt lost. Then they began to sing, "Holy, Holy, Holy." I joined in with gusto the hymn I have sung since childhood. Me in English and everyone else in Mandarin Chinese. I couldn't remember the third verse, so I improvised: "Holy, Holy, Holy, I am glad to be here today. Early in the morning I would like to sing Chinese to thee, but I don't know the right words to say. If only I had learned Chinese I could sing praises like the rest of these. Amen." The young lad next to me grinned as if he were taking English in school. We were from and in the same kingdom. He understood and so did I.

As I attended a healing and communion service for retiring and on-furlough missionaries, I watched them sing and commune and receive the laying on of hands for healing their worn-out bodies. I thought, here are the stewards of grace and peace. They are the beautiful people of God who struggle — and, because of it, are transformed like a cocoon into a monarch butterfly. The stillness in that sanctuary thundered God's presence as those pious old saints shuffled forward, stressed and beleaguered, seeking rest. Then they sweetly sang, "Hold me in your mercy." And God really did! For this was God's kingdom, which had broken into our hectic lives.

---

1. At the time of this writing there are a few reigning kings. Some of the most familiar are: Karl XVI Gustaf of Sweden, Juan Carlos de Borbon of Spain, and King Mswati of Swaziland. Other countries like Denmark have monarchies, but they have Queens at the present time. I remember Ethiopian King Haile Sellassie and King Hussein of Jordan. Both are now deceased. Best known kings of the Bible would be Solomon, David, and Herod. Burger King and *Larry King Live* do not qualify!

www.ingramcontent.com/pod-product-compliance
Lightning Source LLC
Chambersburg PA
CBHW082040230426
43670CB00016B/2719